Wittgenstein
AND Judaism

STUDIES IN JUDAISM

Yudit Kornberg Greenberg
General Editor

Vol. 1

PETER LANG
New York • Washington, D.C./Baltimore • Bern
Frankfurt am Main • Berlin • Brussels • Vienna • Oxford

Ranjit Chatterjee

Wittgenstein AND Judaism

A Triumph of Concealment

PETER LANG
New York • Washington, D.C./Baltimore • Bern
Frankfurt am Main • Berlin • Brussels • Vienna • Oxford

Library of Congress Cataloging-in-Publication Data

Chatterjee, Ranjit.
Wittgenstein and Judaism: a triumph of concealment /
Ranjit Chatterjee.
p. cm. — (Studies in Judaism; v. 1)
Includes bibliographical references and index.
1. Wittgenstein, Ludwig, 1889–1951. 2. Wittgenstein, Ludwig,
1889–1951—Knowledge—Judaism. 3. Judaism—Influence. 4. Wittgenstein,
Ludwig, 1889–1951—Religion. 5. Postmodernism. I. Title. II. Series:
Studies in Judaism (New York, N.Y.); v. 1.
B3376.W564C483   192—dc22   2003027177
ISBN 0-8204-7256-5
ISSN 1086-5403

Bibliographic information published by **Die Deutsche Bibliothek**.
Die Deutsche Bibliothek lists this publication in the "Deutsche
Nationalbibliografie"; detailed bibliographic data is available
on the Internet at http://dnb.ddb.de/.

Cover design by Sophie Boorsch Appel

The paper in this book meets the guidelines for permanence and durability
of the Committee on Production Guidelines for Book Longevity
of the Council of Library Resources.

© 2005 Peter Lang Publishing, Inc., New York
275 Seventh Avenue, 28th Floor, New York, NY 10001
www.peterlangusa.com

Printed in Germany

To the memory of my mother,
Bani Chatterjee
1923-1998

Table of Contents

Preface

This study is not based on new evidence, but on new interpretation of evidence. If a diary of Wittgenstein's were to be found saying "My philosophy is Christian" or "I've written as a covert Jew all my life," the author hopes that the present reading would remain valid; the question of interpreting such avowals would still arise. I have sought only to suggest that the pointing function of all Wittgenstein's work was towards Jewish tradition. For the facts to support a more positive report perhaps no longer exist.

The late Arnaldo Momigliano reminded us presciently that we are 'interpreters of interpreters.' I have nevertheless tried to cleave to the best sources and information in constructing my reading.

It may be objected that scant evidence has been provided of Wittgenstein engaged in Jewish studies. This is true only if one ignores lifelong study of the 'Old Testament' and of writers treating Jewish matters like Ernest Renan and Oswald Spengler. One would also have to discount the possibility of implicit allusions to Maimonides. Among Sephardim, who experienced European racist persecution during the expulsion from Spain and the Inquisition, it is no novelty for a thinker without Hebrew learning to assert intellectual Jewishness.

If plain evidence existed, there would be no puzzle, and the supposition here is that Wittgenstein wanted to leave behind, like Maimonides, a puzzle of some profundity, whose solution only leads to more puzzles.

Wittgenstein's life had cinematic aspects unusual for a philosopher—the grand life of his family in turn-of-the-century Vienna, dauntless soldiering in the Great War, early aeronautics, life in a hut by a Norwegian fjord, the *milieu* of Jewish intellectuals like Freud and Sraffa, Cambridge debates with Bertrand Russell, a trip to Stalinist Russia, the coming of Hitler, taming wild birds on the Galway coast, England in World War II—worthy of a David Lean or Merchant Ivory. So in the course of a long journey through Wittgenstein's writings and Jewish thought, I occasionally daydreamed of presenting my results as a film script or prose fiction.

Regardless of any merit this book may have, working on it has brought its author into contact with traditional Jewish thought and thinkers. Should the result be the same for some readers, he will feel successful. Perhaps Wittgenstein had a similar wish for his readers. Jewish thought does not proselytize, and is therefore of interest to Jew and non-Jew alike.

I ask the forgiveness of errors that despite my best efforts doubtless remain. I alone am responsible for them.

It is a pleasure to recall the kindness of friends in Chicago and Jerusalem and of the members of my family in Washington, D.C. and Maryland. My debt to you is difficult to repay. For constant support I am indebted to my Series Editor, Yudit Greenberg.

R. C.
Hyde Park, Chicago

The risk, then, is the Jewish reading.
—Jacques Derrida, *Glas*

CHAPTER I

The Dimensions of Wittgenstein's Thought

> I ought to be no more than a mirror, in which my reader can see his own thinking with all its deformities so that, helped in this way, he can put it right.
> —Wittgenstein, *Culture and Value*

> Thought serves man as a mirror: it shows him the ugliness and the beauty within him.
> —M. Ibn Ezra, *Shirat Yisrael* (12th c.)

Wittgenstein was modestly confident of the worth of his writings, containing "a lot of froth, but a few *fine thoughts*"; hidden in "feeble remarks," he saw "great prospects." His first biographer Norman Malcolm records that Wittgenstein "did not think of the central conceptions of his philosophy as possibly in error."[1] In attempting to uncover the great prospects, think the fine thoughts, it may be helpful to keep in mind that Wittgenstein is concerned not as much to say things as with the possibility of saying. He is not presenting the results of thought but illustrating a way of thinking, placing it at the disposal of his reader: "I am in a sense making propaganda for one style of thinking as opposed to another. I am honestly disgusted with the other."[2] What these styles of thinking might be, the one he is disgusted by and the one he finds worth propagandizing for, will of course be a major concern in this investigation. In any event, Wittgenstein is best read actively—eventually to confront oneself, not to absorb information.

We find ourselves in this endeavor already on the route to paradox. The paradoxes in Wittgenstein's life and work are highly intriguing but effective guides to the dimensions of his thought. As if exemplifying Karl Kraus's saying that the whole man must move together, Wittgenstein sought a unity between his life and his work, and this he achieved to the extent that it is difficult to separate the biographical paradoxes from those that relate to his *oeuvre*. Scion of one of the wealthiest families in the Austro-Hungarian Empire, he lived a spartan, even ascetic life, preferring nature and crude simplicity to civilized comforts. Recognized as a philosopher of genius, he turned his back on the "profession" to teach little children in unglamorous surroundings, moving from metaphysics to the nuts and bolts of pedagogy. Drawn to the study of science very early, Wittgenstein mastered modern physics and several engineering applications of mechanics. Yet the spirit of his philosophy is stoutly set against—other appropriate prepositions here would be after or above or even *before*—science.

The ascetic Wittgenstein was nevertheless a cultured animal, sensuously responsive to painting, architecture, sculpture, photography, drama, fiction, poetry, and above all to music. Yet he constantly dwelt on the inadequacy of the positive means—the language—in which all this has to be expressed. Of all things, the cultured sophisticate approached philosophy like his businessman father, seeking clarity, decision, agreement. The consummate European, terrified at the prospect of dying in the United States on being taken ill during a visit to Ithaca, New York, also wrote: "...I have no sympathy for the current of European civilization and do not understand its goals, if it has any" (*C&V*: 6ᵉ).

Paradoxes of a clearly intellectual nature also abound. The man who asked "What has history to do with me? Mine is the first and only world!" (*Notebooks*: 82) did not place himself beyond the pale of Western thought without a deep study—among other things—of the historiography of Oswald Spengler.[3] Wittgenstein advocated and by all accounts constantly demonstrated a high seriousness in philosophy. He advised people to do whatever they did *seriously*. Yet he could conceive of a book of philosophy consisting entirely of jokes, or of questions (Malcolm 29). Reflecting on his own work, he was struck by the thought, "'I destroy, I destroy, I destroy—'."[4] In the *Philosophical Investigations* too he mentions the apparent tendency in his work to "destroy everything interesting"(§120), and reassures his reader that he is destroying only "houses of cards." But elsewhere he tells himself: "...you have got to assemble bits of old material. But into a building"(*C&V*: 40ᵉ). While G.H. von Wright, Wittgenstein's student, friend, biographer, and literary executor, believed that "the later Wittgenstein...has no ancestors in the history of thought. His work signalizes a radical departure from previously existing paths of philosophy" (von Wright 15), the man himself denied that he had "ever invented a line of thinking, I have always taken one over from someone else. I have simply straightaway seized on it with enthusiasm for my work of clarification. That is how Boltzmann, Hertz, Schopenhauer, Frege, Russell, Kraus, Loos, Weininger, Spengler, Sraffa have influenced me"(*C&V*:19ᵉ).

The last remark was apparently written in 1931, before the so-called "later

Wittgenstein" von Wright speaks of was yet a gleam, as it were, in the early Wittgenstein's eye. Again paradoxically, two years earlier he had said: "It's a good thing I don't allow myself to be influenced!"(*C&V*: l^e). Von Wright may have had some "Western" conception of thought and philosophy in mind; to defend his remarks one would also have to interpret the "old things" of *C&V*: 40^e ("In fact you must confine yourself to saying old things—and *all the same* it must be something new!") as not philosophy proper, rather something like "the wisdom of the ancients." Whether this was what Wittgenstein meant, or whether a more productive reading would result from taking this as a covert reference to traditional Jewish teaching (as this book suggests), notice that between the "old things" and "something new," "philosophy," or Greek-derived Western metaphysics, dissolves into irrelevance. Looking closely at Wittgenstein's words, yet another defense of von Wright's view would be to distinguish between the claims that he was influenced in the senses (a) that he borrowed or adapted someone else's thought into his own, or (b) that he "seized on" the work of others "with enthusiasm for [his] work of clarification." Sense (b) is quite defensible: there is overwhelming evidence of Wittgenstein finely distinguishing his own position from those of his favorite moderns.

Anyhow, along with some of the paradigms plotted here, the list of names Wittgenstein provides is an excellent introduction to the dimensions of his thought. For it includes an architect, three philosophers, two "social critics" (who in their own time were simply journalists), an historian, an economist, and two physicists. At another point Wittgenstein might have included the names of Tolstoy and William James, whose *The Varieties of Religious Experience* he particularly liked.[5] The list of disciplines would then expand to include psychology and literature, and within it would dwell the spirit of philosophical religion represented by Kierkegaard, Tolstoy and James.

The gauging of dimensions can be continued with profit by simply extending that list backwards and forwards in time—backwards to those who influenced Schopenhauer, and forwards to those thinkers and disciplines that have in turn been influenced by Wittgenstein. Before Schopenhauer one must then append the names of the Buddha, Jesus and Augustine, and after Wittgenstein come Thomas Kuhn and Michel Foucault. The line from the Buddha to Schopenhauer extends to Nietzsche, whose name must link obviously—though on another axis, as it were—to Derrida. If the reader will bear with this name-dropping for a moment and the fog it might create, it may be granted that Freud and Heidegger, too, are readily associated with Nietzsche.

Our list now includes people who could be labeled mystical, moralistic, reflective, analytical, obscure, systematic, subversive or with any combination of these adjectives. These qualities are reflected in Wittgenstein's own writings by traceable if rarely explicit intellectual osmosis and intertextuality. The process can also be imaged as a vein of thought mined by different thinkers through the centuries. This might clarify why Wittgenstein's thought appears to extend through time, drawing on old sources but auguring the future. This quality is not accidental. A remark from 1944 or later runs: "My account will be hard to follow: because it says something new but still has egg-shells from the old view sticking to it"(*C&V*: 44ᵉ); again, in 1948, this time with a touch of mystery, Wittgenstein notes: "It may be that what gives my thoughts their lustre on these occasions [when he is in a 'poetic mood'] is a light shining on them from behind. That they do not *themselves* glow"(*C&V*: 66ᵉ). Whatever the source of such a light may have been, in these remarks that are neither quite personal nor public is this recurring sense of continuity, of reference to thought more powerful perhaps and better organized than his own, but in the same vein. I hope here to explain what has only been observed, however rarely; for instance, David Pears notes: "*Old ideas take root in his mind and begin a new life. In the Tractatus the most striking example is his treatment of solipsism, which he connects with his theory about the limits of language*" (74, emphasis added). Also, diffused through the voluminous records of struggle, a deliberate lack of motion, a sense of stillness not quite expected in a body of writing seen as disturbing traditional Western thought: "Where others go on ahead, I stay in one place."

Let me pick two figures in these backwards-and-forwards connections for closer attention—Augustine and the Buddha. Augustine is an essential representative of Christian doctrine, and he figures directly and prominently in the *Philosophical Investigations* itself. His presence there has been taken by commentators, on the basis of a report by Norman Malcolm, to serve as the subject of a reverential critique: "He [Wittgenstein] told me he decided to begin his *Investigations* with a quotation from the latter's *Confessions*, not because he could not find the conception expressed in that quotation stated as well by other philosophers, but because the conception *must* be important if so great a mind held it" (Malcolm 71). Later I will offer some suggestions on Augustine's place in Wittgenstein's teaching.

The case of the Buddha and his methods (his philosophy or religion) in their relation to Wittgenstein's is an issue for contemporary thought that we need only touch on here. Fortunately, it has already been treated at book length (Gudmunsen, *Wittgenstein and Buddhism*). The author is lucid on the arguments over whether or not knowledge of Buddhism was transmitted to Wittgenstein through the agency of Schopenhauer, although neither answer substantially affects the present study. What needs restating within Anglo-American philosophical circles is that Buddhism was founded by a rebel against prevailing orthodoxies who claimed his methods were entirely empirical, requiring no faith, independent of any historical specificities, yet aiming to generate at their best a perspicuous morality of compassion and service. To many, possible parallels between Wittgenstein and Buddhism will not seem worth exploring. But for others, a careful reading of a compact collection like *Culture and Value* juxtaposed with a modern work of Buddhist exegesis—Murti's *The Central Philosophy of Buddhism* fits the bill well—might prove to be a profitable exercise. To them, much of the "later" Wittgenstein will appear lucid and commonsensical, like a vegetarian course for philosophical gourmets. Wittgenstein did, after all, inveigh against the dangers of a one-sided diet in doing philosophy (cf.*PI* §593). For the reader familiar with Wittgenstein, Murti, writing in 1954 unacquainted with the *Investigations*, is a stimulating source of parallelisms to Wittgenstein in *Madhyamika* philosophy. A critical common feature is the *via negativa* of the dialectic. As to Wittgenstein's remarkably deliberate articulation of the "old in new" in his work, Gudmunsen's major thesis, that "much of what the later Wittgenstein had to say was anticipated about 1800 years ago in India," should stimulate historiographers of thought. Gudmunsen adds that he has "tried to show that substantial parallels can be traced because the same movement of thought occurred for broadly the same reasons" (113)—a very Spenglerian formulation.

At the "forward" end of our chain of thinkers and disciplines we find Thomas Kuhn, representing the history and philosophy of science, Foucault, representing "perspectivist" history and archaeology of thought and its institutions, and Derrida, once Foucault's student, promulgator of deconstruction, representing at least continental philosophy—his early work on Husserl's *The Origin of Geometry* is of course in the philosophy of mathematics, an area to which *Remarks on the Foundations of Mathematics* is one of Wittgenstein's contributions. Leaving Kuhn aside for the moment, the path from Schopenhauer to Wittgenstein, and on to Foucault and Derrida, must pass through the colossal and heroic legacy of Nietzsche. As alienated from the Europe of his time as Wittgenstein was from his, this extraordinary European anticipated Freud in several respects, produced a dazzling critique of language and science, and was, as Benjamin Elman has cogently argued, an intellectual Buddhist *malgré lui*.

Nietzsche is the immediate inspiration of both Foucault's perspectivism and

Derrida's deconstruction. Wittgenstein refers to Nietzsche several times in his manuscripts. He must have absorbed additional influences from those of his favorite writers, such as Spengler, who had internalized Nietzsche.[6] At least one research article asserts that Foucault was much indebted to Wittgenstein.[7] In Derrida's case it is not so much indebtedness as striking parallels in practice, partially observed by many writers, including Richard Rorty and Henry Staten.

Kuhn's work is an excellent instance of the "trickling down" effect of Wittgenstein's thought. Kuhn has studied Wittgenstein closely, and is intellectually allied to others who have.[8] His work has certainly debunked the alleged procedural rationality of science, transforming scientific reason from a "given" to a fit object of inquiry. This reverse alchemy of the mind—not searching the philosopher's stone, but understanding how grammatical processes can con one into believing in the search for it—has a liberating effect of the kind that was dear to Wittgenstein. He remarked that science—the view of science adopted by an intellectual era now drawing to a close—is a way of putting man to sleep, when what is necessary is that he awaken to wonder (*C&V*: 5). Making use of Wittgenstein's tool chest, "[h]istory", says Kuhn in the first sentence of his major work, "if viewed as a repository for more than anecdote or chronology, could produce a decisive transformation in the image of science by which we are now possessed" (1). *A picture holding us captive* is Wittgenstein's image of the predicament he is trying to pry us out of.

The awakening and preservation of wonder is traditionally in Western culture the poet's task. Wittgenstein, who put part of his huge fortune into a trust to help poets—Rilke and Georg Trakl among several others—with anonymous stipends, wanted his philosophy ideally to be poetic (*C&V*: 24[e]). Even before the *Tractatus* had appeared—before he could have become his "early" self—in a letter to the publisher Ludwig von Ficker Wittgenstein said of his manuscript: "The work is strictly philosophical and literary at the same time..." (qtd. in Janik and Toulmin 192). Reflecting on this conception of philosophy would help reduce the baffled feeling Kuhn expresses, "that Cavell, a philosopher mainly concerned with ethics and aesthetics," should have been able to guide him through major problems in the philosophy of science (Kuhn xi). Cavell is an outstanding Wittgenstein scholar, the author, apart from longer works, of a perceptive and oft-cited essay on the "later" philosophy.[9] The seamless web of science, aesthetics, ethics, and philosophy *shown* in the Cavell-Kuhn relationship is typical of the uncharted dimensions and effects of Wittgenstein's work, of a piece with the patterning of his own life.[10]

In speaking of Wittgenstein and Kuhn, one must also refer to the work of

Feyerabend and Toulmin. Feyerabend wrote a helpful "review as rewrite" of the *Investigations* soon after its appearance. Like Wittgenstein, he claims Kierke-gaard among his ancestors (Feyerabend in Pitcher 163). Feyerabend makes more explicit than does Kuhn their joint debt to Wittgenstein: "It was *Wittgenstein*'s great merit to have spotted and criticized this procedure [of discussing formulas and simple rules] and the mistake that underlies it and to have emphasized that science contains not only formulas and rules for their application but entire *traditions. Kuhn* has expounded the criticism and made it more concrete" (Feyerabend, *Science* 66, original emphasis). Feyerabend has recounted his approach to questions about paradigms under the direct influence of Wittgenstein, presented to von Wright and Elizabeth Anscombe in the latter's house in Oxford where Wittgenstein sometimes stayed (67n.). To Toulmin's work we have referred and will continue to do so, particularly to his book with Allan Janik, *Wittgenstein's Vienna*, responsible for so many of our early "background" notions about Wittgenstein. Like Feyerabend, Toulmin was among Wittgenstein's students.

Apart from the problem of there allegedly having been more than one of him, Wittgenstein, while active, invariably disagreed with interpretations and "applications" of his work, even by people who considered themselves his followers. Accordingly, and perhaps tiresomely, I desist from implying that the work of these three philosophers—or anyone else's that might be mentioned—captures the "essence" of Wittgenstein's work, that he would support or approve of their writings. But I do claim this: Wittgenstein's philosophical tools and methods have proven to be an often unnoticed enabling force in the fundamental transformation of areas of thought, in the uncovering of startling new avenues of discussion. Von Wright has suggested that the historic significance of such men "does not manifest itself in their disciples, but through influences of a more indirect, subtle and, often, unexpected kind"(19).

To prefigure some possibilities in our exploration, let us observe how Feyerabend brings out the relevance of meaning and reference (an eminently linguistic issue exhaustively treated by Wittgenstein) to the incommensurability question in the philosophy of science: "...we certainly cannot assume that two incommensurable theories deal with one and the same objective state of affairs (to make the assumption we would have to assume that both at least *refer* to the same objective situation. But how can we assert that "they both" refer to the same situation when "they both" never make sense together? Besides, statements about what does and what does not refer can be checked only if the things referred to are described properly, but then our problem arises again

with renewed force)" (70). This is an early indication of the exhaustive probing, as a result of Wittgenstein's work, of the terrain of language and communication on which all edifices of thought—including mathematics and
science—rest.

   ❧   ❧   ❧

Wittgenstein hinted that his work had a mirroring function (*C&V*: 18). Held to
one's face, a mirror can be used for ethical self-scrutiny, or for vanity's sake.
Held at an angle, it can reflect practically anything. We have here in summary
form all the problems and possibilities in interpreting Wittgenstein. A mirror
is best used, not expanded upon. Wittgenstein's work is in fact tremendously
useful, the usefulness continually at risk in the arena of academic argument
and "culture." Few hold Wittgenstein's mirror up to their own natures in the
foul atmosphere of careerism and commerce. This he foresaw. The academy,
especially academic philosophers, he hated intensely. But his early audience
was inevitably an academic one. Inevitably, too, their response revealed their
own limited capacities, not Wittgenstein's. One is put in mind of aphorisms by
two of Wittgenstein's favorite authors. Georg Lichtenberg remarked that a
book was like a mirror: if an ass peered into it, one could not very well expect
an angel to peer out.[11] Karl Kraus was equally disconcerting: "Why does a man
write? Because he does not possess enough character not to write" (qtd. in
Janik and Toulmin 201). This must apply to the great as to the humble.
Wittgenstein's particular excuse for inflicting his writings on us (in the publication of which he was restrained to a fault) would have been that he was "not
fit for anything else" (*ibid*. 206; given the evidence of his extraordinary competence in a number of unrelated areas, this is manifestly untrue and should not
be taken at face value). By forcefully directing his best students into useful pro-
fessions like medicine and cautioning those that he couldn't channel about the
danger of dishonesty in the professional academic world, he sought to avoid
breeding philosophical progeny.[12]

 This attitude is in danger of being overlooked as a mere quiddity of Wittgenstein's. Permeated though it may be with his thought, professional academic
output has been characterized by intradisciplinary fragmentation in the decades
since his death. More powerful effects are possible when reader, expositor and
text are agents deployed in Wittgenstein's grand goal of intellectual liberation,
"the battle against the bewitchment of our intelligence by means of *our* lan-

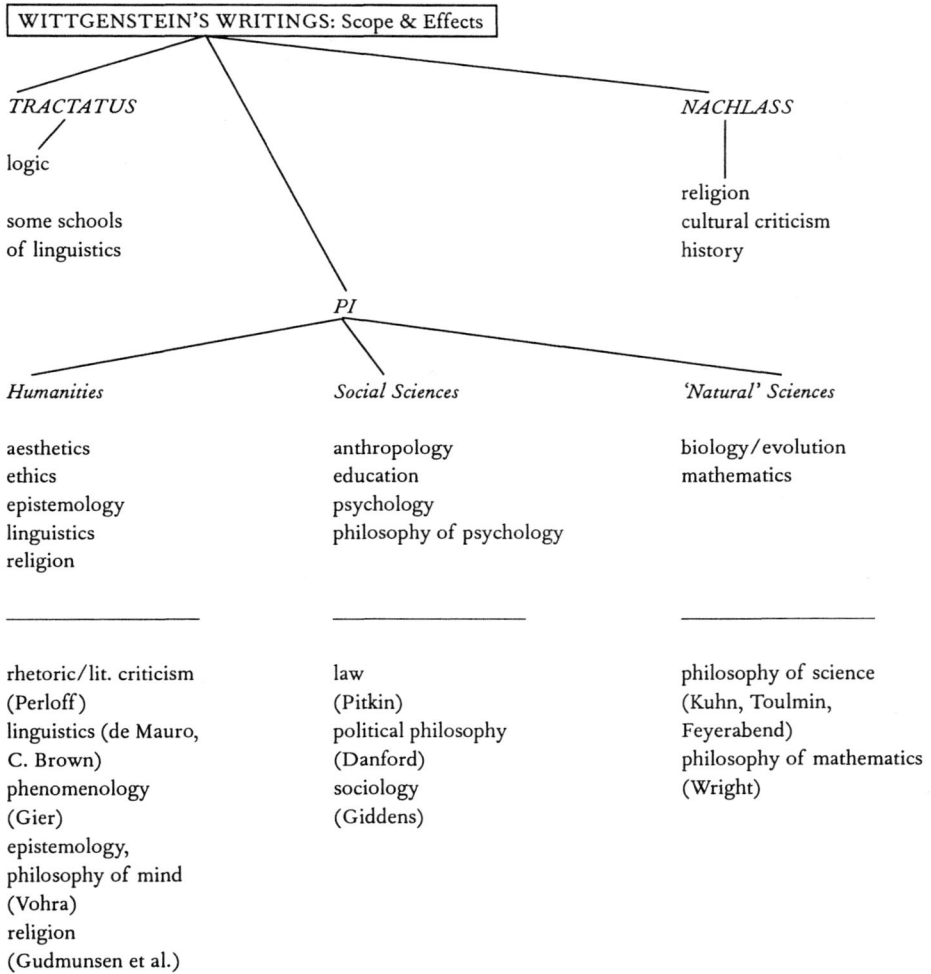

| WITTGENSTEIN'S WRITINGS: Scope & Effects |

TRACTATUS

logic

some schools
of linguistics

NACHLASS

religion
cultural criticism
history

PI

Humanities

aesthetics
ethics
epistemology
linguistics
religion

Social Sciences

anthropology
education
psychology
philosophy of psychology

'Natural' Sciences

biology/evolution
mathematics

rhetoric/lit. criticism
(Perloff)
linguistics (de Mauro,
C. Brown)
phenomenology
(Gier)
epistemology,
philosophy of mind
(Vohra)
religion
(Gudmunsen et al.)

law
(Pitkin)
political philosophy
(Danford)
sociology
(Giddens)

philosophy of science
(Kuhn, Toulmin,
Feyerabend)
philosophy of mathematics
(Wright)

FIGURE A

guage" (*PI* §109, translation modified; the German text reads "*ein Kampf gegen die Verhexung unsres Verstandes durch die Mittel unserer Sprache*"; Anscombe renders the last phrase of this famous remark as "by means of language," dropping *unserer* and somewhat diluting the implication of ethical responsibility *on us* for having bewitched *our*selves with our language). Although emphatic about the truly important things being unsayable, Wittgenstein obviously deemed intellectual liberation an achievable goal; when achieved, it opens up the possibility of the unsayably important being *realized*. This goal therefore becomes the standard to judge "Wittgensteinian" influences in intellectual life. Should it appear vague or unduly lofty, a second, weaker criterion will serve, to wit, whether or not a certain application of Wittgenstein's methods and procedures results in a *transformation* of an area of discourse towards making it less a congeries of techniques and more a means of raising the ethical issues that were his overriding concern and of his favorite writers and artists. Those dealing professionally with language—semioticians, structuralists, rhetoricians, grammarians, analysts of discourse, textual theorists—are at an advantage. They are likely to find that Wittgenstein's problems are also their own deepest ones.

Schematically, then, we can consider Wittgenstein's influence in the following way, preserving for the moment the traditional division into "early" and "later" Wittgenstein. Respecting the fact that there were only two works that he wanted to publish, his *oeuvre* falls into three divisions: the *Tractatus*, the *Philosophical Investigations*, and the *Nachlass* (voluminous manuscripts, of which selections have appeared and continue to do so). I ignore here letters, the *Notebooks 1914–1916* (published in 1961), and variant texts of the *Tractatus*, though the first two at least are certainly of great interest. Not strictly *Nachlass* are notes dictated by Wittgenstein and students' reconstructions of lectures (e.g., *The Blue and Brown Books, Lectures and Conversations on Aesthetics, Psychology and Religious Belief*). These are subsumed under the *PI* branch of Figure A. The *Nachlass* itself is taken here to include all the manuscripts, including excerpts now familiar as *Zettel, On Certainty, Remarks on the Foundations of Mathematics*, as well as recent collections like *Culture and Value* and *Remarks on the Philosophy of Psychology*. Note that these themes and titles originate with editors; rarely are they Wittgenstein's, and may thus wrongly convey the impression that he saw himself contributing to different "fields," while actually he was just pursuing his ethico-philosophical investigation, all too easily sicklied o'er with the pale cast of other people's academic thought. This brings to our attention a tension between the two—Wittgenstein's circling path of inquiry, and the more or less incidental disciplinary fallout at points along the route that can be applied by social scientists in their narrow areas of competence.

Descending from the lower node in the figure are the areas impacted by the respective writings—first Wittgenstein's own, then expositors'. Only representative book-length expositions are selected, no completeness is claimed. On some questions the relevance of Wittgenstein's writings has not yet been explored.

We see that it is what is considered to be the later Wittgenstein that has had the most widespread influence. The line from the *Tractatus*, because of the interpretation of this work by the Vienna Circle (on which see Fann, especially 25–28, and Janik and Toulmin) has led so far only to analytical philosophy and certain trends in linguistics. But the later work either directly touches on many issues in the humanities and social sciences—not to mention science "itself"— or has been so interpreted by writers in these areas. Philosophy itself is left out of the *Humanities* column in the figure; only its branches are mentioned.

The "absent presence" of ethics and aesthetics (declared to be one in the *Tractatus*) in Wittgenstein's writings makes a critical impact on the humanities, and is of tremendous consequence in understanding Wittgenstein's thought on language. In the *Lectures and Conversations on Aesthetics, Psychology and Religious Belief* (not his title!; henceforth *LC*) we find informal and intimate records of his "style of thinking" in action (the phrase is used five times on p.28 alone). Questions and issues are linked such that answers and trends of thought in one area light up others. This requires the engagement of the reader's intellect. For instance, *explanation* in psychology, aesthetics and other areas comes up several times (p.19, for instance). Wittgenstein says: "People still have the idea that psychology is one day going to explain all our aesthetic judgments, and they mean experimental psychology. This is very funny—very funny indeed." We are all interested in the hilarious. But for those who are not already laughing, this question is linked with our expectation of a certain form of answer that appears right. He goes on: "Supposing it was found that all our judgments proceeded from our brain. We discovered particular kinds of mechanism in the brain, formulated general laws, etc....(Mechanisms for English language, etc.). Suppose this were done, it might enable us to predict what a particular person would like and dislike. We could calculate these things. The question is whether this is the sort of explanation we should like to have when we are puzzled about aesthetic impressions....Obviously, it isn't this, i.e. a calculation, an account of reactions, etc., we want—apart from the obvious impossibility of the thing" (20).

From music (top of p.19), we are led to neural mechanisms for language. Explanations are based on *people agreeing to accept* particular sets of reasons as explanations for particular things. Someone might agree, on hearing syncopation in Brahms, that it was the 3/4 time that "makes me wobble"; "*on the other hand, if he didn't agree, this wouldn't be the explanation*" (*LC*: 20–21; emphasis added). Another explanation, satisfactory to questioner and explainer alike, has then to be found. Simple examples of this sort pile up quickly. An explanation for a poem sounding old-fashioned could be: no one would use a certain word any more; this in turn could be "verified" in a dictionary, and if the parties involved are satisfied with it, it is the explanation; nevertheless, Wittgenstein remarks, "I *could* point out the wrong thing and yet you would still be satisfied." This is actually what we do with children, sometimes believing an explanation to be the right one, but often just fobbing one off on the child. *It is the possibility of agreement* that enables explanations to be advanced. Our linguistic practices are already in place, and one of the things we know they can do for us is to obtain the agreement of Smith, Jones and Robinson (21; in America one would want to include Novak, Yu, Washington, Schindler, Gutierrez *et al.*).

Wittgenstein points to the distinction between cause and motive in law. Motives are conscious things. We are expected to know things. But we don't know much, strictly speaking, about the internal causes of our actions and re-actions, even though it is said, "No one can see inside you, but you can see in-side yourself." The kind of explanation we seek for aesthetic inclinations is neither causal, nor empirical, nor statistical (p.21)—it has in fact been pre-sented in an earlier conversation three pages before in the text: "You have to give the explanation that is accepted. This is the whole point of the explana-tion" (18). The explanations of Freud have already figured in these dialogues. His name floats in again, as if by accident. Wittgenstein had tremendous re-spect for Freud; during this period, he spoke of himself as a "disciple" and a "follower" of Freud (41), which puts him in a rather select set. Wittgenstein's favorite sister, Margarethe Stonborough, was analyzed by Freud. Neverthe-less, Freud received a critical reading, and as Hallett wryly notes, with such fol-lowers one has no need of critics (765; one might safely assume that Wittgenstein *always* read his favorite writers critically, particularly if they were scientists or philosophers presenting theses. As noted, however much he valued those he felt akin to in certain ways, in his practice they were spurs to thought and never authorities to be accepted and expounded. (This is one rea-son why he never bothered with conventional scholarly apparatus; see the *Preface* to the *PI*, p.vi).

Wittgenstein's attention to weaknesses and conflicts in otherwise impres-sive texts is strongly suggestive of deconstructive practice, which needs a text to wreak post-structuralist havoc, questioning its metaphysics in the margin, as it were. The reading of Freud by Wittgenstein is a case in point. As the psychologist saw a fundamentally neurotic human psyche, so the linguistic philosopher saw language as a repository of intellectual ailments. As the psy-choanalyst attempts to reflect the patient's repressed conflicts into his or her consciousness, so Wittgenstein tried to make his work reflect his reader's dis-eases of thought back to the reader. In general, Wittgenstein approached philosophical problems as if they were diseases, much as Freud approached his patients (cf. *PI* §255: "The philosopher's treatment of a question is like the treatment of an illness")—but he vehemently rejected the suggestion of a real congruence between his work and Freudian psychoanalysis, and this is important. There is a final uncanny resemblance, possibly inspired by Freud's approach. Wittgenstein notes, for all the world as if he were writing a textbook of psychotherapy, that "...we may not terminate a disease of thought. It must run its natural course, and *slow* cure is all important. (That is why mathematicians are such bad philosophers.)" (*Zettel* §382).

So what does this disciple and follower of Freud's have against his guru? Well, *in general*, that he was too much under the influence of physics as the ideal of science, of the frame of mind that says "There *must* be some law"—whereas, Wittgenstein says, "to me the fact that there aren't actually any such laws seems important" (*LC*: 42; this statement of the "fact" that there aren't any psychoanalytical laws is in fact a pointer to a deeper, more pervasive set of arguments in Wittgenstein's later writings that challenge at bottom most notions of "law" or "rule," including those held in mathematics and linguistics; see Kripke, *Rules*, Chatterjee, "Linguistics"; "[t]he incurable illness", said Wittgenstein, "is the rule, not the exception"—*Last Writings* I: §110). Freud further does not say what the right solution to, say, a problem manifested in a dream might be—it could be one that satisfies the patient, or one the doctor knows to be "correct," overruling the patient if necessary. In the event the patient is cured, the proffered analysis is a shoo-in as the "right" one. But *in particular*, Wittgenstein held that Freud's deterministic explanations, reductions of the form "X is only Y", were doing something "immensely wrong"—cheating the patient (*LC*: 24). A beautiful dream is identified as bawdy *au fond*, as if we were to insist that perfumes made from disgusting materials were in fact disgusting. Wittgenstein argues that "obviously" it is not the case that Freud was "fond of bawdy"; a serious possibility is that the sorts of connection he made have a charm for people—they are interesting. "'If we boil Redpath [one of his listeners] at 200°C, all that is left when the water vapour is gone is some ashes, etc. This is all Redpath really is.' Saying this might have a certain charm, but it would be misleading to say the least" (24). Wittgenstein claims that the "misleadingness" magnified in the hypothetical reduction of Redpath is present in all explanations of the same structure, even if, as often in the natural sciences, they happen to tally with experience. "The *attitude* they express is important. They give us a picture which has a peculiar fascination for us" (25–6). This idea of certain pictures that are almost fatally fascinating is a recurring theme in Wittgenstein, always in the thick of the battle against linguistic bewitchment. More often than not he is interacting with his own earlier form of expression. An instructive passage is *PI* §114. He draws attention to a key idea in the *Tractatus*, citing the passage where he had claimed that "the existence of a general propositional form is proved by the fact that there cannot be a proposition whose form could not have been foreseen (i.e. constructed). The general form of a proposition is: This is how things stand" (*Tractatus* 4.5; the last sentence appears translated in the self-citation as "This is how things are"). One soon gets into a rut constantly repeating this formula. Inevitably, "one thinks that one is tracing the outline of the thing's nature over and over again, and one is merely tracing round the frame through which we look at it." Fascinated by the product of the medium, we forget the medium's inherent problems and thus give them a Protean existence: "a *picture* held us captive. And we could not get outside it, for *it lay in our language and language seemed to repeat it to us inexorably*" (*PI* §114–15; emphasis added). A simple but sobering set of problems lurk in the little word *is* that we use so confidently in these formulaic claims: "This is what Redpath really is," "X is only Y," "This is how things are" (*two* uses of "to be" packed into a little five-word sentence here!) and so on.

From discussing some very specific things—Freud's analysis of a beautiful dream, a possible interpretation of a case of stammering (*LC*: 23, 25)—we are nudged by Wittgenstein to reflect on some general characteristics of thought and language. There is a constant refrain of "it ain't necessarily so" in the air as we are conducted through case after particular case of the forms of explanations we are wont to accept. There are rhetorics of explanation that we fall for. If depth analysis convinces someone of a certain "hidden" motive, Wittgenstein suggests that for the sake of the greatest philosophical clarity we consider this a matter of persuasion and rhetoric rather than discovery of an actual motive (*LC*: 27). This distinction is easy to lose as our intelligence is lulled by words like *cause, explanation, unconscious*, and so on—words pertaining to the general "scientific" mode as well as to particular disciplines. Wittgenstein is quick to clarify that what he is doing is also persuasion: "If someone says: 'There is not a difference,' and I say: 'There is a difference' I am persuading, I am saying 'I don't want you to look at it like that'" (*LC*: 27).

The repeated stress on difference becomes significant. Wittgenstein considered using a line from *King Lear* ("I'll teach you differences," I: iv, 94) as his *motto* for the *Philosophical Investigations*. Following Derrida's reading of de Saussure, an anticipation of the deconstructionist stress on *difference* as a feature of textuality can be recognized. The attention to rhetoric is akin to the focusing on figures or metaphors in Derridean reading to expose the contradictory metaphysics of particular texts. Wittgenstein's readings make these methods less obscure. Such intertextual illumination—or textual interillumination—is not only helpful in itself, it also informs us of Wittgenstein's place and role in contemporary, even future thought. To go back to Freud, the critical reading that Wittgenstein extended to him in 1938 (the year of most of the *LC*) is no aberration. A reading far ahead of its time in the long history of interpreting Freud, it has been independently re-enacted more than once. Wittgenstein put his finger on Freud's claim to being scientific as a key problem with his work (*LC*:42–4). His career of research and publication began in the nineteenth century. The physics of that time was for him, as for many, the ideal of science.[13] Norman O. Brown, an insightful and influential neo-Freudian, writing some twenty years after the *LC* took place and seven years before their publication, observes in his *Life Against Death: The Psychoanalytical Meaning of History*: "On this point [human language as a disease] Freud was not unaware of the implications of the line of thought he started; nineteenth-century science, with which he identified himself, was not critical of its own instruments. But if psychoanalysis is carried to the logical conclusion that language is neurotic, it can join hands with the twentieth-century school of linguistic analysis—a depth analysis of language—inspired by that man with a real genius for the psychotherapy of language, Wittgenstein" (70–71). The key thought here is of a science "critical of its own instruments." The chief instruments of any science are its formulae and concepts, all built on the ground of language—ultimately the basic instrument of any science is its language, and the critique of language is eminently Wittgenstein's *métier*. But in anticipation of arguments to come in Chapter IV, we must note here this highly significant opinion of Wittgenstein's: "Psychoanalysis as represented by Freud was irreligious" (Drury 151).

Apart from Brown, other recent and powerful forces on the late twentieth-century intellectual scene have confirmed Wittgenstein's insights in regard to his fellow Viennese. Lacan and Derrida have both read Freud creatively, but Derrida's reading is closer to Wittgenstein's. He points out that Lacan reinstates a commitment to truth with its concomitant, *explanation*, in his version of the Freudian unconscious. Without quoting Derrida in his playful prolixity, suffice it to note that he too, like Wittgenstein and Brown, notices the complicity of metaphysics and positivism in Freud's discourse, yet endeavors to highlight its path breaking features that escape the containment of "a certain linguistics" ("Freud and the Scene of Writing," in *Writing and Difference*, 198–99). In other words, Derrida likes and exploits Freud's ability to escape the confines of "scientific" language. But his comment on Lacan parallels Wittgenstein's view of Freud most closely. Lacan's dictum is: the *Unconscious is struc-tured like a language*; he speaks of symptoms having a cause in the unconscious. To Derrida, this is stressing the less adventurous side of Freud. Wittgenstein similarly picks up on the idea of a language of dreams. If it can be translated into ordinary language, the process should be reversible, but Freud acknowl-edges that this can never be done. While Freud tends to ask what makes one hallucinate something, Wittgenstein suggests that there may not be any causes at all in one-to-one relations to hallucinatory effects.[14]

Those all too easily persuaded by theories in areas not as "soft" as psycho-analysis—such as Darwin's theory of evolution—also came in for a grilling from Wittgenstein. He notes of the "Darwin upheaval" that, although one group responded with "Of course!" and another with "Of course not!", his style of critical thinking could say the same thing against both of them (*LC*: 26). But Wittgenstein's strongest jabs hit the "Of course!" mental attitude and provide a good example of his blunt conversational mode:

> Why in the Hell should a man say "of course"?...Did anyone see this process [of monocellular organisms becoming more and more complex] happening? No. Has anyone seen it happening now? No. The evidence of breeding is just a drop in the bucket. But there were thousands of books in which this was said to be the obvious solution. People were certain on grounds which were extremely thin. Couldn't there have been an attitude which said: "I don't know. It is an interesting hypothesis which may eventually be well confirmed"? This shows you how you can be persuaded of a certain thing. In the end you forget entirely every question of verification, you are just sure it must have been like that. (*LC*: 26–7)

So he returns to rhetoric and persuasion. In his *Wittgenstein and Phenomenol-ogy*, Nicholas Gier mentions the psychologist B.F. Skinner whose "uncritical effusion about the achievements of Darwin is embarrassing for philosophers familiar with the serious theoretical problems of Darwinism in all of its forms. Skinner claims that the key word in Darwin's great work is 'origin'...and yet Darwin himself admitted that the origin of flowering plants was a great mys-tery to him. In the contemporary debate it is still questionable whether or not natural selection itself is able to explain the development of new species. Even with the genetic reforms of later Darwinism, which place great emphasis on mutations, there are serious problems with the so-called 'hopeful monster' the-sis" (242–43n.; Darwin is also discussed at length by M.O'C. Drury in *The Danger of Words*, the author's attempt to lay out the urgent implications of his close friend Wittgenstein's philosophy). With Darwin, Wittgenstein again put his finger early on a problem, which has not been resolved a half-century later. It is worth recording that in an informal conversation he was even more explicit about Darwin: "I have always thought that Darwin was wrong: his theory doesn't account for all this variety of species. It hasn't the necessary multiplicity" (Drury, "Conversations," 174). This contradicts Staten's remark (*Wittgenstein and Derrida* 96–7) about "a profound convergence...between Wittgenstein and Darwin."

In the next two pages of the *Lectures and Conversations* Wittgenstein turns on James Jeans' *The Mysterious Universe* (a cosmological work), and on a mathematical proof by Ursell, a student, which he says he had pulled to bits. Ursell responded that the proof had a certain charm for him. If we are in a receptive frame of mind for what Wittgenstein is trying to persuade us of, we might realize with a mild shock that *charm*, a thoroughly aesthetic concept, is what is common to arguments in psychology, evolution, mathematics, cosmology, and aesthetics. To Ursell's defense that his proof has charm, Wittgenstein can only respond, quite naturally, "It has no charm for me. I loathe it" (*LC*: 28). The "objectivity" of proof has been subjectivized.

         ∽   ∽   ∽

All citations essentially from two slim volumes of aphorisms and conversations barely adding up to a hundred and fifty pages, minutely and relentlessly pursued, these are themes, along with others, throughout Wittgenstein's later writings. The three branches of the *PI* node in Figure A are still loaded with fruit. The humanities branch, for instance, bears "rhetoric and literary criticism," among others. As to the social sciences, Wittgenstein made a direct contribution to anthropology in the form of a scathing critique of Frazer's *The Golden Bough*.[15] Those remarks date from the years just before the *LC*. Criticism is again directed at Frazer's naïve and presumptuous "explanations" of the ritual actions of primitive peoples. Wittgenstein's other contributions to the social sciences—always by way of doing philosophy, let us remember—are his minute and detailed critiques of psychology, now published in several volumes under the rubric "the philosophy of psychology." Indirectly, the disciplines of political science and sociology have been affected through the books of Danford, Giddens and Winch, while Pitkin's *Wittgenstein and Justice* explores consequences in the area of law and justice. De Mauro and Brown have sought to relate Wittgenstein to the linguistics of our times.

For the rest of this chapter I would like to switch back to that area between the biography and the writings that we began with. One of the most significant, recurring but still unexplored connections in Wittgenstein, I would like to suggest, is between religion, hints of a Jewish sensibility, and the philosophy of language. We have touched on religion. Wittgenstein's attitude is a subtle and positive reticence, and effectively intriguing. He says that "an honest religious thinker is like a tightrope walker. He almost looks as though he were walking on nothing but air. His support is the slenderest imaginable. And yet it really is possible to walk on it" (C&V: 73ᵉ). One might be justified in arguing that Wittgenstein was thinking of himself; but this is not necessary. We need only recall how much Wittgenstein was drawn to the kind of writer between philosophy and religion who strove, with art and argument, to walk this very tightrope. He often spoke of what he valued using the metaphor of depth. For instance: "Religion is, as it were, the calm bottom of the sea at its deepest point, which remains calm however high the waves on the surface may be" (C&V:53ᵉ; cf. also 74).

Bartley is one of the few writers to have explored the theme of Wittgenstein as a Jew. But it is really in material made public since the appearance of his book that we see how Wittgenstein felt. Speaking only of people of his own time and place, his impulse for moral emancipation through work—writing, teaching, art—is akin to Mahler's. The obsession with language and communication is reminiscent of Kafka and Walter Benjamin. Wittgenstein identified himself with the intellectualist mode of Jewish tradition: "The Jew is a desert region, but underneath its thin layer of rock lies the molten lava of spirit and intellect" (C&V:12ᵉ–13ᵉ; the last phrase is the translator's rendering of *die feurig-flüßigen Massen des Geistigen*—the English typically splits up into *spirit* and *intellect*, *spiritual* and *intellectual*, the concept so seamlessly united, in Wittgenstein as in the German language, in *Geist, geistig*). George Steiner, in his *Leslie Stephen Memorial Lecture*, thinks that "One need hardly stress the Judaic character of the entire movement, philosophic, psychological, literary, cultural-political which I am addressing, or the tensed overlap between this movement and the tragic destiny of European Judaism. From Roman Jakobson, Freud, Wittgenstein, Karl Kraus, Kafka or Walter Benjamin to Lévi-Strauss, Jacques Derrida and Saul Kripke, the *dramatis personae* of our enquiry take on a larger logic" (5). Nietzsche and Mikhail Bakhtin seem to be part of this "entire movement," while Chomsky's linguistics, as opposed to his politics, is not. So while there may be exceptions to Steiner's generalization, they need not detract from the importance of the link that he suggests.

Among the people on Steiner's list, only Freud, Kafka and Benjamin, to my knowledge, derived inspiration for their work and art from Jewish sources such as the Kabbalah. (I leave Derrida out here as a complex case to be discussed in a later chapter). The evidence for Wittgenstein will emerge in the following chapters. He did not apparently wish his predominantly Jewish descent to be revealed, according to Bartley (184). But his wide reading in religious literature certainly allows for first hand acquaintance with some main Jewish texts in the languages he knew. Bartley, although he gives no source, says that Paul Engelmann, known to be Wittgenstein's closest friend from the years of the Great War, *himself imbued with Jewish tradition*, thought Wittgenstein's attitude towards language was "typically Jewish" (65). I will leave the question here for now after citing two rather pertinent remarks with George Steiner's authority behind them: "The Freudian view and use of human speech, of written texts (with its unmistakable analogues to Talmudic and to Kabbalistic techniques of decipherment in depths, of revelatory descent into hidden levels of etymology and verbal association), radically dislocates and undermines the old stabilities of language"(3). With regard to Wittgenstein on Freud, Steiner says: "No ascription of meaning is ever final, no associative sequence or field of possible resonance ever end-stopped (Wittgenstein's dissent from Freud seizes upon this very point"(4).

Drury, one of those students directed away from being a philosopher, has left us the opinion that the texts of the later Wittgenstein are rendered banal if not seen continually to point away from themselves. If we are to take Wittgenstein at his word, that his work is a mirror, then his texts point to us. Until they have changed us—having given us as an instrument of change an acutely developed awareness of the hold of language—nothing has changed. That is a possible reading of Wittgenstein's skepticism about the idea of progress, expressed in the motto from Nestroy's *Schutzling* he chose for his last work: "It is in the nature of every advance, that it appears much greater than it actually is." The affinity of mood and spirit to the motto of the *Tractatus* is apparent: "...and whatever a man knows, whatever is not mere rumbling and roaring that he has heard, can be said in three words" (Kürnberger).

CHAPTER II

The Whole Man Moves Together

His idea of his book is not that anyone by reading it will understand his ideas, but that some day someone will think them out again for himself, and will derive great pleasure from finding in his book their exact expressions.
— Frank Ramsey, letter to his mother from Puchberg am Schneeberg, September 20, 1923

So much has been written about Wittgenstein that a book claiming to add something new to the interpretation of his entire philosophy must begin by pointing out the limitations of previous explorations, and, developing an alternative route, must conclude by showing its distinct advantages over others, illuminating the seemingly disparate concerns partly visible in that philosophy. These concerns have been rather well defined in isolation by one or the other work of commentary and interpretation. Light on the peaks, however, does not mean that the entire landscape is made the less mysterious.

Not that there is such a thing as "a philosophy of Wittgenstein"—a new structure, an elaborate system, a positive statement. Wittgenstein pursues a strategy of minimalism: minimum publication, minimum clarity about intention (note his remark on the difficulty of understanding not what he was saying, but the point of his saying it), minimum explanation, minimum possibility of a posthumous "school" founded by disciples causing distortions to set in. Conversely, this minimalism involves a maximum volume of writing (apparently designed for different degrees of exposure: circulation among friends, notebooks to survive his death, notebooks to be destroyed, letters to single recipients, publication), maximum assumption by the author of preunderstanding on the reader's part, maximum transferring of interpretive workload (preface to the *Investigations*: "I should not like my writing to spare other people the trouble of thinking. But, if possible, to stimulate someone to thoughts of his own"). Wittgenstein's role in his own texts is—if the reader can understand—to hint at being a challenging and extreme other. This other has been given various names by commentators, depending on the *Zeitgeist*—positivist, radical behaviorist, Buddhist, Christian (Catholic) ethicist (cf. Cyril Barret's book)—names that can be seen as attempts to put Wittgenstein into a category acceptable to the western world view. However, each of these naming moves can only apply to part of his work. Few would suggest that the term "positivist" covers the *Investigations* and the *Tractatus*, or that both are the writings of a Buddhist, or of a Christian ethicist. So far, then, the labelings of Wittgenstein's thought have had this weakness in common, that they require the sundering of one part of his work from another.

Wittgenstein's thought travels a fine line between the analytic philosophical culture in which he worked (Russell, Moore, Frege) and the later developments from Nietzsche and phenomenology (Husserl, Heidegger, Derrida; see Cornel West on this in *Why Nietzsche Now?*). Although it may be in many respects akin to the latter, the self-contained (one might say, post-academic) nature of Wittgenstein's subversion of philosophy makes it more accessible, less convoluted, more stark in its ethico-religious clarity than the two movements it travels between. And for this very reason—fewer entanglements in the politics of scholarship—it is easy to ignore. Wittgenstein strove *not* to found a school, perhaps the first philosopher to so strive. If an alliance between this detached subversion and the ethico-religious consequences of the work of thinkers like Rosenzweig, Levinas and Derrida can be shown, contemporary thought may be focused differently, achieving in some way Wittgenstein's aim of forcing the old into combination with the contemporary, requiring the artist in the intellect (as Russell once described him) to show—by arguments enmeshed in contemporary interests—the unchanging relevance of the old.

Wittgenstein strikes us as a writer whose insight and message are so pressing that for him the traditions and conventions of "philosophy" have no value in themselves. Like Nietzsche, he must deliver his concern partly by mocking them, partly by confrontation. After that there is no positive "philosophy" to state, only hints and allusions for the individual readers to pick up according to their knowledge and ability, and the hope that one or the other of them will be endowed with pre-understanding of all this. Since it is the hints and allusions that are important, and not the arguments, which share the limitations of all arguments, these latter often appear hilarious, or their author thinks them to be so. With arguments that are mocked and undermined by their propounder, and hints so veiled as to be incapable of general recognition, it is no surprise that the "wholeness" or "relatedness" of the writings has proven elusive.

Philosophy is not just the set of statements in the medium of language put out by philosophers—it is also the undermining, at least the critique, of the very medium that purports to carry those statements. Since this was not the general understanding among academic readers of Wittgenstein, a great deal of energy and intelligence has been applied to extrapolating isolated theories and principles from his work—the Picture Theory of Meaning, the Principle of Verification, the Private Language Argument, the Use Theory of Meaning, and so on—and putting them to work in analytical philosophy or in humanistic and social science disciplines sympathetic to analytical philosophy. The "early" vs. "later" division is really *a part of the rhetoric justifying this piecemeal extrapolation*. If each phase constituted a whole philosophy, it could more legitimately be "applied" without regard to the lifelong, overriding concerns of the writer. Such a fate is usual even for the philosopher who is trying to establish a controlled and predictable "school." Realizing that he would not escape it either, Wittgenstein, investing no energy in building a "school," wrote for the pleasure of the one reader who already understood. It is not unusual, when engaging say a biologist-philosopher of science or a psychologist in conversation about Wittgenstein, to hear them say, "Well, that's the part that's useful for me. As to what he really said or meant, I don't know, I'm not interested." Such a person's reaction to his remark written in 1930 ("Each of the sentences I write is trying to say the whole thing, i.e. the same thing over and over again; it is as though they were all simply views of one object seen from different angles," *C&V*: 7^e) would be disinterested and uncomprehending. He or she may well prefer to ask of Wittgenstein, well, what is the one thing? If you know what it is, why don't you say it, in *one* sentence? The entire critique of language subsumed in this statement about all his sentences, the implication that the most important things cannot be said, that if something could directly be said it would not touch his ethical concerns, these things would escape such a reader. Notice that Wittgenstein's remark dates from mid-career—while not excluding the *Tractatus*, it embraces all the writing in progress and to come, bridging various phases of his effort.

There are other passages in Wittgenstein whose bridging role has not been made clear by commentators. In this regard the *Preface* to the *Tractatus* was meant by the author to bear a heavy responsibility. Assuming they were able to understand it, perhaps its first positivist readers were made uncomfortable—they ignored it, and, with very few exceptions, ignoring it became traditional. One recent exception: "In any longer study of the *Tractatus*, the preface would have to be quoted in full and discussed in detail, for it seems intensely earnest in intent, yet it reads like an incredible joke—a serious joke coterminous with philosophy itself" (Dominick LaCapra, *Rethinking Intellectual History*, 111–112). If the preface were treated as LaCapra suggests, perhaps the rest of the work would be redundant, as indeed it would also be for Wittgenstein's ideal reader who had already thought the thoughts himself, seen their limitations and used them as a ladder. One of the reasons Wittgenstein was unhappy with Russell's introduction to the *Tractatus* may well have been that, although Russell dwelt on mysticism at some length, no mention was made of the prefatory framework, which along with the conclusion Wittgenstein considered the most important parts of the book. As Wittgenstein wrote to his friend and prospective publisher Ludwig von Ficker, "...the book will say a great deal that you yourself want to say. Only perhaps you won't see that it is said in the book. For now I would recommend you to read the *preface* and the *conclusion* because they contain the most direct expression of the point of the book" (*Ludwig Wittgenstein, Briefe an Ludwig von Ficker*, 35, qtd. in Janik & Toulmin 192, original emphasis). Wittgenstein was very finicky about his preface, making several detailed comments to Ogden about the English translation, and pointing out that if he gave the publishers all publication rights "then they ought to print my preface in German too!!! *For the preface is part of the book.*" He suggested that printing it in German "would make the sense of the preface and the book plainer" (*Letters to C.K. Ogden*, 48, 55).

Important as the preface obviously is, at this point in our account it remains baffling. There seems to be a missing link in the suggestions to Ficker, perhaps a subtlety the author does not want to divulge. Why, if the book says much of what Ficker himself wants to say, would he not be able to find it there? Why does Wittgenstein seem to have concluded, despite the congruence between his thoughts and Ficker's, that he is not the one ideal reader being sought? Provisional explanations include the possibilities that Wittgenstein merely wanted to emphasize that Ficker would miss the point of the book if he did not pay special attention to the preface and the conclusion, or that he would miss the point even if he did, because *the whole book alludes to some tradition or code* of which Ficker was ignorant, since it was not practicable simply to tell him what this was. Paul Engelmann has a third suggestion:

> To the ordinary reader, even if versed in philosophy, Wittgenstein's basic thoughts, as stated in the *Tractatus Logico-Philosophicus*, often seem incomprehensible, because "too complex." That they are not; but they are incomprehensible owing to the absence of the psychological conditions from which alone such thinking can spring and which must exist, though to a lesser degree, in the reader's mind as well. (*Letters*, 94)

This is hardly less obscure than the preface itself. Engelmann does not specify "the psychological conditions from which alone such thinking can spring." Later in his book, however, in a section on Wittgenstein's family, he claims that in the Anglo-Saxon world Wittgenstein's personality cannot be understood without reference to "the soil that nurtured his intellectual roots." Wittgenstein comes to life when seen in *the environment of the Austrian-Jewish spirit* (119). If by psychological conditions and nurturing environment Engelmann means something that has to do with the Jewish spirit and intellectual tradition, then we have the earliest claim, made tentatively and with a certain indirectness characteristic of both writer and commentator, that the *Tractatus* is a work best understood as a "Jewish" book performing a traditional intellectual role, its preface a cornerstone in the structure. Regardless of the implications of this suggestion, to which we must return later, the preface to the *Tractatus* emerges in truth as *the preface to all Wittgenstein's work*. A prefatory formulation suggesting that the reading and understanding of the book that follows it is not the author's wish, rather his goal is the provision of pleasure to one single reader who already understands, may be suspected of questioning the ordinary conception of communication and understanding. While this may have been far from clear to academic philosophers in the Europe of the 1920's, and may still be so in some segments of the philosophical world, such questioning has a much better chance of being listened to sympathetically today, when diverse thinkers have been pointing in the same direction. The lesson for us at this point is a smaller one, however: that *the attitude towards communication and ethics implicit in the* Tractatus *and its preface were already those Wittgenstein held and maintained for the rest of his life*. The preface and conclusion of the *Tractatus* are nowhere refuted, and there is no contrasting preface to the later work heralding some new purpose.

The theme of the reader's pre-understanding persists through to the time of Wittgenstein's return to Cambridge and the beginnings of the *Philosophical Investigations*—again a feature bridging rather than separating the two periods of activity. Reflecting once again on the relationship of introductory material to the rest of a book, he wrote: "The book must automatically separate those who understand it from those who do not. Even the foreword is written just for those who understand the book" (*C&V*: 7ᵉ). The function of separating out his readers had not been emphasized in the preface to the *Tractatus*, but the paradoxical procedure of writing *only for those who already understood* remained unchanged a decade later. Indeed, there is a clear attempt to make the contrast between saying and showing more explicit in the very first sentence of the sketch of another foreword: "The danger in a long foreword is that the spirit of a book has to be evident in the book itself and cannot be described" (*C&V*: 7ᵉ).[1]

LaCapra senses "a serious joke coterminous with philosophy itself" in the preface to the *Tractatus*. Engelmann feels that Wittgenstein's adversary "in the *Tractatus* is philosophy itself" (*Letters* 124). Mysticism also is the adversary of rational philosophy; Engelmann suggests that Wittgenstein derived his logic from his mysticism, rather than, as usually believed, mysticism from his logic—a very important distinction. The mysticism thus predates the logic and philosophy. In Jewish tradition, mysticism has been defined as "that aspect of the Jewish religious experience in which man's mind is in direct encounter with God." The writer, Louis Jacobs, an authority on the subject, goes on to say that "[i]t is necessary to speak of the mind in this context since it is undoubtedly true that in most varieties of Jewish mystical experience there is a strong intellectual content" (Jacobs, *Jewish Mystical Testimonies*, 1). The question arises: if philosophy is the adversary in the *Tractatus*, what is the adversary in the *Philosophical Investigations*? One clue suggesting that there had been no change, only a willingness to be more explicit, is this remark from the time of the conception of the later work: "Philosophy is an instrument whose only use is against philosophers and against the philosophers in us" (Ms. 219:11, 1932/ 33, qtd. in Hallett 382). Philosophy remained very much the adversary.

There seems to be some overlap, some thread of connection, between jokes, mysticism, and the hatred for traditional philosophy. Pre-understanding, probing the boundaries of reason, inexplicability to those who do not "already" understand, the need for prior experience and agreement, the bonding effect of sharing something implicit, these would appear to be common to both humor and mysticism. The acts and comments of Irishmen, Scotsmen, Frenchmen, Englishmen *et al.* only draw guffaws because Americans, for instance, do not need any explanation as to what these nationalities stand for in the jokes. The answer to the question, what's the difference between a Northern woman and a Southern woman? (a Northern woman says "You can!" A Southern woman says "Y'all can!") is based on historical stereotypes that one either knows or does not know when the joke is heard, and all present are automatically sorted out into two groups. Wittgenstein seems to have sought in his work this kind of sorting effect: "The book must automatically separate those who understand it from those who do not" (*C&V*:7ᵉ). Some jokes call into question a serious formulation while attempting to represent it:

There was a young lady named Bright
Who traveled much faster than light
She set out one day
In a relative way
And returned on the previous night

Here the gap between the theoretical concept of relativity and everyday life is exploited. Wittgenstein is reported to have had the following exchange with the philosopher C.D. Broad, who proposed: "Either God exists, or He does not." "Couldn't he half exist?" Wittgenstein asked. Broad walked out of the room. As Wittgenstein wrote in a manuscript in mid-career, "I am always inquiring into the impossibility of expression, which is the real ground of the problem" (Ms.108: 269, 1929–30, qtd. in Hallett 210).

Another of the paradoxes of "normal communication" is put this way by Wittgenstein in the *Tractatus*: "The meanings of primitive signs [=names, *Urzeichen*] can be explained by means of elucidations. Elucidations are propositions that contain the primitive signs. So they can only be understood if the meanings of those signs are already known" (3263). Tullio de Mauro, calling this a limpid and irrefutable paradox, says that language is clearly a closed circle. Referring to Wittgenstein's suggestion that his book could only be understood by someone who has already thought it out himself, de Mauro says: "The extreme stand he reaches in the *Tractatus* is expressed in these words. Only a mystic communion of souls (that is, a communion non [sic] demonstrable empirically or rationally) guarantees that the meaning of a phrase be understood by someone other than the person uttering it" (*Wittgenstein*, 27). But to say or to claim something like this has a hint of the absurd—it is trying to *say* what must be manifest in a work, what can only be shown. Wittgenstein was therefore careful to negate his propositions, to hope that his (one) true reader would realize they were nonsense and yet use them as a ladder. It might be asked, why write the book at all, since the hoped-for reader has already thought out the contents for himself? There is reason to believe that Wittgenstein, with the great value he placed on silence, would have considered not writing, or at least not publishing, preferable. He was doubtless familiar with Karl Kraus's trenchant and troubling question and answer: "Why does a man write? Because he does not possess enough character not to write" (qtd. in Janik & Toulmin 201).[2] Perhaps Wittgenstein's inscription on the fly-leaf of Moritz Schlick's copy of the *Tractatus* has a similar thrust: "Each of these sentences is an expression of an illness." The philosopher's work shows illness, although it may itself be treatment for the illnesses of others, and for the great illness of misunderstanding the logic of our language. Wittgenstein remarked more than once on the vanity of writing: "An example that shows how monstrously vain wishes are is the wish I have to fill a nice notebook with writing as soon as possible" (*C&V*: 36ᵉ), and he once accused *Kraus himself* to his face of vanity (McGuinness, *Wittgenstein*, 281).

Wittgenstein probably justified his writing and publishing in two ways: with the feeling that his thoughts were not really his own, but were taken from a tradition for refurbishing and commentary, and with an attitude he so admired in a dedication of Bach's: "'To the glory of the most high God, and that my neighbour may be benefited thereby.' That is what I would have liked to say about my work" (Drury, "Conversations," 182). Note, in any case, that the extent of his philosophical publication, some 75 pages in an entire lifetime, is surely the least of any "major" philosopher.

If we think of a joke as a primitive sign, it too can be explained by elucidations. But elucidations contain whatever makes up the point of the joke. Therefore an elucidation is redundant—it can be understood only if the joke is. Hence the embarrassment of "explaining" humor—itself having the effect of unintended humor—or the ridiculousness of a person displaying the "tubelight effect" in understanding a joke. A fool is said to laugh three times—before the punch line, then when everyone else laughs, and again when he actually understands the joke. While we may grant that he *does* understand the joke at the last try, the fool he has made of himself at the first two attempts somewhat vitiates his success. Ordinary, non-mystical "communication" is of this kind. Ordinary traditional or academic philosophers, those Wittgenstein so consistently despised, display similar patterns in practicing their calling. Their responses to the joke or riddle of existence, like the fool's, consist of several stages, often known as their early, middle and late philosophies. A thinker's second phase of writing is often fueled by surprise at being so wrong the first time, and there is a natural temptation to fit Wittgenstein into this common pattern. On first beginning systematic reading in philosophy, however, he expressed "the most naïve surprise that the philosophers he once worshipped in ignorance are after all stupid and dishonest and make disgusting mistakes" (Pinsent's diary, May 1912, qtd. by McGuinness, *Wittgenstein*, 104).

Far better for the fool not to laugh at all, to admit that he has not understood. With no indication that he was deliberately posturing, this indeed seems to have been Wittgenstein's way, the way of the fool whose honesty gives him wisdom. Engelmann records: "When some passage from philosophical literature was quoted or related to him, he would often say with utter seriousness and genuine modesty: I do not understand it" (Engelmann, *Letters*, 107). Explanations in jokes or in philosophy are equally redundant in this "early" Wittgensteinian view—the explanation must be manifest in the narration or description.[3] This aim in philosophical writing, at least, will be recognized in Wittgenstein's later work as a major theme, acting again as a bridge to the earlier: "We must do away with all *explanation*, and description alone must take its place."[4] §109 of the *Investigations* continues: "And this description gets its light, that is to say its purpose—from the philosophical problems. These are... solved...by looking into the workings of our language, and that in such a way as to make us recognize those workings: *in despite of* an urge to misunderstand them." The preface to the *Tractatus* says somewhat more succinctly: "The book deals with the problems of philosophy, and shows, I believe, that the reason why these problems are posed is that the logic of our language is misunderstood." Nothing has changed at the core, but we see how the "chapter heading" style of the *Tractatus* occasionally becomes more explicit ("Broad was quite right when he said of the *Tractatus* that it was highly syncopated. Every sentence in the *Tractatus* should be seen as the heading of a chapter, needing further exposition. My present style is quite different; I am trying to avoid that error." To Drury, 1949, in his "Conversations", 173).

We have linked philosophy as a joke, or philosophy by jokes, to a mystical tradition which enables one to understand texts in that tradition *before reading them*. Wittgenstein sought just such a reader for the *Tractatus*. (Note, by the way, that there is never any way of "checking" or "verifying" someone's claim to be such a reader, because the means of verification would constitute a refutation of the mystical attitude. Such taking of things on faith, as it were, has analogies in Wittgenstein's attitude to the existence of God—it could not be proven: to ask for proof was to immediately show the absence of faith—in contrast to the Roman Catholic Church's dogma, for instance, that the existence of God could be proven by natural reason, which by itself ruled out for him the possibility of being a Catholic; see Drury, "Conversations," 123). The "one reader as addressee" theme was not some conceit or trope of Wittgenstein's; in his comments on the English translation "if there were one person" (for part of the sentence in question), he remarked: "...I real[l]y meant one single [i.e. by the German *Einem*] but it sounds very odd in English and rather clumsy..." (Wittgenstein, *Letters to Ogden*, 49).

A recent argument with "proof" that the *Tractatus* is a joke—from a professional philosopher, Tim McDonough of the University of Illinois at Urbana-Champaign—may be found at *http://www2.uiuc.edu/unit/reec/Wittgenstein*.

There is an old precedent for Wittgenstein's attitude to the reader in his preface, giving another justification for calling this attitude truly mystical. The preface is a kind of user's guide to the book, and to it, as we have seen, he referred prospective readers like Ficker. In the twelfth century, Maimonides wrote a prefatory section to his *Guide for the Perplexed* that is translated as *Instruction with respect to this Treatise*. There the renowned Talmudist and medieval philosopher speaks of "...giving satisfaction to *a single virtuous man* while displeasing ten thousand ignoramuses—I am he who prefers to address *that single man* by himself, and I do not heed the blame of those many creatures. For I claim to liberate *that virtuous one* from that into which he has sunk, and I shall guide him in his perplexity until he becomes perfect and finds rest" (Maimonides, *Guide*, vol. I, pp.16–17, emphasis added).

In Wittgenstein's case, the search for, the stress on the single reader continues well into the "later" phase. After World War II, when the *Philosophical Investigations* was taking the shape it would have at the author's death, he took to reading it sentence by sentence with Norman Malcolm. "The reason I am doing this," he told his first biographer, "is so there will be at least one person who will understand my book when it is published" (Malcolm, *Wittgenstein*, 51). The preface to the *Investigations* speaks of bringing "light into one brain or another." This model of one-to-one transmission of "secret" knowledge or doctrine continuing from the *Tractatus* is typical of several esoteric traditions, found in Buddhism, Judaism, and Hinduism. Indeed, the essence of esotericism, leading to alternative methods of transmission, is deep skepticism about normal "rational" language. Such skepticism is justified, the basis of the entire tradition validated, when there is transmission of the teaching to one single person. The fact that it can be transmitted, if not precisely communicated, is affirmed, while the need for mass communication, typical of exoteric religion, is eschewed in a gesture of self-confidence. The philosophical distinctiveness of the esoteric faith as well as a deep critique of language and communication are made manifest by the process of singulary transmission itself.

The above discussion suggests that the mystical characteristics of the *Tractatus*, especially of its preface, are deep and well thought out, neither an embellishment nor a pose. They are best understood by these words with reference to Maimonides: "Communication expresses objectivity. The esoteric is subjective: it vanishes as soon as it is translated into the realm of the objective and the ordinary" (Faur, *Homo Mysticus*, 33). The negative dialectics flow from this distinction and are not the discovery of a logical investigation. The work is embedded in mysticism, which comes before and after it, both in the sense of the preface and of the conclusion, and in the sense that mysticism was in Wittgenstein's being before and after the writing of the *Tractatus*, including the years when the *Investigations* was composed. We have two works embedded in the same kind of ethico-religious mysticism, rather than one written by a positivist logician, and another, its refutation, by the same man after turning mystic. There are other ways of indicating the self-sufficient nature of each work, whose potency, however, is increased if it is read in tandem with the other. These ways have to do with Wittgenstein's own remarks and attitudes as well as the contents of the books. For instance, there is a certain tentativeness in the author's attitude to the *Tractatus* that belies its reputation as a finished, frozen, crystalline work. When his hesitation and skepticism are not emphasized, the *Tractatus* is seen as a definite statement definitely rejected, creating the impression of a total disjunction, if not worse, between the earlier and the later author. And yet, on having reread the book with his close friend Nicholas (the brother of Mikhail) Bachtin in the 1940's, Wittgenstein noted: "It suddenly seemed to me that I should publish those old thoughts and the new ones together; that the latter could be seen in the right light only by contrast with and against the background of my old way of thinking" (preface to the *Investigations*, x^e). Two points are easily overlooked: the *Tractatus* is internally self-refuting or self-rejecting; it was *written to be rejected*, the preface and the conclusion from all indications having been part of the conception from the very beginning; so the implications of any external rejection by the author must be read carefully—the rejection of a rejection can be an affirmation, and thus a joke on those who the author felt did not understand the book. Second, the doubts and hesitations are part of the mental energy feeding into the work that came later. These were not doubts and suppressed insights about which something could be done—by revising the book, for instance; rather, they were *strategically deployed* as nagging questions in the *Tractatus* and opportunities for clarification in the *Investigations*. Imagine Wittgenstein well in charge of his project, with enough arguments and a pesky question or two in place, concerned about the length of his book—that it be no longer than artistically appropriate—and displaying a detached nonchalance. Such a picture is provided by his correspondence with C.K. Ogden over the translation and publication of the *Tractatus*. Instead of a man who had poured his all into a book, we see someone who has carefully regulated his effort and is planning for the possibility of having to produce another one some day. Wittgenstein's reply after Ogden had apparently written asking for material (supplements or *Ergänzungen*) that might lengthen the book is worth quoting at some length:

I am very sorry indeed I cannot send you the supplements. There can be no thought of printing them. What they contain is this: when I had finished the book *roughly* there remained certain prop[osition]s—about a hundred—about which I was doubtful whether I should take them in or not. These prop[osition]s were—partly—different versions of those now contained in the book; for it had happened that I had written down a proposition] in many different forms, when the same thought had occurred to me in different ways during the long time I worked at that business. Another part of the supplements are merely sketches of prop[osition]s which I thought I might someday take up again if their thoughts should ever revive in me. That means: the supplements are exact<e>ly what must not be printed....As to the shortness of the book I am *awfully sorry for it: but what can I do?*....(Rather than print the Ergänzungen to make the book fatter leave a dozen white sheets for the reader to swear into<o> when he has purchased the book and can<n>t understand it.) (Wittgenstein, *Letters to Ogden*, 46)

This suggests that there was a residue of thought extending to the later work, as has already been argued—both works directed towards a common goal, written eventually in contrasting styles. Wittgenstein may have been saying to himself: "Let me see if this brief, cryptic version works; if not, I can use some of the left over material with a different approach." He had noted a tendency of his as early as 1914: "one often makes a remark and only later sees *how* true it is" (*Notebooks* 10e), returning to the thought some sixteen years later: "...my head often knows nothing about what my hand is writing" (*C&V*: 17e). In a conversation with Drury already quoted we find an attestation to this relationship between the "early" and the "late": "Every sentence in the *Tractatus* should be seen as the heading of a chapter, needing further exposition. *My present style* is quite different. I am trying to avoid that error" (Drury, "Conversations", 173; emphasis added). Wittgenstein thought of himself as using two different styles in his work—the *Tractatus* compressed, other writings, freer, expansive, though not necessarily straightforward. He regarded the *Tractatus* as having erred in terms of style, not substance. The style was not fathomed by his readers; its substance was not wrong, but unapproachable. As he had feared even before publication: "It's galling to have to lug the completed work round in captivity and to see how nonsense has a clear field outside! And it's equally galling to think that no one will understand it even if it does get printed!" (Wittgenstein, 1919, *Letters to Russell*, 70). The parsimonious author of the *Tractatus*, refusing to lengthen it, thought well enough of the old work to want it reprinted with his new book.

What was galling to imagine must have been really galling when it came true. Wittgenstein plays self-consciously with the word *nonsense* in a remark to Ogden in response to a suggestion that the book be called "Philosophic Logic":

"There is no such thing as philosophic logic. (Unless one says that as the whole book is nonsense the title might as well be nonsense too.)" (1922, *Letters to Ogden*, 20). This was cutting very close to the bone, for after all the ideal reader had been invited to understand his propositions as nonsensical. Awareness of the very thin line between "my nonsense" and "the nonsense outside" encouraged the flippant attitude Wittgenstein often took towards his work, complementing the jokes inside it. Of what was to be the *Investigations* he wrote in 1937: "This book is a collection of wisecracks. But the point is they are connected, they form a system. If the task were to draw the shape of an object true to nature, then a wisecrack is like drawing merely (just) one tangent to the real curve; but a thousand wisecracks (lying close to each other, closely drawn) can draw the curve" (ms. 119, qtd. in Hilmy, *Later Wittgenstein*, 22).[5] As we have seen, Malcolm records Wittgenstein as saying that a serious and good philosophical work could be written that would consist entirely of jokes or of questions (*Memoir* 29). In the same spirit he imagined a religion without any doctrines, in which nothing would be said. The suggestion in each case is a subversive one—philosophies made up of jokes or questions, bypassing answers, theories and constructs, mute religions without dogma or commandment, bypassing language. The object of mockery is conventional discourse, with its investment in the "telementation" model of communication. This model relies on the possibility of a stable grammar and semantics, such as was put forward tongue-in-cheek in the *Tractatus*. In the *Investigations*, we are reminded again as a continuation of Tractarian themes: "The problems arising through a misinterpretation of our forms of language have the character of *depth*. They are deep disquietudes....—Let us ask ourselves: why do we feel a grammatical joke to be *deep*?" Without answering, he adds: "And that is what the depth of philosophy is" (§111). This is reminiscent of LaCapra's phrase "a joke coterminous with philosophy itself," also of Wittgenstein's response in the conversation with Broad: couldn't God half exist?—a semantic joke if not a grammatical one. As soon as such a joke leads to the realization that "existence" is only linguistic, a human concept like all others, that God need not be bound to it any more than He is to wearing dark clothing on formal occasions, the irreverence or absurdity of the joke has paid off, the ladder can be kicked away. This is the point of LaCapra's phrase about a coterminous joke. If misleading philosophy comes to an end, is dissolved, so is the joke. The only remaining problem is how to fill the void, to enable the inauguration—not conceptualization—of ethical behavior. Engelmann put it simply: "ethical propositions do not exist; ethical action does exist" (Engelmann, *Letters*, 110).

And that is what Wittgenstein rather ruefully emphasized in the preface to the *Tractatus*: "how little is achieved" when the problems of philosophy are solved. Yet they must be solved before the world can be seen aright.

What of "mistakes" in the *Tractatus*, spoken of by many commentators, and by Wittgenstein himself? In response, it seems appropriate to ask G.E. Moore's famous question "What exactly do you mean?" about any term in philosophical discussion: "What exactly do we mean, 'mistake'?" Wittgenstein's own usage is likely to have been a little wry. The *Tractatus* was certainly not so mistaken as not to have its uses. Wittgenstein told Anscombe about the book no earlier than 1942, when she first became his student, that it was not a bag of junk, but more like a clock that did not tell the right time (Hunnings 235). The remark is typical in continuing the disparaging terminology of over two decades ago ("nonsense"), but also provides an elaborate simile placing the book in the context of its readership and comparing it to an intricate mechanism. From an engineer who knew his physics, "a clock that doesn't tell the right time" is a usefully ambiguous comparison. No clock tells the "right" time, but a clock is useful when constantly checked against other clocks. In this sense the *Tractatus* points away from itself, asking the reader to find other texts that will make it useful. What we need to know about any clock is its rate of gain or loss with respect to other timekeeping devices, not its "rightness". This secret of its usefulness cannot be expressed—"said"—by the clock, or for that matter by a text; it must be worked out by its reader. By being "incorrect" a clock hints at other things about the universe, about our notions of time and motion. This is a function similar to the "nonsense" of the *Tractatus*, of which its author need no more be ashamed than a clock of its "inaccuracy". Each flaw reveals a lesson—about the relativity of time, about intertextuality and the circularity of texts. Evidence, if evidence be needed, that Wittgenstein was fully aware of these implications of talking about inaccurate clocks and so on is in the *Tractatus* itself: "We cannot compare a process with 'the passage of time'—there is no such thing—but only with another process (such as the working of a chronometer). Hence we can describe the lapse of time only by relying on some other process" (63611). The comment made to Anscombe about the *Tractatus* was thus actually developed from a formulation already within the book—an instance of the acute self-consciousness of his methods on Wittgenstein's part.[6]

In another figure about the *Tractatus* in the same—last—decade of his life, already briefly mentioned, Wittgenstein spoke of every sentence in it as "the heading of a chapter, needing further exposition." So it is a limited mechanism that needs other perhaps more special equipment, pulleys and levers, as it were, to make it work. "My present style is quite different," he added to Drury, as we noted above; "I am trying to avoid that error" ("Conversations" 173). The implications are of a *rhetorical or stylistic misjudgment* in the *Tractatus* sought to be corrected by a *rhetorical or stylistic change* in the *Investigations*. However, other misjudgments in this area not present in the earlier might creep into the later work. Hence the idea of publishing the two books together, so that *what he was trying to do in both may emerge despite the stylistic/rhetorical misjudgments in either*. Unlike the mistakes he found in or objections he made to, for instance, the work of Russell or Frege, Wittgenstein's omissions, side-steppings, and stylistic choices were as if by design not crucial to the enterprise. When Russell realized the thrust of Wittgenstein's objections to his work in logic, he wrote to Lady Ottoline Morrell: "I saw he was right and I saw that I could not hope ever again to do fundamental work in philosophy" (referring to events of 1913, in a letter of 1916; see McGuinness, *Wittgenstein*, 176). There is nothing like this in the reverse direction: Wittgenstein completely stymied by Russell's objections.

No argument or piece of evidence can make the *Tractatus* collapse, because it seeks to point beyond the language of evidence and argument. This is not elitism or arrogance, because the idea is never the joy or gloating over understanding a secret doctrine, but *ethical action, in which sphere all are equal*: "And a 'higher' ethics for the select must be rejected, particularly from Wittgenstein's point of view" (Engelmann, *Letters*, 110). Stressing this might highlight the religio-ethical nature of the *Tractatus*, or lead to its rejection by the rational-minded, or (and this was perhaps the most typical reaction) selected "doctrines" it seemed to enshrine may be adopted and misapplied, thus allowing its overall "pointing" or "ladder" function to go by the board. The second possibility is the fate of most religious texts, and at least one commentator has noted the impression of being a sacred text that the *Tractatus* gives: "a work of impressive subtlety and power which presents difficulties of interpretation not less than and indeed very similar to those sometimes presented by a sacred text" (G.J. Warnock, qtd. in Gier, *Wittgenstein and Phenomenology*, 6).

To write, to speak, then, without being clear about the logic of our language in Wittgenstein's sense is to make mistakes. Hence the great valorization of silence. The unenlightened reader, and the enlightened author as reader of his own work, can freely judge a text to harbor mistakes, but the two are not thereby saying the same thing about the text in question.[7] One is referring to some imagined truth or rightness which the text fails to attain, the other is playing a negative dialectics of hinting and pointing. I suggest that Wittgenstein's own view, internal to himself and something he could never say openly, was that the *Tractatus*, by its ending, insured itself against internal mistakes. Alongside this, he had a definite conception of the *use* of the book—it was definitely not user-friendly, but the manufacturer could provide a certain level of technical support. As he told both Russell and Ramsey, the written "chapter headings" could be given detailed oral commentaries. After the writing of his second book, the author's offer of support changes somewhat: take either the *Tractatus* with its ending, or the *Investigations* as it is, and you have the same philosophy. The reader would have to make a similar input, reach the same point on his own, if with a different ladder. Since the *Tractatus* was still a fact when the *Investigations* appeared, there was a complicating intertextuality. This Wittgenstein tried to handle by alluding to it, in a limited way, as "mistakes", with the positive value of raising the interest level of the later work. This is not to deny that there may have been mistakes in some "real" sense as well, only to claim that these have no impact on the message or the philosophy of the *Tractatus*.[8] They are of serious interest only to those whom that philosophy eludes. The others understand Wittgenstein's propositions, mistakes and non-mistakes alike, to be nonsense, and not worth quibbling over; the wonder of the *Tractatus* is that the quibbling done by Wittgenstein himself satisfied, convinced and impressed those who were of opposite mind to his—the positivists of Vienna.

Wittgenstein never directly repeated anywhere else the themes of singular transmission, pre-understanding and silence from the preface to the *Tractatus*. Does it mean they were "mistakes"? More likely by the time of the *Investigations* they were part of the "deep background" of Wittgenstein's life and work that the discerning would not ignore; if indeed his two works were to be published together, as he had hoped, everybody, even the not so discerning, would have all his important formulations in one place. The similarities between the two books would then be part of the author's full impact; stressing the differences has tended to generate a two-headed monster expressing more the capacities of his readers than Wittgenstein's.

Let me give an example of something that may well be considered a "mistake" from the point of view of the later work—the so-called Picture Theory of Meaning. At the beginning of the 'thirties, in lectures transcribed by Alice Ambrose, Wittgenstein said: "I once said that a proposition is a picture of reality. *This might introduce a very useful way of looking at it, but it is nothing else than saying, I want to look at it as a picture*" (Ambrose, ed., *Lectures*,108n., emphasis added). This remark shows clearly the heuristic and hypothetical purpose of the deployment of many, perhaps all, of Wittgenstein's analogies and illustrations. For, as emphasized in the later work, philosophy can in no way interfere with the actual use of language, it leaves everything as it is (*Investigations* §124). Furthermore, this technique is freely deployed in the later book in the continuing battle against the bewitchment of our minds by means of our language, to wrest our minds out of the uncritical linguistic ruts they have lain in. This is why, as he also said in the Ambrose lectures, he was willing to give up any illustration if it drew an objection from a listener. The examples did not matter, were not essential to his message; therefore they could not really be mistakes. At the same time, Wittgenstein could not say this without sabotaging his own method and losing his audience—although he did emphasize that it would be easy to understand what he was saying, the examples, and so on, but not *the point* of his discourse. Since all his sentences were trying to do the same thing, and were not engaged in building different aspects of some elaborate structure whose strength depended on the "correctness" of every example, he would be willing to risk the misunderstanding, misuse or rejection of particular examples to gain the larger prize—the transmission of his overall point.

Ignoring the distinction between the depiction of some possibility—here, a proposition as a picture—and a commitment to that possibility on the author's part has impeded the understanding of Wittgenstein's methods. He told Malcolm "he really thought that in the *Tractatus* he had provided a perfected account of a view that is the *only* alternative to the viewpoint of his later work" (*Memoir* 69), a lucid enough statement, but sometimes read as if suggesting that he had found the earlier *work* wrong. Rather, Wittgenstein is saying that in the Tractatus he had presented a certain view. He had presented it so well ("a perfected account") that it was taken to be the book's view, as a thesis the author was advocating, while of course he detached himself from his particular propositions before taking the reader's leave. The view that the positivists found so congenial was *undermined* in the *Tractatus*. The undermining was continued in the later work. So the account contained in the *Tractatus* is the only possible alternative to the viewpoint of the later work, *and* to a part of the *Tractatus* itself. The "perfected account" includes the Picture Theory of Meaning, which is under attack throughout. "I want to look at it as a picture" suggests an autonomous act of the will directed to making some other point; here the separation between what he is saying (a proposition is a picture of reality), and the point of his saying it (perhaps to get the reader to ask, isn't that an ab-

surd idea?) is naturally crucial. This is why, as Malcolm also records him saying, "he did not think of the central conceptions of his philosophy as *possibly
in error*" (60)—note, not just of his "later" philosophy. The alternative provided in the *Tractatus* was a controlled and deliberate one, for a practical as
well as a stylistic purpose, and not to be seen as a "mistake" later demolished by
the author's own arguments. In the hopes of clarifying all this, "he definitely
wanted the *Tractatus* to be republished jointly with his newer writings" (Malcolm 69). So the "picture theory" was not a mistake, nor was it a theory. Rigged
up to show the ultimate absurdity of such a conceptualization, it was an illustration of how language might be conceptualized. The trouble is it was rigged
up too well, not for Wittgenstein, but for his first readers.

In the Ambrose lectures (1932–1935), Wittgenstein makes a revealing
statement about mistakes as well as about his method: "My method throughout
is to point out mistakes in language. I am going to use the word 'philosophy'
for the activity of pointing out such mistakes" (27). Of significant interest are
two things: that this again is not a "new" method for the "later" phase, but *my
method throughout*; secondly, that since the method consists solely of pointing
out mistakes, it allows for no approving descriptions of language use. There is
nothing to prevent our concluding that in language—certainly in our understanding of the logic of language, where philosophical problems arise—there
are only mistakes. Only silent inward reflection in consequence of this will lead
to *deep* resolution of ethical problems. To the place of such mystical insights in
understanding Wittgenstein we will return in later chapters. Now let me add
two more examples suggesting how the question of "mistakes in the *Tractatus*"
may be viewed.

Take the well-known story, encountered by all students of Wittgenstein in
expository books about him, of the exchange with Piero Sraffa during a train
ride. Sraffa made a Neapolitan gesture, it is said, and asked—sarcastically, one
imagines—what its logical form was. The force of this question is said to have
demolished Wittgenstein's early work and forced him to start afresh, acknowledging his mistakes. Doubts have been cast over this account by Bartley, who
calls it a "legend," and adds: "Wittgenstein is said to have attributed the change
to his realization that he could not 'analyze' a Neapolitan gesture made by
Sraffa. But even if the anecdote is genuine, it explains the change in Wittgenstein's outlook about as much—and as little—as the story about the apple explains Newton's theory of gravitation" (*Wittgenstein*, 1st. ed., 144). There is a
question to himself in the *Notebooks 1914–1916*, placed some fifteen years before the conversation with Sraffa, which clearly shows the deliberate nature of

Wittgenstein's not having done what he was challenged to do: "But why do you never investigate an individual particular sign in order to find out how it is a logical portrayal?" (18ᵉ). This is precisely Sraffa's question, asked by an "interlocutor" (in the mode familiar to us much later in the *Investigations*).[9] Wittgenstein knew the logical view of language he was presenting in the *Tractatus* would not hold up to his own questioning. Its purpose, as I have been suggesting, was to parody the efforts of those who thought such a view possible. To turn philosophy away from this view was the purpose of the *Tractatus*, to show how ethical problems could not be approached until it was abandoned. But the parody was as good as the real thing for those who were set to find a logical, scientific view of language—a story well told in Janik and Toulmin's *Wittgenstein's Vienna*.

Where Bartley speaks of "the change in Wittgenstein's outlook," therefore, it would be vastly clearer to say "the different expression of the outlook." In talking to Sraffa, Wittgenstein had confirmation that an intelligent person might object to the *Tractatus* as he himself would, but without awareness of his overall method. The "read the preface and the conclusion carefully and you'll see through my nonsense" strategy had totally failed. Exchanges with Sraffa and the blinkered behavior of the Vienna Circle (along with other factors) led to *a new rhetorical strategy*, realization that he must pull out new weaponry from his reserve arsenal, including perhaps some of the *Ergänzungen* he refused to give to Ogden, and the thoughts that had come to him as a teacher of children.

Consider next the treatment of science in the *Tractatus*. At the very first mention of natural science, philosophy is cordoned off from it (4111, repeated at 4113). Natural science is separated even from logic (6111). The solution of any problems of natural science is irrelevant to the solution of the riddle of life (64312). And then, on the next page, Wittgenstein seems to give science a critical and praiseworthy role: "The correct method in philosophy would really be the following: to say nothing except what can be said, i.e. propositions of natural science-i.e. something that has nothing to do with philosophy—and then, whenever someone else wanted to say something metaphysical, to demonstrate to him that he had failed to give a meaning to certain signs in his propositions" (653). This way of putting it seems to give approval to natural science for having found with certainty a lasting, non-metaphysical speech. And indeed it was taken this way by the Vienna Circle, as backing for their hyperscientific program. But read on. The very next proposition is the one that undermines all the book's propositions: "My propositions serve as elucidations in the following way: anyone who understands me eventually recognizes them as nonsensical,

when he has used them—as steps—to climb up beyond them....He must tran-
scend these propositions, and then he will see the world aright" (654). The
makings of a highly compressed joke can be discerned in these moves. First,
clear declarations that science has nothing to do with philosophy, and therefore
is of no value to Wittgenstein's enterprise. Then a sudden "setting up" of science—only it can speak—followed immediately by a retraction of all the
propositions in the book as nonsense (suggestive, useful nonsense, of course)
when they are eventually understood. The tension built up between the cor-
doning off of science and its seeming valorization is immediately and deci-
sively resolved in the last paragraph. None of Wittgenstein's references to
science are actually pro-science, and this is consistent with his later views, although Vienna positivists for their own purposes took the early Wittgenstein
to be pro-science. When Hilmy, in his *The Later Wittgenstein*, suggests that the
author of the *Tractatus* was not as anti-science as he later became, he is creating a slight distortion in an otherwise very useful study: "...Wittgenstein came
to view the identification of meaningful discourse with empirical propositions
of natural science, an identification which he himself advocated in the *Tractatus*, as involving an 'overrating of science.' Thus his Tractarian speculations
about the essence of language demonstrated a 'scientific spirit' not only qua alleged 'discoveries' but also in their tendency to result in an 'overrating of science'—a glorification of science as constituting the sole domain of meaningful
discourse" (211–12).

This illustrates the habit of readers of Wittgenstein of stopping to read
where they see something they like, or when they reach an understanding of
what he is saying—not pausing to reflect on the *point* of what he is saying. This
has happened with the *Tractatus* and the *Investigations*. Anyone who sees "a
glorification of science as constituting the sole domain of meaningful discourse" in the *Tractatus* simply hasn't given weight to the concluding remarks
that immediately follow, to the subtle dialectics that run through the preface
and the conclusion.

We have inevitably been led to see what Wittgenstein thought we would
see as a result of the *Tractatus*. Limiting talk to the propositions of natural science does nothing to solve the problems of philosophy, for we would then be
plagued, as debates in the philosophy of science have shown us to be plagued,
with the same kind of riddles about the language of science as about language
"itself." Hilmy makes a fine statement at the conclusion of his book: "It would
seem that the intellectual tendency toward 'a scientific way of thinking,' which
Wittgenstein considered a characteristic of our age, *itself* was viewed by him

as stemming from language, from the misleading expressions of language" (*Later Wittgenstein*, 226).[10] Were our age to become non-scientific (whatever that might mean), Wittgenstein's work would not become irrelevant, for, as the preface to the *Tractatus* has it, misunderstanding the logic of our language is the source of our problems—not science. Certainly, too, speaking only in science, as it were, as 653 seems to recommend, does nothing to illuminate ethics, always Wittgenstein's main interest.

It appears, then, that in addition to the "serious joke coterminous with philosophy itself" that LaCapra sees in the preface, the conclusion of the *Tractatus* too has embedded in it a joke, this time on the linguistic or rhetorical aspect of science, where it is as vulnerable as ordinary language. In this way the interwovenness of science with language, and of ethics with both, is brought home.

It may be well to point out that while Wittgenstein suggested in 1930 that science puts man to sleep (*C&V*: 5ᵉ), and used rather strong expressions such as "our disgusting soapy-water science" in later years (1946, *C&V*: 49ᵉ), his target was not so much science itself as the people who practiced it and its effects on their (and our) outlook. What science would be like were there to be change here is hard to imagine; certainly Wittgenstein was not interested in reforming science, but in the *deeper* job of making clear our misunderstandings of language. David Pears says that Wittgenstein's attitudes to science result in the build-up of a parallelogram of forces of which the later philosophy is the resolution (*Ludwig Wittgenstein*, 186). This image suggesting deliberate design is compatible with the general argument here. We shall see later how Wittgenstein's resistance to science can be seen in a way not before considered. In the meantime, Pears's account, suggesting a greater explicitness in the later book, is the same tendency we have been seeing in several other issues. Some of what the reader was expected to do on reading the first book is done by the author in the second, much as a considerate teacher, on finding some lessons beyond the pupil's capacities, may help with the hardest ones.

Wittgenstein seems to have been prepared for a multi-level encounter, mediated by him, of the *Tractatus* with its readers. His feelings ranged from despair that not a single person would understand the book to the hope that it would be recognized generally as having solved the problems of philosophy, clearing the way for harder problems (of ethics) to be tackled. At one level, he sought the famous "single" or solitary reader who read the book with understanding. His earnest inquiry of Engelmann as to what Karl Kraus thought of it suggests that Kraus was such a prospective reader. Wittgenstein appears to have hoped that there would be more such among the general anonymous readership a work could hope to find. Lastly, he was prepared to personally tutor selected readers who showed serious interest or capacity—Ramsey, Russell and Moore led the list, paralleled by Malcolm and Drury for the later book. Such people would be given the expansion of "chapter headings," the oral commentary on the written text, and so on, which he mentioned in letters and conversations. None of this seems to have turned out as desired. Kraus's reaction has not been recorded; with Russell he early lost hope of an understanding in philosophy, confirmed by Russell's introduction to the *Tractatus*; Moore and Ramsey he felt to be severely limited for his purposes. The complaint of being misunderstood seems to have prevailed for the rest of his life, goading Wittgenstein to write continuously, to refute indirectly those who misconstrued him.

There was never an early Wittgenstein; there was only a Wittgenstein who had found something to say early on, and then tried the rest of his life to say it in different ways, with some regard to the revealed capacities of his immediate audience.

Janik and Toulmin have asked the question, why did Wittgenstein remain silent in the face of the misrepresentation of the *Tractatus*, and they have rightly suggested that to explain this "might well require an exercise in psychobiography that would involve laying bare the whole development of his personality" (201). Without attempting anything so ambitious, we can put forward some possibilities here. No doubt, as Janik and Toulmin also suggest, Wittgenstein would have shared Kraus's hunch that a man writes because he does not possess enough character not to write. In addition, however, we might recall the *Tractatus* unobtrusively noting that "those who have found after a long period of doubt that the sense of life became clear to them have then been unable to say what constituted that sense" (6521). We may take this as a claim, or an admission, that the author had had such an experience, which he nevertheless struggled to communicate, the *Tractatus* being the result. On his return to philosophical activity, he wrote: "If you have a room which you do not want certain people to get into, put a lock on it for which they do not have the key. But *there is no point in talking to them about it*, unless of course you want them to admire the room from outside!" (*C&V*: 7e, 1930; emphasis added). So there was something planned, part almost of Wittgenstein's writerly temperament, that prevented responses to the uncomprehending. Lastly, however, and somewhat in conflict with the last point, Wittgenstein, always plagued by the thought of being comprehended by no one, deployed hints and clues throughout his writings, published and unpublished, including a hint that his manuscripts would be of use to a certain type of person: "(I believe it might interest

a philosopher, one who can think himself, to read my notes. For even if I have
hit the mark only rarely, he would recognize what targets I had been cease-
lessly aiming at)" (*On Certainty* §387, 50ᵉ). These hints, and Wittgenstein's discussion of hints, will have to be taken up later.

This chapter concludes with recapitulating that Wittgenstein was one
philosopher. He became this one philosopher very early, before the writing of
the *Tractatus*. The following exchange with Drury occurred in 1948: "DRURY:
'It is remarkable that Kant's fundamental ideas didn't come to him till he was
middle-aged.' WITTGENSTEIN: 'My fundamental ideas came to me very
early in life'" ("Conversations", 171). Drury repeats this remark in his *The
Danger of Words*, adding: "I can vouch for the accuracy of the words" (ix).[11] So
we are further confirmed in our view that Wittgenstein had only one set of fundamental ideas, which came to him very early in life, and which were therefore
the only ones he developed for the rest of his life. The task then is to clarify
these ideas further, to track their origins as far as possible, and to measure the
consequences of these interpretive activities in our understanding of Wittgenstein. This we shall now attempt to do.

CHAPTER III

The Jewish Man's Burden, or,
Clarification with Courage

What makes a subject hard to understand—if it's something significant and important—is not that before you can understand it you need to be specially trained in abstruse matters, but the contrast between understanding the subject and what most
people want to see. Because of this the very things which are most obvious may become the hardest of all to understand. What has to be overcome is a difficulty having
to do with the will, rather than with the intellect.

—Wittgenstein, *Culture & Value*

What I do think essential is carrying out the work of clarification with COURAGE:
otherwise it becomes just a clever game.

—Wittgenstein, *Culture & Value*

HOW TO READ WEININGER

Whenever genius is discussed, I think of the *schnorer* who became the talk (and mar-
vel) of his profession when he stood up on a busy street in Berlin during Hitler's
reign, with dark glasses, a tin cup, and this sign, which made coins from the *Herren-
volk* drop in a veritable shower:

> I DO NOT ACCEPT
> MONEY FROM JEWS
>
> —Leo Rosten, *Hooray for Yiddish*!

Weininger writes as though, if I recognize what is Jewish in my thought and feeling,
I have a sense of guilt, of something I would overcome if I could. In Wittgenstein
there is nothing of this.

—Rush Rhees, Postscript to *Ludwig Wittgenstein:Personal Recollections*

Earlier we mentioned Kraus's suspicion that the man who writes does not have
enough character, not to write. Knowing this, why did Wittgenstein write?

One answer could lie in demonstrating *how* he wrote, and we hope eventually to do this. For now, let us reflect that although a man may write because he does not possess enough character, not to write, nevertheless he possesses enough character, to write; the writing reveals the content of his character to each critical reader. The writer who is aware that writing at all—as opposed to silence or not writing—reveals an insufficiency of character, may be expected somehow to deflect, defer, disguise any easy recognition of his writing as writing, and among his tools to this end would be hints, allusions, gaps, subterfuges. Another tactic may be simply to deny that he is writing: "I do have enough character, not to write; so if I write, it's not from any lack of character, it's because my writing is not really writing—it's nonsense. (If you can understand *that*, you don't need to read me"). I want to argue that Wittgenstein wrote within some such simple yet cryptic framework, extended by other allusions and subterfuges.

An example, greatly misunderstood, is the use of Weininger and his book *Sex and Character.* Otto Weininger, a lone and obsessive scholar, published his book in his early twenties and committed suicide soon afterwards. He had the posthumous distinctions of his book being translated into numerous European languages, going into several editions, enjoying great influence, and he himself being cited approvingly by Hitler as the only good Jew.[1] Wittgenstein was in the habit of recommending a reading of *Sex and Character* to people close to him, among them Moore, Drury and Anscombe. This has led to asking the question, typically by Monk: "...what could he *possibly* have learnt from it?" (23).

The question is poorly framed. Someone like himself, who sprang from the soil and breathed the antisemitic air of Austria-Hungary, had nothing to learn from Weininger. But with appropriate guidance, the book could be instructive about European philosophy, culture and ethics for the non-Jews, perhaps also for assimilated Jews. Those with intellectual investments in Greek thought, Kant and Schopenhauer, Christianity, the culture of male dominance and European ("Aryan") superiority might recognize themselves and their culture for what they were—*this* was what Wittgenstein thought a reading of the book might encourage. However, to understand his commendation requires preconditions which did not exist and have not existed by and large among Wittgenstein's readers—the assumption that he was reading Weininger not as someone who felt at home in the European belief system, but as a Jew; that as a religio-ethical thinker, rather than a philosopher *in sensu stricto*, he considered it vital for his colleagues and students to understand the legacy of stereotyping and prejudice in their own vaunted culture, much as he wanted each individual to look into himself to detect the nastiest that could be found there. His alienation from Europe and his trust in a scattered cosmopolitan audience he once put explicitly, in terms whose closest parallels are Jewish: "the fact remains that I have no sympathy for the current of European civilization and do not understand its goals, if it has any. So I am really writing for friends who are scattered throughout the corners of the globe" (*C&V*: 6ᵉ; the phrasing is in part reminiscent of Isaiah 11:12: "...And gather together the scattered of Judah/From the four corners of the earth"). Remarks of Sander Gilman's about *Sex and Character* support the understanding that Wittgenstein did not have anything to learn from the book, while he may have thought highly of its pedagogical value for those he lived among: "Weininger's suicide shortly after the publication of his book helped to publicize his ideas, *but they were hardly new ones to his contemporaries. The appeal of Weininger's work was not innovation but summation.*...It reflects the general view of antiSemitic racial science about the special nature of the Jew" (*The Jew's Body* 133, 137; emphasis added). In general, then, the book Wittgenstein was urging people to read was not a collection of sensational new ideas, but a distillation of attitudes from the readers' own culture.[2] For instance, Weininger's proud list of anti-Semites reads like a "Who's Who in Europe"; it includes even Pascal (to whose thought von Wright has compared Wittgenstein's).

The handling of *Geschlecht und Charakter* by Wittgenstein is illuminating in several areas, including his method of reading, his relation to Jews and Judaism, the presumed influence on him of other thinkers, his ability to reveal his thoughts while covering up his route to them, and his use of the kind of subterfuge that risks misleading commentary on the way to eventual clarity. His fundamental ideas, as we have seen (Ch. II, p. 42), had come to him very early in life, and Weininger's book is to be seen not as constituent of his early ideas, but as a means of clarifying them by subtle contrast, of making sure that the seamy side of European culture not escape attention in the dialogue of philosophy. A known and believing Jew would scarcely expect those close to him to think that he agreed with Weininger, but someone in a position of concealment such as I attribute to Wittgenstein would be in danger of being taken for an anti-Semite by constantly recommending Weininger's book. Wittgenstein took that risk to see what the reactions would be, while at the same time clearly detaching himself from Weininger. G.E. Moore wrote him a letter after reading the book. Wittgenstein responded:

> I can quite imagine that you don't admire Weininger very much, what with that beastly translation and the fact that W. must feel very foreign to you. It is true that he is fantastic but he is *great* and fantastic. It isn't necessary or rather not possible to agree with him but the greatness lies in that with which we disagree. It is his enormous mistake which is great. I.e. roughly speaking if you just add a "~" to the whole book it says an important truth. However we better talk about it when I come back. (*Letters to Russell, Keynes and Moore*, 59).

Wittgenstein did not and could not expect a person of Moore's background to read Weininger and appreciate him the way he did himself—"W. must feel very foreign to you." Nevertheless, Weininger was a direct product of the Euro–Christian malaise, and it is a fact of enormous interest that philosophers of ethics did not recognize this.[3] While for Wittgenstein "it isn't...possible to agree with him," millions in Europe had been persuaded. So *Sex and Character* plays the role of a trial balloon in Wittgenstein's attempts to reveal to the English upper middle class his peculiar *Weltanschauung* deriving from the Viennese *Zeitgeist*. Weininger had got everything wrong—and then committed suicide; it has been said, on realizing that he had turned into a monster; and *this* was his moral greatness.[4] Of course, it did not occur to the millions who were persuaded by the book to emulate its author's action or even renounce the book. Rush Rhees records a rather chilling story from the time of the German entry into Prague.[5] To honor the Czechoslovakian Minister Beneš a German refugee newspaper had printed a "liberal" speech by him about individual rights, opposite a page from Hitler"s *Mein Kampf* about the need for ruthlessness. Thinking that they were well done, Rhees showed Wittgenstein the opposed pages. "When he'd read them he paused and then, nodding reflectively: 'At the same time this [pointing to the *Mein Kampf* page] is much more *business-like* than that one" (Rhees, *Ludwig Wittgenstein, Personal Recollections*, 225). Wittgenstein "liked" Weininger the same way he "liked" Hitler. It would appear that in Wittgenstein's system of priorities, texts like Weininger's and his admirer Hitler's deserve our attention more than "liberal" writings. It would be analogous in a way (to Wittgenstein's suggestion that his friends read Weininger) to suggest the reading of *Mein Kampf* by undergraduates today. Such an exercise would test the moral worth of each undergraduate; with some experienced guidance, a great advance in moral education might result. The more "nasty" the source, the more it grows out of the darker realities of our own society, the more effective its reading potentially is, as Wittgenstein noted himself: "I ought to be no more than a mirror, in which *my reader can see his own thinking with all its deformities* so that, helped in this way, he can put it right" (*C&V*: 18^e, emphasis added: cf. also *Tractatus* 5511). Such an attitude is reflected in at least one old Jewish source: "Thought serves man as a mirror: it shows him the ugliness and the beauty within him" (M. Ibn Ezra, *Shirat Yisrael*, 12th century). (Both quotations served as epigraphs for the first chapter).

Among the friends who read Weininger was Maurice Drury. A discussion (with Wittgenstein) touched afterwards on women: "And then with regard to Weininger's theme that women and the female element in men was [*sic*] the source of all evil he exclaimed: 'How wrong he was, My God he was wrong'" (Drury, "Notes," 106). Misogyny is a major component of Weininger's book, and Wittgenstein rejects it head-on, just as the remarks to Moore show he thought "the whole book" had to be negated before it could teach an important truth. It is therefore not persuasive to suggest, as Monk does, that "there is much in Weininger's work that chimes with attitudes we find Wittgenstein expressing time and again....So much so, that there is reason to believe that of all the books he read in adolescence, Weininger's is the one that had had the greatest and most lasting impact on his outlook" (25).[6] One could reasonably hold that the book had an impact on the expression of unpublished thoughts—because he seems to be arguing against it implicitly at various times, as we shall see. But the thought of the *Tractatus* and the *Philosophical Investigations* owes nothing to Weininger.[7] The questions about him indicate the importance of keeping in mind an agricultural—and feminine—metaphor of Wittgenstein's about his originality, with a hint of Jewish reproductiveness for good measure: "I believe that my originality (if that is the right word) is an originality belonging to the soil rather than to the seed. (Perhaps I have no seed of my own.) Sow a seed [the Weininger seed?] in my soil and it will grow differently than it would in any other soil" (*C&V*: 36^e; emphasis added). Much later in life, visiting American friends in the post-war years, Wittgenstein affirmed the same attitude to one of them with reference to Kierkegaard: "[H]e got hints. He did not want another man's thought all chewed. A word or two was sometimes enough" (Bouwsma, *Wittgenstein: Conversations*, 46).

Wittgenstein clearly refuted *Sex and Character* directly to the people who read it on his suggestion. But he was quite taken with the book in his own way, for his own purposes. He seems to have carried on a refutation-dialogue with the dead author and his opinions—opinions which, going by the many translations and sales of his book, were latent in the European intelligentsia, and eventually hailed by the Nazis. For instance: Jews have no genius? (Weininger 317, Gilman 134). "Amongst Jews, 'genius' is found only in the holy man. Even the greatest of Jewish thinkers is no more than talented. (I, for instance)"

(*C&V*: 18ᵉ). These three sentences have interesting implications. First of all, the Jewish world is seen as autonomous, with its own standards for genius and talent. Wittgenstein is creating for the Jew a sphere of autonomous discourse, a discourse generally made impossible for him in Western, Christian civilization. Secondly, since in that world the holy man or prophet, who brings the word of God to Israel, is esteemed above all others, in Jewish terms only he is to be deemed a genius.[8] Accordingly, the greatest of the Jews' other—secular—thinkers are merely talented. While they might count as geniuses in the reckoning of the gentile world, Israel must judge genius by her peculiar standards. In keeping with traditional attitudes affirmed repeatedly by thinkers like Maimonides, a clear contrast is implicit between activity for the life and mission of Israel, and everything else, such as art.[9] Thirdly, the inclusion of the author himself in the ranks of talented *Jewish* thinkers is by itself a complete and spirited rebuttal of Weininger's suggestions. Wittgenstein is saying: yes, Mr. Weininger, the Jews do have genius, but of a kind that you with your platonizing Christian sensibility would not recognize if it stared you in the face. Modesty forbade the declaration of his own genius here, but we shall see that elsewhere Wittgenstein shyly hinted at a prophetic self-image. Lastly, *it is hardly conceivable that before calling himself a Jewish thinker, Wittgenstein would not have acquainted himself with what at least some representative Jewish thinkers had thought.* (Based on allusive indications discussed below, one of them most likely was Maimonides).

As for Weininger's stricture that the impulse to lie is stronger in woman (Gilman 134), consider this: "Often it is only very slightly more disagreeable to tell the truth than to lie; about as difficult as drinking bitter rather than sweet coffee; and yet I still have a strong inclination to lie" (*C&V*: 37ᵉ). Not the only time that Wittgenstein identified himself with the feminine.[10]

And women have no genius? "If at some time there should be great musical compositions and great poetry, and if there were a high proportion of women among the great composers—this would not make me think more highly of women. What I'd admire in any woman would be just what I've found in those women whom I've deeply admired in the course of my life. Something I could not find in a man. Something I'd never expect or look for in a man" (Rhees, "Recollections," 207). The concept of genius is male; why should women be held to it?

Jews a disease in the body of Europe? (Gilman 136). "Within the history of the peoples of Europe *the history of the Jews is not treated as circumstantially as their intervention in European affairs would actually merit,* because within this history they are experienced as a sort of disease and anomaly, and no one wants to put a disease on the same level as normal life....We may say: people can only regard this tumour as a natural part of the body if their whole feeling for the body changes (if the whole national feeling for the body changes). Otherwise the best they can do is *put up with it*" (*C&V*: 20ᵉ; first emphasis added). Obviously, the fault for this state of affairs is being ascribed not to the Jews, *but to those who have decided to experience them as a disease and an anomaly.* As Spengler emphasizes, "[t]he Gothic expression '*corpus christianum*' indicates explicitly in its very terms that the Jewish Consensus does not belong to it" (*Decline*, II: 332; in Spengler's terminology a *consensus* is a "nation without a land," 204). Since Jewish history is conceived in the initial rhetoric of anomaly and disease by non-Jews, that anti-Semitic consequences follow is not surprising. Again, even Spengler saw this quite clearly: "the Jews are a peculiar phenomenon in world-history only so long as we insist on treating them as such" (II: 205). Wittgenstein's point, made in 1931, was not different from internal Jewish understanding, and both were put this way by Gilman sixty years later: "The continuity between the Torah and the Gospels, the Christian demand that the Jews of the Torah prefigure (and thus are replaced by) the Christian experience removes the discourse of the Jews about their own history from their own control" (18). This early religious conflict is reinforced eventually by European *Nationalgefühl*, which Wittgenstein goes on to characterize in the same passage as precisely the force that cannot disregard, as an individual might, the rhetoric of disease, for *not* disregarding such myths is what makes a nation. The whole feeling for the body must change. That is asking a lot of people constituted as nations—but also just what will eventually be necessary. Having disarmingly accepted the opponent's premises, Wittgenstein exposes the complicity of those premises with nationalism, and indeed comes up with the "international-Jewish-cosmopolitan" type of argument much despised by the European right wing. His is not the stance of an anti-Semite, attributed to him by Monk *on the basis of these same remarks* (314–316). Few commentators have emphasized that Wittgenstein was not just offering amateur speculations about Jews. We know for certain that he had undertaken considerable reading in Jewish history and the "intertestamental" period (books by Eduard Meyer, Ernest Renan's *Histoire du Peuple d'Israël*, and of course Spengler's copious treatment of such matters) to all of which he brought his detachment, prescience, and awareness of the weaknesses and excesses of the writers concerned. To such parts of his reading as are unrecorded, too, he would have brought the same qualities.

Wittgenstein's involvement in the anti-semitism issue through Weininger has other interesting aspects. The latter's great notoriety and influence meant that other Jewish writers also had to respond to him. How did they do so? An instructive parallel is suggested by Ritchie Robertson: "...it seems likely that Canetti drew on *Geschlecht und Charakter* in his portrayal of the Jew and of women in *Die Blendung*. This is not to say that *Die Blendung* is merely fictionalized Weininger; but, like Kafka's *Das Schloß* (*The Castle*) *it does seem to derive from Weininger the initial assumptions which it then examines and qualifies*" (92, emphasis added). Canetti created in the novel a character, Fischerle, a Jew, but one very different from himself. Robertson speculates that "Canetti's identity as a Sephardic Jew gave him enough detachment from the Viennese 'Jewish question' to use stereotypes as a means of exploration." Wittgenstein, though hardly a Sephardi, had a different kind of detachment or cover: a record of family achievement, conversion, and assimilation that even the Nazis were unable or unwilling to question. The use of stereotypes to explore or refute would come just as easily to him as to the differently marginalized Canetti.

Another instructive parallel is provided by Otto Rank, of the original Freudian psychoanalytical circle and at one time its secretary. Rank was interested in Weininger's attack, in his thirteenth chapter, on the Jews' "feminine" concern with matchmaking, their failure to comprehend asceticism. In his *Jewish Origins of the Psychoanalytic Movement*, Dennis Klein reports that "[h]aving once accepted Weininger's polemic as an expression of his own contempt, Rank reversed Weininger's tone in his Jewish essay. He believed that instead of being destructive, sexuality and matchmaking were the foundations of an elevated state of existence, one undisturbed by repression or asceticism. Rank regarded matchmaking as a positive expression of naturalness" (173–4n.6). Recall Wittgenstein's rebuttal to Drury of Weininger's misogyny: "How wrong he was, my God he was wrong" (Drury, "Conversations," 106). Drury once related to Wittgenstein how on a visit to the temples of Luxor in Egypt he saw "on the wall a bas-relief of the god Horus with an erect phallus in the act of ejaculation and collecting the semen in a bowl!" Wittgenstein's response: "Why in the world shouldn't they have regarded with awe and reverence that act by which the human race is perpetuated. Not every religion has to have St. Augustine's attitude to sex. Why even in our culture marriages are celebrated in a church, everyone present knows what is going to happen that night, but that doesn't prevent it being a religious ceremony" (Drury, "Conversations," 162). This attitude of Wittgenstein's, if it cannot be called Jewish, is certainly antithetical to Weininger's asceticism, his hatred of marriage and matchmakers, and cold disinterest in the perpetuation of the human race.[11]

If more evidence is sought for responses to Weininger analogous to those of Wittgenstein, Canetti and Rank, it can be found also in the case of a non-Jew, von Ficker, whom Wittgenstein once turned to as a prospective publisher of the *Tractatus*. According to Allan Janik, "...Scheichl asserts that the kind of animosity towards the Jews which is represented in Weininger's work actually helped Ludwig von Ficker to affirm brotherhood with Jews in 1937 when the vast majority of people who thought about the issue were doing just the opposite" (*Essays on Wittgenstein and Weininger*, 144). If Janik's source is right in his assertion, then von Ficker is a shining example of Weininger backfiring in the way Wittgenstein hoped he would with all those to whom he recommended *Sex and Character*.

Before leaving the discussion of Weininger and the remarks about Jews published in *Culture and Value*, it would be helpful to take all of them into account and follow their implications in Wittgenstein's intellectual selfperception. At the outset we might distinguish between *Wittgenstein's personal conception of Jewishness*, as it were, and *Judaism's*; we are trying to describe the former, and to see to what degree it coincides with the latter. Wittgenstein's conception can be seen in his "extraneous" remarks, as well as in his "core" philosophical work; hopefully there are no conflicts between the two regions; after—or as—his view is worked out, it can be compared with the traditional conception or conceptions expounded by ancient and modern authorities.

A remark from 1930 contains these two sentences: "What Renan calls the 'bon sens précoce' of the semitic races (an idea which had occurred to me too a long time ago) is their *unpoetic* mentality, which heads straight for what is concrete. This is characteristic of my philosophy" (*C&V*: 6ᵉ). If these remarks are characteristically syncopated, we must try to reconstitute what was left out. A long time before this, Wittgenstein is telling us, independently of Renan and perhaps of any other secondary source, he had reflected generally on precocious semitic good sense. He was forty-one at the time of writing, so this takes us back some ten or fifteen years to the period 1915–20. By some time before or during the composition of the *Tractatus*, then, Wittgenstein was acquainted with a semitic source important enough for him to be confirmed in at least one characteristic of his thought. He could only have reflected on the basis of some text or texts, and since the passage treats both philosophy and religion, the source must have pertained to these areas. At a time when he was supposedly formulating a new way of thinking, the phrase "characteristic of my philosophy" refers unambiguously to the *whole* of his philosophy, without any suggestion of there being more than one philosophy—this is significant for the argument in the last chapter that one philosophy is all there ever was. Finally, Wittgenstein, not with pride but with a sense perhaps of workmanlike satisfaction, attests that the un-poetic semitic good sense of the concrete is characteristic of *his whole philosophy*. These conclusions are not relatable to anything in *Sex and Character*; they are antithetical to the negative and virulent spirit of that book. My argument about Wittgenstein's treatment of Weininger is closely parallel to one made by Edward Timms for Karl Kraus, whom Wittgenstein felt such affinity for and whose *Die Fackel* he constantly read: "His aim was to turn the tables on the anti-Semites by deconstructing their own rhetoric" (197).

INTRODUCTION TO CONCEALMENT

> "A favorite strategy of the *converso* (and of those writing under the specter of perse-cution) is to produce a polysemic text, where different meanings interlace, disguising one another, thus creating diversionary movements and the possibility of multiple interpretations."
> —José Faur, *In the Shadow of History*

> "...J.F.M. Hunter has...contend[ed] that Wittgenstein 'contrived his most forthright statements in such a way as to conceal the point he wished to make.'"
> —S. Stephen Hilmy, *The Later Wittgenstein*

> "...it would seem that there exists a tradition in Jewish thought, forged in the crucible of persecution, to write in such a way that what is being expressed is veiled."
> —David Bakan, *Sigmund Freud and the Jewish Mystical Tradition*

> "I know I did say to him: 'I am Jewish, and I have often missed the chance to come out with it in time to stop others from revealing their profound dislike for Jews in gen-eral. Anyhow, the English are shrewd. I assume they know about me, they probably know about you....' I was moved to see that he looked up hopefully."
> —Fania Pascal, "Wittgenstein: A Personal Memoir"

A remark of Wittgenstein's made in 1931 reads: "The Jew is a desert region, but underneath its thin layer of rock lies the molten lava of spirit and intellect" (*C&V*: 13ᵉ). Here the Jew is first of all identified with the biblical desert, in the traditional manner with the biblical *tout court*, thus refuting a tendency in anti-Semitic usage to distinguish the modern, fallen and decadent Jew of Europe from the stout "Hebrews" of the Bible. The image of something life-affirming hidden behind thin rock is surely not accidentally reminiscent of Moses himself. The Jew is conceived in Mosaic terms. Nevertheless, the Jew is not directly cognizable; there is that opaque layer of rock, however thin, with the dry exterior on one side and the inward, flowing intelligence on the other. Some act of involvement or participation must occur before the interior can be "accessed." Suggestions of secrecy, concealment, masking already inhere in this conception. It is instructive to compare what one might consider Wittgenstein's occasional and "amateur" remarks with those—in a totally different context—of a scholar and rabbi, Abraham Joshua Heschel:

> Usually *the Jew of the past shied away from disclosing his personal religious concern and experience, and as a result his reticence has been mistaken frequently for spiritual apathy.* The truth is that the soul was never silent....*Beneath the calm surface of creed and law the souls were astir.* Our task, then is to go beneath the tranquility of creed and tradition in order to overhear the echoes of wrestling and to recapture living insights. (*God in Search of Man: A Philosophy of Judaism*, 30–31, emphasis added.)

Wittgenstein's single figurative sentence accords well with the historically informed description of Heschel, a descendant of several generations of Eastern European rabbis and *tzaddikim*. Both are speaking of the same Jew, conceived in congruent terms—reticent about religion to the point of concealment, yet astir with concern and spirit. This is the natural context in which to read Wittgenstein's phrase "*die Heimlichkeit und Verstecktheit der Juden*," rendered rather frighteningly in English as "the Jews' secretive and cunning nature."[12] "The secrecy and hiddenness of the Jews" would be a more defensible translation and have the advantage of Wittgenstein's German in not attributing a "nature" to the Jews. The point anyhow is that Wittgenstein is not talking about Jews concealing themselves in gentile society to subvert it and spread contagion—as Monk extrapolates—but, in the manner of Heschel, of their tendency to remain inward. While not caused by persecution, the tendency has helped them to survive persecution and not become extinct. Not being—unlike Christianity or Islam—a proselytizing religion committed to propagating itself among non-adherents, Judaism has no cause to explain itself to the outside world. This alone can lead to the charge of secrecy. Wittgenstein adds that he does not mean to commend the capacity for secretiveness. The simple converse of this observation is that had the Jew not been characterized by inwardness in his religious life, his chances of surviving persecution would have been greatly reduced. Rousseau, whose character Wittgenstein suggested "has something Jewish about it," spoke in a Jewish mode for many writers when he wrote in his *Confessions*: "I would love society like others, were I not sure of showing myself not only at a disadvantage, but as completely different from what I am. The part that I have taken of writing *and hiding myself* is precisely the one that suits me" (see Derrida's *Grammatology*, 142).

Any remaining suspicion that Wittgenstein was from beginning to end naïvely under Weininger's sway, accepting of racial and national stereotypes and generalizations—a possibility that runs completely counter to his linguistic investigations, stressing as they do the bewitchment of our minds by means of our language—can be dispelled by another source. In strongly opposing the attribution of a certain "national character" to the British by Norman Malcolm, Wittgenstein wrote to him: "...you made a remark about 'national character' *that shocked me by its primitiveness*. I then thought: what is the use of studying philosophy...*if it does not make you more conscientious than any journalist in the use of the* dangerous *phrases such people use for their own ends*" (Malcolm 39, emphasis added). The plain claim here is that it is precisely by studying (his) philosophy that one gains insight into the dangerous use of phrases; that his philosophy is a means of combatting primitive ideas about "national character." If it be countered that Wittgenstein's ideas about national character applied only to Europeans, that he may well have been a racist in other contexts, here is another example provided by Drury. He, Skinner and Wittgenstein were caught for days in a rainy spell in Ireland, during which they tried to divert themselves by reading aloud from Prescott's *History of the Conquest of Mexico*. "During the reading he would from time to time stop me and exclaim at Prescott's condescending attitude towards those whom he referred to as 'the aborigines of the American continent.' Wittgenstein found this superior attitude very offensive, pointing out that at the time Prescott was writing, slavery in the Southern States was still legally enforced" (142). Inconceivable therefore to the point of ridiculousness that the manifest danger of Weininger's notions completely eluded Wittgenstein. Anyone who claims he accepted them must also see Wittgenstein as a believer in the widely prevalent "racial thinking" of the time—in the "Aryan vs. Jew" context and everywhere else. This is clearly not the case. So the argument here is that Wittgenstein played ironically with Weininger's distillation of anti-semitic rhetoric, and, like Canetti and Rank, used it for his own purposes of clarification, although almost certainly none of the three knew what the others were doing. Thus each provides some independent validation of the reading or use of Weininger by the others. To look for the *use* made of Weininger, and not for any automatic or given meaning residing in his text, is very helpful in clarifying Wittgenstein's remarks.

SOME VERSIONS OF YIDDISHKEIT

In reading these thoughts of Wittgenstein's involving Jews, a point to note is that he is not discussing or describing the Jews in general as an anti- or even philo-Semite might (!). Rather, the observations are tightly linked to religion, to his work and to his person, as if he were asking himself: how am I and my writing linked to the Jews and religion? What answers—not necessarily truths or generalizations—will help me "get clear" about these links? *This is why the remarks are so tightly concentrated within a couple of years*, 1929–31, with apparently nothing after that period—not because, as has been suggested, he was ashamed or confused about what he had written.

We have seen that Jewish standards of genius admit only the holy man; he (Wittgenstein) is merely talented. The peculiar Jewish service is not to create or invent, "rather to make a drawing of the flower or blade of grass that has grown in the soil of another's mind and to put it in a comprehensive picture" (*C&V*: 19^e). In a passage that could serve as a model of clarity, it is suggested that this is not a fault as long as what is being accomplished is quite clear. Only when this is not the case is there any danger, "when the nature of a Jewish work is confused with that of a non-Jewish work," something that the author of a Jewish work may himself allow to happen. The *coup de grâce* comes in the last sentence: "It is typical for a Jewish mind to understand someone else's work better than he understands it himself." These remarks are not Weiningerian. They are not negative. They do not denigrate the Jewish to the glory of the Aryan. They show, rather, something unexpectedly different—from an apparent outsider a description of the nature of Jewish intellectuality that accords with descriptions of the "inside" view; Wittgenstein gives a "syncopated" account—fully in keeping with traditional or scholarly ones—of Jewish intellectual work in relation to non-Jewish. The reason why this has not been noticed before may well be that readers of predominantly secular humanist orientation have not made the appropriate historical connections, being unaccustomed to investigating religious implications except vaguely under the rubric of the "*Judaeo-Christian tradition*" [on this see Cuddihy, 173 and end of text], while Judaic matters are often best studied separately.[13] Instead of situating Wittgenstein within the circles of influence generated by Schopenhauer, Weininger and Spengler, then, it may be useful to explore some features of Judaic tradition in their discreteness from any other, including the Christian.

The peculiarities of Jewish tradition, the life of the people of Israel, have been conditioned from their beginnings by separateness, revelation, covenant, scripture, and commentary. These and other motifs in Jewish existence give a cast to intellectual life very different from the Graeco-Christian background of non-Jewish Europe and the West. For the present approach to Wittgenstein's remarks, it would be best to consider four items other than revelation and the covenant, as they apply directly to contemporary intellectual life—Jewish separateness, the book, writing, and commentary.

Since its inception, as a condition of the covenant at Sinai, Israel is enjoined to be separate from "the nations." The Hebrew word for this apartness is *kadosh*, or "holy." *Goy kadosh*, a holy people, is *a people apart*. The Jew cannot forget to be apart without also forgetting to be holy. The separateness in principle is made necessary in practice by the existence of multiple directives, laws or commandments (*mitzvot*, sg. *mitzvah*), generally reckoned as 613 in number—pertaining to diet, clothing, hygiene, prayer, sex, marriage and other aspects of life—that inhibit contact with non-observant people. The concept of *mitzvot* has been described in this way: "The moralists saw each *mitzvah* as incorporating a particular teaching of *musar* or ethics, the theologians saw them as the path of discipline leading man away from this-worldliness towards spiritual perfection. Performing *mitzvot* was *imitatio dei, it was the distinctive task of the Jew marking him off from the gentile*, it sanctified him as a member of 'a kingdom of priests and a holy nation'" (Unterman, *Jews: Their Religious Beliefs and Practices*, 30, last emphasis added).

The Jew behaves differently, eats different food, has a different understanding with God, reads a different book; far from implying the superiority typical of nationalist myths, these differences are tied to readiness, in humility, to serve God as teacher, guide or "light unto the nations", claims more likely to draw persecution than anything else. The Hebrews' attitude as "people of the Book" to creative or "original" writing, to Euro-Christian thinking, is also very different—limiting and involved, if also *précoce*. José Faur, a rabbi and literary scholar, describes the traditional posture: "...'writing' and the 'people of the Book' are mutually exclusive....The Hebrews became the 'people of the Book' by accepting the full implications of the Book: *they abstained from writing books*. Or, to put it differently: their book is the Book because they abstained from writing books. Rather than play 'the insane game of writing,' they heeded the advice of King Solomon...'of making many books there is no end'" (*Golden Doves*, 16; emphasis added). The Jewish author's Jewishness, his acknowledgement of the book that is his patrimony, preclude him from seeing anything that he writes as anything but a response, however distant or indirect, to that one book. "The Jewish mind," consequently, is a mind that focuses all its powers on commentary, clarification, and analysis of biblical texts—or those "created" by others—at any level from the literal to the mystical and esoteric.[14] Other than in this sense, the concept of art, artistic *creation* in literature or other media, is entirely absent.[15] Faur describes the extraordinary role of commentary and interpretation in the lives of the people of the Book: "The entire basis of the rabbinic movement, and the subsequent survival of Judaism as we know it, rests on *interpretation*. Without interpretation, the entire edifice of Judaism would have vanished into naught: the political, juridical, and religious institutions, the justification for their own peculiar history and destiny, the hopes for the future, the system of values, etc., are the effect of interpretation" (*Golden Doves*, 60).

By noting that the romantic-gentile concept of genius can be located amongst Jews only in the holy man, Wittgenstein in the passage on geniuses and holy men is affirming the traditional Jewish direction of the intellect towards the holy, conceived of as the Bible. Anything else, forms of art or independent thinking not linked to the holy, for instance, can aspire only to be seen as talent. To the extent that greatness and genius are equivalent, the standards of admission are very strict. Prominent moderns are rejected: "The less a person knows and understands himself, the less great he is, no matter how great his talent may be. Hence our scientists are not great. Hence Freud, Spengler, Kraus, Einstein are not great" (Man. 130, qtd. by Hallett, *Companion*, 765). The third sentence of the "genius" passage, including himself "for instance" in the class of talented Jewish thinkers who are not geniuses, is a compromise between the wish to identify openly as a Jewish thinker and the immodesty of declaring himself a genius in the Jewish religious sense. Being a thinker (or philosopher) at all seems to preclude the Jew from entering the ranks of Jewish genius.

Having established his self-identification or classification, Wittgenstein's next sentence exhibits the technique of refuting by acceptance and "clarification"; while appearing self-deprecatory, it actually affirms his Jewishness even if seen in gentile terms as a tendency to reproduce: "There is some truth, I think, in my idea that I am only reproductive in my thinking. I don't believe I have ever *invented* a line of thinking." Freud reproduced Breuer's germ of psychoanalysis: is that an example of Jewish reproductiveness? he asks, and then immediately mentions *his own* inventions as limited to similes. The only work of "art" he produced—a sculpted head of a woman—was a clarification of someone else's. And what is essential in such activity? "...carrying out the work of clarification with COURAGE: otherwise it becomes just a clever game." In fact, Wittgenstein's idea of originality was courage (*C&V*: 36ᵉ).

THE MEANING OF A JEWISH MIND IS ITS USE

I have been using *reproduction, commentary, clarification, interpretation*—to which *repetition* can be added—in overlapping, perhaps interchangeable, senses. This is occasionally true of Wittgenstein also: consider *clarification* and *reproduction* here. In rabbinic thought, reproduction or repetition can never be identical with the original: "...repetition involves encoding the original event. Thus the original is always changed: the encoded message is not identical with the original" (Faur, *Golden Doves*, 52). This is important in understanding Wittgenstein's posture. Since for him reproduction is an intervention, changing the original, it is writing without writing. Thus we provide Wittgenstein another option in answering the Krausian charge that if he had enough character, he wouldn't write. The first was to say: "...my writing is not really writing—it's nonsense"; now he can say: "It's not really writing at all—it is *reproduction!*" This connects up in what seems an illuminating way with an understanding of the role and meaning of silence in Wittgenstein. Drawing again on Faur's exposition: "silence is realized first by *repeating* the words of others (the Mishna), and second by studying (that is, commenting upon) the commentaries of others (Talmud). Accordingly, *silence* may be defined as speech on a speech (effected either by repetition or by comment)" (116–17, 145). The frequently noticed pointing function of Wittgenstein's writings, a function which has nevertheless remained puzzling because of the difficulty in deciding what he was pointing to, may also be understood as silence in this sense—a writing silently drawing attention to an age-old tradition, but itself lacking in content. Remarks written in 1941 tend to confirm this reading: "You must say something new and yet it must all be old. In fact you must confine yourself to saying old things—and *all the same* it must be something new!" (*C&V*: 40ᵉ).

To write in *this* reproductive manner, reminiscent of ancient rabbinic scholarship, is what defines a Jewish thinker, a Jewish mind, phrases Wittgenstein deploys with a confidence that belies the possibility of their being produced by shallow prejudices or borrowed unreflectively from the vulgar pool. What is called *the Jewish mind* by him "rightly or wrongly" forms itself in freedom, through a process of being educated in a holy tradition. The individual who develops a Jewish mind is perfectly free—especially after Spinoza's championing of the secular life for Jews—to "change his mind," as it were: "Freedom as an absolute category...is a basic biblical doctrine (Deut. 30: 15, 19), particularly essential to Judaism, that teaches the absolute responsibility of man.... Man's freedom is perfect. He is free even when facing God" (Faur, *Doves*, 67; see further the examples from Scripture there, as well as Wittgenstein's high admiration for a passage from the Renaissance scholar and Kabbalist Pico della Mirandola describing and extolling human freedom: "Oh the unlimited generosity of God the Father, Oh the boundless good fortune of man: to whom it has been granted that he may have what he chooses and be what he desires," Drury, "Notes," 111n.).

About the mind Wittgenstein speaks of there is nothing racial or genetically determined. After all, a Jewish thinker with a Jewish mind, seeing himself as an original creator in the gentile sense, may easily fall into confusion about the nature of his Jewish work (*C&V*: 19ᵉ). On the other hand, recall that Wittgenstein was prompt to rebut in writing and with some heat the ethnic stereotyping of non-Jewish nations such as a naive young Malcolm once strayed into (Malcolm, *Memoir*, 32). Of course an interesting question would be: did Wittgenstein have anything more direct to say about anti-Semitic prejudices in Europe, or about Nazi propaganda? Nothing seems to exist on record, and there is a possibility that, finding it all so shameful, he never mentioned Nazi anti-Semitism. The remarks we are discussing were personal and remained unpublished for a quarter century after his death.[16] However—although to ask the question, was the young Wittgenstein well aware of antisemitism? is somewhat like asking if a black child in Chicago is aware of racial prejudice—we do have an account, related later in life to his friend Arvid Sjögren, of an early experience of prejudice in Vienna by the boy Ludwig.[17] His elder brother Paul and he were trying to select a "health club" or gymnasium to join. These establishments, then and later, were "extremely nationalistic and Aryan origin was usually required." The one they would have liked to join certainly was; "Ludwig thought they should simply pretend to it; Paul, older and more realistic, saw that they would never get away with it" (McGuinness, *Wittgenstein*, 49).

By his pre-adolescent years, then, Wittgenstein had encountered the need, if not the necessity, of having to pass for a gentile. His later remarks about Jews display certainly an ambiguity at first reading, especially for the post-war gentile reader who hardly feels comfortable with phrases like *Jewish thinker*, *Jewish mind* and *Jewish reproductiveness*. Contextualizing them in a traditional perspective removes the ambiguity and shows how Wittgenstein, while using the language of the outside world—even the language of hostile elements in that world—drew a traditional picture. (It is worth mentioning in this connection that Wittgenstein suffered through another common experience of European Jews: prejudice on account of language and nationality. The distinguished philosopher Alfred North Whitehead, for instance, cut himself off from Wittgenstein at one point because he "was Teutonic, spoke German, etc." (Bouwsma, *Wittgenstein*, 49).

Wittgenstein goes on to depict the Jewish mind with an analogy. He says one might think of it, rightly or wrongly, as not having the power to produce even the tiniest flower or blade of grass. There is a catch here right away, for what mind has such power? In any case, the Jew with a Jewish mind, not concerned with creation/production, makes a drawing ("reproduction") of the speck of vegetation that has grown in the soil of another's mind. *He then locates it in a comprehensive picture*, says Wittgenstein.[18] More catches! "Comprehensive" is a big word; in a comprehensive picture a tiny blade of grass may not be very significant among other reproductions the Jewish "artist" has chosen. The "Jewish" approach, when taken by anyone, puts the reproductive artist in control, purely by *the clarifying or explicatory nature of commentary*, and avoids the hubris of a claim to creativity. No wonder that the application of such methods may result in the understanding, as Wittgenstein says is typical of the Jewish mind, of someone else's work better than the author himself. The experienced reader exerts interpretive control over the creative work. In the *Philosophical Investigations*, interpretation is linked not to "mere" reproduction but to creative and ethical action: "To interpret is to think, to do something" (p.212d). Commentaries on or interpretations of the Hebrew Bible traditionally have created more meaning than the text itself, which has only consonants, and in that sense is unreadable. Plentiful evidence exists of Wittgenstein's thinking on interpretation. No less than as if it were in a consonantal text, "[a]ny sentence still stands in need of an interpretation," and that is to say, "no sentence can be understood without a rider" (*Zettel* #229). In the *Blue Book*, "originality" and interpretation are put on a par by this reasoning: "Whenever we interpret a symbol in one way or another, the interpretation is a new symbol added to the old one" (33). The thinking applied to a specific text led to the following opinion on Albert Schweitzer's *The Quest for the Historical Jesus*, for instance: "it shews how many, many different ways people can interpret the Gospel story" (Drury, *Conversations*, 121). To bring this point to a focus, one can hardly do better than reproduce a formulation of Moshe Idel's: "The Kabbalistic reading is an act of cooperation with God, or a co-creation of the Torah."[19] If reading is cooperating with God, who needs to write? It would be an insane game indeed. If reading is co-creation of the Torah, who needs originality or creativeness?

In considering creation vs. reproduction, Wittgenstein touches also upon the question of pride vs. humility: a Jewish author who falls into confusion about the nature of his work may look as proud "as though he had produced the milk himself" (a reference to a line from a poem by Wilhelm Busch). One of his memorable similes about philosophy suggests that its greatest achievements are like our rearrangements on a shelf of a disordered pile of books; "(t]he onlooker who doesn't know the difficulty of the task might well think in such a case that nothing at all had been achieved" (*Blue Book*, 44–45). Here too the juxtaposition of works by other people is at the heart of this "Jewish" method. We know that in his writing there are many pictures of the creations of others, for instance the theories of Augustine, Frege, Russell, Moore, Weininger. His remarks on Jewish intellect, therefore, are quite likely not the stray Sunday observations of a self-hating Jew or anti-Semitic diarist; they are better seen as the well-considered clues deployed by an authentic Jewish writer about the tradition that provides the illumination to match his work.

Between these remarks and all of Wittgenstein's writing another important relationship likely exists. The end of the *Tractatus* introduces, as we have seen, a well-known proposition about philosophy:

> The correct method in philosophy would really be the following: to say nothing except what can be said, i.e. propositions of natural science—i.e. something that has nothing to do with philosophy—and then, whenever someone else wanted to say something metaphysical, to demonstrate to him that he had failed to give a meaning to certain signs in his propositions. Although it would not be satisfying to the other person—he would not have the feeling that we were teaching him philosophy—this method would be the only strictly correct one. (653)

The core idea here is: to do philosophy by not writing or saying anything that has to do with philosophy.[20] This is a voluntary restraint, something learnt, perhaps, by experience of other ways of doing philosophy, or from the *bon sens précoce* of tradition. One makes a contribution to philosophy by seizing on the works of others with enthusiasm for the task of clarification. And one of the great difficulties—psychological, if not intellectual—of this *modus operandi* is that the "other" person, who is disposed to "acquire knowledge" or to learn to be a creative philosopher, feels frustrated in several ways and may turn on his teacher and his reticent method by means of several stereotypical accusations. To avoid this it may be necessary to construct a temporary edifice and have the reader bring it down, or to post a warning like this one at the end of one's book: "My propositions serve as elucidations in the following way: anyone who understands me eventually recognizes them as nonsensical, when he has used them—as steps—to climb up beyond them."

NOTES AND THE *TRACTATUS*

The temporary edifice of the *Tractatus*, the ladder to be kicked away when higher regions have been reached, are not unlike the thin layer of desert rock that must be broken to release the riches of intellect and spirit when its deceptive thinness has been gauged. To these images of illusion and concealment still more can be added from the remarks published in *Culture and Value*. The characters in Karl Kraus's writings are suggestive of stylized human types that could be put on stage in masks. Such masked theatre is, anyhow, the manifestation of an intellectualistic character: "[a]nd for the same reason perhaps it is a theatrical form that will attract only Jews" (*C&V*: 12^e). The Jewishness of Karl Kraus's writing is recognized; abstract character types in masks connect Kraus with Jews and intellectualistic theatre, again a connection with no hint of discredit to anyone. Wittgenstein held Kraus quite high in esteem generally and found in his writing weaknesses common to his own. Paul Engelmann was convinced "that the way of thinking [Wittgenstein] found in Kraus's writings exercised a decisive and lasting influence on the objectives of his philosophical activity" (*Letters*, 123). Although he once accused Kraus of "insufferable vanity," in the tone of this inquiry to Engelmann high regard is apparent: "But I would dearly like to know what Kraus said about it. If there were an opportunity for you to find out, I should be very glad. Perhaps Loos knows something....Do write to me" (*Letters*, 15; emphasis added). The "it" is the still unpublished *Tractatus*, freshly declined by Jahoda, publisher of Kraus's one-man journal *Die Fackel*, of which Wittgenstein was a constant reader. McGuinness says simply that Wittgenstein saw the *Tractatus* as "a contribution to the aims of *Die Fackel*" (266). In their book on the "Viennese" background of Wittgenstein's work, without any Jewish considerations in mind, Toulmin and Janik wrote: "If the world-view of the *Tractatus* is *au fond* the world-view of Kraus, Wittgenstein's conception of philosophy is also Krausian" (199). And to exemplify this congruence they quote *Tractatus* 653, which appears above. There is in fact rather extensive scholarship on Kraus's relation to Judaism, confirming Wittgenstein's reading of Kraus. It includes *Karl Kraus ʒum 50. Geburtstag*, a contemporary essay by Berthold Viertel (published in Vienna in 1924), and later work published by Gerhard Scholem and Susan Handelman. Anti-semitism and self-hatred are hard to reconcile with Wittgenstein's seeing Jewish qualities common to him and the esteemed Karl Kraus. Wittgenstein speaks freely of hiding and concealing in his own work—putting a mask on his face as a writer, as it were, although his simile is different. Telling people what they don't understand is pointless, he says, even if you tell them that they won't be able to understand, which often happens with a loved one. This is a continuation of the thought that you can only tell someone what he or she *already* understands (discussed in the last chapter, 40–41). People have to be kept out of a room containing something they won't understand by putting a lock on the door for which they do not have the key (*C&V*: 7ᵉ). *Recogniʒing the failure of understanding immediately results in a search for the key* by those who really want to know the significance of the room's contents; others may not even see *the lock*: "The honorable thing to do is to put a lock on the door which will be noticed only by those who can open it, not by the rest" (*C&V*: 8ᵉ). Seven years later he notes laconically: "When something is well hidden it is hard to find" (*C&V*: 29ᵉ; 1937). Earlier he has bewailed, with an almost audible groan, the "great temptation to try to make the spirit explicit" (*C&V*: 8ᵉ, 1930). Perhaps there is some hint here of *apophatic knowledge*, described by one authority as "superior to common rationality and inferior to prophecy", and the master key to Maimonides (Faur, *Homo Mysticus*, 20; Maimonides used the lock-and-key metaphor himself in speaking of "a key permitting one to enter places the gates to which were locked"' *Guide of the Perplexed* I, 12a, Vol. I, p.20—one of several clues suggesting that Wittgenstein had in fact read this work).[21] Another nine years into his life and four years before his death, in 1946, a reprise: "Yes, a key can lie for ever in the place where the locksmith left it and never be used to open the lock the master forged it for" (*C&V*: 54ᵉ). In any case, from the talk of locked rooms and keys and pre-understanding, of the book automatically separating "those who understand it from those who do not" (*C&V*: 7ᵉ), Wittgenstein's readership cannot but subject itself to a triage: those few (perhaps only one person), who have thought its thoughts before and have read with pleasure; those who notice the locks on certain chambers and can also find the key to open them; and those who fail to notice the locks, not being equipped to negotiate the text at all. Practically all his life, and certainly with regard to the *Tractatus*, Wittgenstein was adamant that no one had understood him. How many of his exegetes and commentators would he have admitted into the second group?[22]

While apparently making references to esoteric modes of Jewish textual practice, Wittgenstein remained firmly rooted during the 1930's in the increasingly grim realities of Jewish existence in Austria. In the passage exploring the trope of the Jews as a tumor in the European body, he also takes up the belief that they do not have any sense of property. This may be true, he says (an acceptance move) and even compatible with Jews' liking to be rich, "since for them money is a particular sort of power, not property." Then, as if anticipating the many ransoms and bribes that would be necessary in the years ahead, his thoughts turn immediately to his own family: "For instance I should not like my people to become poor, since I wish them to have a certain amount of power." Even in the exceptional circumstances of 1930's Vienna, his endorsement of money as power is not unqualified: "Naturally I wish them to use this power properly too" (*C&V*: 21ᵉ). He is speaking, as it were, of a distinction between the kosher and non-kosher uses of power. Not to be overlooked is Wittgenstein's identification with the so-called Jewish qualities he is discussing.

SOMETHING UN-JEWISH

We have looked at most of the substantial remarks about Jews in *Culture and Value*. One that remains, from 1929, suggests that "[y]ou get tragedy where the tree, instead of bending, breaks. *Tragedy is something unJewish*" (*C&V*: 1ᵉ, emphasis added: *tree* is conceivably used here as a symbol of Judaism; in any case, Jews have not broken; a breaking of the covenantal relationship may count as a tragedy). The same year he used a significantly different formulation of this thought in speaking to the then recent acquaintance Drury, who had announced his desire to be ordained as an Anglican priest: "For a truly religious man nothing is tragic". *Jewish* in one's personal notebooks is translated as *truly religious* in speaking to the stranger. Then in 1931: "*In this world (mine) there is no tragedy*, nor is there that infinite variety of circumstance which gives rise to tragedy..." (*C&V*: 9ᵉ, emphasis added). Here it could be justly construed that Wittgenstein is telling himself (and any reader to come) that the world in which he lives is a Jewish world. Of how he might have conceived the incompatibility of tragedy—after serving in World War I and living through the suicides of three of his brothers—with a Jewish world view there is little direct evidence. His key religious experience, in the theatre, ironically, had the *Leit-*

motiv of complete security, above "that infinite variety of circumstance that gives rise to tragedy."[23] *Hubris* is essential to tragedy, and humility before God perhaps the *sine qua non* among Jewish virtues. Wittgenstein committed himself to eliminating his pride and vanity, seeing religion as the sole means of doing so (*C&V*: 26[e], 48[e]). It is unlikely, though, that the unJewishness of tragedy was arrived at on the basis of some personal deliberations on his part, invented by himself rather than taken over from somewhere else; the thought must be stimulated by some traditional account, such as this one transmitted by Heschel: "Revelation means that the thick silence which fills the endless distance between God and the human mind was pierced, and man was told that God is concerned with the affairs of man; and not only does man need God, God is also in need of man. *It is such knowledge that makes the soul of Israel immune to despair*" (*God in Search of Man*, 196). This Hebrew conception cannot be found among the Greeks; Aristotle's God is inert and immutable. The pessimism of Greece, not immune to despair unlike the soul of Israel, was described in some detail by William James in one of Wittgenstein's favorite books, *Varieties of Religious Experience* (125n.). (He wrote in 1912: "Whenever I have time I now read James's 'Varieties of religious experience'. This book does me a lot of good").[24]

The remarks on tragedy, a Greek invention inconceivable in a Jewish world, provide a link to the next question in our study: what does Wittgenstein indicate about the posture of his thought towards the Greek heritage in Western intellectual tradition? In the background may be heard an older question: what are the necessary contradictions between Judaism, as represented by rabbinic thought, and the discourses of the Greeks, taken over in large measure by Christianity?

ARE WE GREEKS? ARE WE JEWS?

> "Any thought of an objectivity, or a Platonic self-subsistence of ideas, be it the idea of beauty or of justice, is alien to the prophets"
>
> —Heschel, *The Prophets*

Wittgenstein's view of Judaism and Hellenism is ambient in our account, which focuses rather on his views about classical Greek thought, Plato and Aristotle—something that has hardly received any notice. The background question has been often and ably, sometimes controversially addressed by scholars such as Thorleif Boman, Emmanuel Levinas, Susan Handelman and José Faur in recent years.[25] Heschel, in his book on the philosophy of Judaism, refers to stark differences between the Greek and the Hebrew. Important treatments of the "Athens and Jerusalem" theme were written earlier by Lev Shestov, the Russian Jewish philosopher living in Paris who influenced existentialism, and by Leo Strauss, author of works in political philosophy and of *Persecution and the Art of Writing*.[26] These writers generally agree in their perception of Hebrew-Greek differences. Earlier still, in the nineteenth century, in Chapter IV of his *Culture and Anarchy* (1869), a less sophisticated, schematic depiction of "Hebraism and Hellenism" was introduced into Anglo-American culture by Matthew Arnold. Arnold opposed what he called Hebraic "strictness of conscience" to Hellenic "spontaneity of consciousness." In his view these two, although opposed, are not contradictory, their common aim corresponding to man's native desire to combine reason and the will of God in "the universal order."[27] It appears that Arnold got his conception from Ernest Renan, the same writer whose idea of Semitic *bon sens précoce* had been anticipated by Wittgenstein, although it has also been suggested that Heinrich Heine, familiar to Wittgenstein too, of course, was Arnold's source.[28]

The basis of rabbinic thought on a different linguistics, on non-Greek realities such as revelation, writing and commentary, is absent from Arnold's formulation. His eclectic homogenization works to efface the very differences that Israel feels committed to preserving, that Wittgenstein recalled in his remarks on Jewish minds and Jewish books, and that were, according to John Murray Cuddihy, in the form of Hebraism "a major theme of alienated Diaspora intellectual Jewry" (*Ordeal of Civility*, 183). Current interest is well indexed by the fact that this formulation of Arnold's from *Culture and Anarchy* occurs as an epigraph in both Derrida's "Violence and Metaphysics" on the thought of Emmanuel Levinas, and in Susan Handelman's *The Slayers of Moses: The Emergence of Rabbinic Interpretation in Modern Literary Theory*: "Hebraism and Hellenism,—between these two points of influence moves our world. At one time it feels more powerfully the attraction of one of them, at another time of the other; and it ought to be, though it never is, evenly and happily balanced between them." According to Handelman, "The history of philosophy...is ultimately an argument between Jews and Greeks....In Levinas, Derrida finds an attempt to 'dislocate the Greek logos' and thus to dislocate our identity and the principle of identity in general, *which is a summons to depart from Greece*, to liberate our thought from the 'oppression' of the same and the one, an 'ontological, or transcendental oppression,' which Derrida claims is the source of all oppression in the world" (*Slayers of Moses*, 170–71, emphasis added). It was written of the *Tractatus* as early as 1921: "the conception of identity is subjected by Wittgenstein to a destructive criticism from which there seems no escape"—the judgment of Bertrand Russell in his introduction. On more detailed inspection, how does Wittgenstein, whose project was to battle against the bewitchment of our intelligence by means of our language, align himself in this scenario?[29]

WITTGENSTEIN AND THE GREEKS

When the Aristotelian Society and Mind Association held their Joint Session at Cambridge in the summer of 1946, Wittgenstein gave deep offense by ostentatiously leaving town on the very day the session was to begin.
                                              —Stephen Toulmin in *Wittgenstein's Vienna*

About this time we sat on a bench and he began to talk about reading Plato. Plato's arguments! His pretense of discussion! The Socratic irony! The arguments were bad, the pretense of discussion too obvious, the Socratic irony distasteful—why can't a man be forthright and say what's on his mind? As for the Socratic method in the dialogues, it simply isn't there. The interlocutors are ninnies, never have any arguments of their own, say "Yes" and "No" as Socrates pleases they should. They are a stupid lot. No one really contends against Socrates. Perhaps Plato is no good, perhaps he's very good. How should I know? But if he is good, he's doing something which is foreign to us. We do not understand. Perhaps if I could read Greek!
                                              —Wittgenstein in conversation with Bouwsma, Oxford 1950

Traceable as far back as the *Notebooks 1914–16*, Wittgenstein mentions the distinction between the "Ancients" and the "Moderns," although it is not clear what exactly he meant by the former term. In the literary sense, the distinction connotes "progress and the rationalistic spirit of inquiry versus reverence for Classical rules and precepts" (Cuddon's *Dictionary of Literary Terms*). The comments, reprised in *Tractatus* 6371–2, are clear in the claim that "the whole *Weltanschauung* of the moderns involves the illusion that the so-called laws of nature are explanations of natural phenomena." Indeed, in the familiar "modern" intellectual world, everything, including gas clouds at the farthest reaches of the universe, the smallest processes of the human brain or changes in the weather, is potentially explicable by laws of nature, seen "as if they were rails, along which things had to move" (Man.FW 1, qtd. by Hallett, *Companion*,

297). We see the origins of this attitude in the efforts of the ancient Greeks, typified, say, by Archimedes, to arrive at principles of astronomy, physics, biology.[30] Science makes everything knowable—"with the new system it is supposed to look as if *everything* had a foundation"—while "[t]he older ones [*Die Alten*] are indeed clearer in that they acknowledge a clear terminus." But who are *Die Alten* here? It is not clear that the ancient Greeks acknowledged a clear terminus to human knowledge. Wittgenstein mentions God and fate as such termini, and fate is certainly Greek; but Jewish tradition does explicitly say, in the words of Maimonides, that "man's intellect indubitably has a limit at which it stops." The very things that current science is engaged in determining are mentioned as outside this limit: "the number of the stars of heaven and whether that number is even or odd...the number of the species of living beings, minerals, plants..." (*Guide of the Perplexed*, I, 31). In counseling restraint in the search for knowledge, Maimonides adduces passages such as *Proverbs* 25: 16: "Hast thou found honey? Eat so much as is sufficient for thee, lest thou be filled therewith and vomit it." While delicately clarifying that the intention of these texts set down by the prophets and the sages is not to ban speculation or cut the intellect off from what it *can* apprehend (I, 32), he interprets the Babylonian Talmud as linking this restraint with man's regard for the honor of his Creator. This is also the bearing of a passage in the Reform Jewish *Union Prayer Book* version of a traditional motif recognizing the limits of reason: "Help us, O God, to banish from our hearts all vainglory, pride of worldly possessions, and *self-sufficient leaning upon our own reason*...May we never forget that all we have and prize is but lent to us, a trust for which we must render account to Thee" (emphasis added). The theme of a limit to human knowledge is not confined in Wittgenstein to the early notebooks or even to the *Tractatus*. In *Zettel*, which contains some of his last writings, it recurs in the form of a probing question: "'Why do you demand explanations? If they are given you, you will once again be facing a terminus. They cannot get you any further than you are at present'" (#315). The question is tied up both with the "explanation vs. description" issue and with ethics. Searching for explanations is the way of science, leading by way of the "grand unification theory" of physicists to a theory of everything, idolizing the "laws of nature". Wittgenstein chooses instead the way of description, minutely exposing the workings of language, including theoretical terminology, and the futility of linguistic explanations, scientific explanations being also linguistic. Our craving for generality, the hunt for explanations, seems to have been a particular distraction from attending to ethics, the true end of Wittgenstein's work.

Whether or not by *Die Alten* he means the prophets or the rabbis—part of Hebrew tradition—acknowledging a terminus to the intellect has the same role in their thought as in his. The moderns are the philosophers descended from the Greeks rediscovered in the Renaissance, in his time Bertrand Russell, Gottlob Frege, G.E. Moore, and the rest of academic philosophy he consistently and painfully separated himself from. Heidegger, Levinas, Derrida, Handelman, Faur—to name a few—all equate philosophy itself with Greece: a series of footnotes to Plato. How far was Wittgenstein opting out of this company, this tradition, and, keeping in view his denial of any basic originality, with what part of the ancient intellectual world did he feel his thinking compatible?

PROPAGANDA FOR ONE STYLE OF THINKING

For a man who claimed that no one had understood him, Wittgenstein made some remarkably focused characterizations of what he was trying to do in or to philosophy. Most important, he was impatient, tired, even disgusted with the past, and although aware of the endless nature of philosophical debate, he wanted to get something done and over with by his own activity. According to Drury, Kant had depicted a great deal of philosophy as one person holding a sieve while another tried to milk a he-goat. As a businessman's son, Wittgenstein probably detected something similar, if not worse, on his own. "Philosophy," he declared in his notebooks, this pride of the Greek mind, "is an instrument whose only use is against philosophers, and against the philosophers in us" (Man. 219, 11; qtd. in Hallett, *Companion*, 382). Philosophy as we have it was only good if it could eliminate itself. He did not think, instinctively, that the subject needed systematic study, no more perhaps than his beloved father Karl, the steel magnate, felt the necessity to acquire a degree in commerce. At age 23 Ludwig expressed "the most naïve surprise that all the philosophers he once worshipped in ignorance are after all stupid and make disgusting mistakes" (Pinsent's diary qtd. in McGuinness 104). This is evidence of his own clarity of intention, his fundamental insights and commitments having already come to him early in life, as he later told Drury. Over method there was no vacillation, and the talents of a driven businessman probably inherited: "I know that my method is right. My father was a businessman, and I am a businessman: I want my philosophy to be business-like, to get something done, to get something settled" (Drury, "Conversations," 125–26). From beginning to end what he wanted to get done (though this was stated variously) was as much a task for a rhetorician as an engineer: to persuade people to change their style of thinking by making propaganda for another style (*L&C*: 28). But just as Wittgenstein cannot be imagined conducting direct and overt propaganda for a nation or a people, including the Jews, a direct assault on the *Urquell* of philosophy is not to be expected; there is not even any general discussion of Greek thought. Both the style of thinking that he is "honestly disgusted with" and the style he wants people to change to, remain discreetly unspecified, style A and style B, for all we are directly told. But it is possible to be less algebraic about A and B and attempt to plug in actual values. In a manuscript dating from 1931, the time of the "Jewish" remarks, some typically tangential comments touch upon the role of the Greeks in philosophy. "One repeatedly hears it said", he observes, "that philosophy does not really make any progress, that the same philosophical problems that already occupied the Greeks occupy us still. But those who say this do not understand why it is so. The reason is that our language has remained the same and continually misleads us into asking the same questions. So long as there is a verb "to be" that seems to function like "eat" and "drink," so long as there are the adjectives "identical," "true," "false," "possible," so long as people talk of the flow of time and the extension of space, etc., etc., they will keep on encountering the same puzzling difficulties" (Man. 1 11, 133–34, qtd. in Hallett, *Companion*, 201, trans. varies in *C&V*:15ᵉ). These are the people who don't see that different verbs, from "to be" to "to drink" have nothing that is common to all, but are linked by overlapping family resemblances and are also heterogeneous. They vary continuously in *use*, a concept that, since it leads to variation and multiplicity, never seems to have found favor with the major philosophers of Greece. The absence of this understanding—of the importance of variance, heterogeneity, difference, multiplicity—results, in Wittgenstein's analysis, not only in stasis in philosophy, but in a *satisfaction of the longing for the transcendent*—because when people think they have reached the "limits of human understanding" in their continuing puzzlement, "they believe of course that they can see beyond these." So we are trapped by words like "being" and "identity," we think we have crossed the limits of understanding when we realize that we are trapped, and this is the real trap, because it is still determined by the language, the words, that were the problem to begin with. Around the same time (1931) Wittgenstein, reading a claim that philosophers are no nearer to "reality" than Plato was, notes that this is a very strange situation—how could Plato have reached so far? Why can't we get any further? Was he so "*extremely* clever"? (*C&V*: 15ᵉ). If so, Wittgenstein would have to be either very impudent to be asking the question, or cleverer than Plato to think he can get us further. Of course, he is neither of these. *Plato just gave us one way of thinking about language* that has dominated our intellectual world ever since. Wittgenstein wants us to change it; he conducted propaganda against it his whole life, and proposed another way, foreshadowed in a line from *King Lear* that he thought of as a motto for the *Philosophical Investigations*: "I'll teach you differences!" (Drury, "Conversations", 171).

LANGUAGE AND DIFFERENCE

> His concern was to stress life's irreducible variety.
> —Ray Monk, *The Duty of Genius*

> ...the theme of difference seems to be typically Jewish, from the Bible to Derrida.
> —Susan Handelman, *Slayers of Moses*

To detect basic opposition to Plato in Wittgenstein is not, of course, an original discovery. He has been recognized before as a fundamental anti-Platonist; for instance Stanley Rosen in *The Limits of Analysis* refers to "those great anti-Platonist enterprises undertaken by Nietzsche and Wittgenstein" (183). Barry Stroud has written of "Wittgenstein's attack on Platonism" in mathematics (Pitcher, ed., 485). Saul Kripke has noted that "[f]or Wittgenstein, Platonism is largely an unhelpful evasion of the problem of how our finite minds can give rules that are supposed to apply to an infinity of cases" (*Rules*, 54). What is offered as unique here is an eventual description of his alternative style of thinking as within the Jewish or rabbinic mode.

How did Wittgenstein want to change the Socrates-Plato style of thinking about language? We will only begin to answer this crucial question here; parts of the answer may fit in elsewhere. As an example of Socratic-Platonic thinking, take this statement from the *Sophist*: "And thus it is with vocal signs as with the things for which they stand; some can be fitted together and some cannot, and those which so fit together effect discourse" (261D-262E, qtd. in Hallett 245). Wittgenstein says: "I cannot characterize my standpoint better than by saying that it is opposed to that which Socrates represents in the Platonic dialogues".[31] Why? In the one sentence from the *Sophist*, there are theoretical commitments to the *identity* of vocal signs with each other (while modern linguistics acknowledges that there can be no phonetic identity between any two speech sounds), and to referentiality between these vocal signs and "the things for which they stand" (an idea proposed early in the *Tractatus* only to show its inadequacy along with other such ideas). Regarding the latter point, most interesting is Stephen Toulmin's claim in 1973 (although he does not give a source) of Wittgenstein acknowledging later that "*the whole* Tractatus *had been...a kind of Platonic myth.*" Finally, in the *Sophist* sentence is the idea of discourse being effected by a fitting together or general unity between sign and thing, or some signs, at any rate, and some things. This assumption or expectation of a kind of generality in the matching of signs, leading to a unity (or, to use his word, surveyability, *Übersichtlichkeit*) of the entire scene of our language has been the source of major troubles in philosophy (see, for example, the *Blue Book*, 17–18; specific mention is made of "the idea that the meaning of a word is an image, or a thing correlated to the word"). Wittgenstein explained why his standpoint is opposed to Socrates: "For if asked what knowledge is I would list examples of knowledge, and add the words 'and the like.' No common element is to be found in them all." In the *Theaetetus*, "Socrates fails to produce a definition of 'knowledge' because there is no definition giving what is common to all instances of knowledge. Because the word 'knowledge' is used in all sorts of ways, any definition given will fail to apply to some cases" (Ambrose, *Lectures*, 96).

Susan Handelman has suggested that "the tendency to *gather* various meanings *into a one* is...characteristic of Greek thought in general: its movement towards the general, the universal, the univocal. The Rabbinic tendency, by contrast, is towards differentiation, metaphorical multiplicity, multiple meaning" (*Moses*, 33). Wittgenstein, too, wanted to teach differences: he is forthright in telling Drury, on a related point, that it has puzzled him why Socrates is regarded as a great philosopher. "Because when Socrates asks for the meaning of a word and people give him examples of how that word is used, he isn't satisfied but wants a unique definition. *Now if someone shows me how a word is used and its different meanings, that is just the sort of answer I want*" (Drury, "Conversations," 131; emphasis added). Whether or not there is a Greek-Hebrew divide in philosophy as described by Handelman and others—I think there is—her depiction of Hebraic thinking does coincide with Wittgenstein's depiction of his own way. This can be seen again in the *Blue Book*. He says of an opponent, misled by forms of expression: "he wouldn't talk as he does if he were aware of this difference in the grammar of such-and-such words, or if he were aware of this other possibility of expression" (28). Examples flow of different uses of the mathematical term *proof*, different meanings of the word *discovery*, differences between the uses of the word *kind—kinds of numbers, kinds of proofs* "as though the word "kind" here meant the same thing as in the context "kinds of apples" (29). As for Plato's "vocal signs and the things for which they stand," in Wittgenstein's phrase "a thing correlated to the word," Handelman calls this the "confinement of meaning within the ontology of substance," something avoided in both rabbinical and Wittgensteinian approaches, which we are claiming to be on the same side of the argument.

Our argument will be strengthened by the demonstration that the expression of anti-Socratic views was not confined to Wittgenstein's conversations with close friends, or to private notebooks, or even to not quite canonical works such as the *Blue Book*. The argument favoring the observation of variations of use as more instructive about meaning than the usual Socratic question, what does this word mean? is everywhere in Wittgenstein, from the *Notebooks 1914–1916* and throughout the *Philosophical Investigations*. In the last book, the apparently indispensable and impregnable notion of identity has its stability destroyed after at least ten discussions beginning early at §215 and recurring throughout. Similarly, the idea of the elements of language standing in a one-to-one relation to elements of the world, of words having reference to things, is set up in the *Tractatus* ("as a Platonic myth") but brought down with other provisional propositions, there as well as in the *Investigations*.

It appears that Wittgenstein did not want any egregious anti-Greek thrust in the works prepared for publication; there is a certain vagueness as to who his opposition is. Outside the canon he made numerous criticisms of Greek philosophers, and clearly said at least once that his approach could be accurately described as opposed to Socrates. Yet at another time he would speak only vaguely of a way of thinking he was honestly disgusted with. When Socrates does enter the stage of the *Philosophical Investigations*, he plays only a minor though very interesting role—the transmitter of the idea in the *Theaetetus* that *names are really simples*, unitary elements of language that are not further analyzable, and also of the less innocent doctrine that "the essence of speech is the composition of names" (*PI* §46). Arguments and results follow from these proposals, as from Augustine's picture of language and its learning—which we will look at closely in the next section. Through minor roles and brief, mostly anonymous references in the *Philosophical Investigations*, many are gently implicated in the collective "bewitchment of our understanding by means of our language" that the book battles against. It is surely part of Wittgenstein's ethical attainment that this trail of what he considered mistakes and those who had left it are treated with enormous and unfeigned respect. While one could easily turn derisive, Wittgenstein never forgot that the promptings leading his predecessors to *their* thoughts and theories were no different from his own: to help and clarify things for their fellow men. He said of using Augustine's view of language at the beginning of the *Investigations*, that the view must be important if so great a mind held it. Exposure of wrong turns it took seemed in no way to affect his estimation of Augustine's mind. In *PI* §340 we are given a little summary of a main principle of the book: "One cannot guess how a word functions. One has to *look at* its use and learn from that. But the difficulty is to remove the prejudice which stands in the way of doing this. It is not a stupid prejudice." That last sentence seems crucial in reminding us that in Wittgenstein's view philosophy is not an intelligence quiz with winners and losers, or a continuous war of theories leaving the stage set for the next army, but a process of clarification in which all can and, indeed, must participate in a Levinasian spirit of continuous openness to the other. The real discovery, for Wittgenstein, is "[t]he one that gives philosophy peace, so that it is no longer tormented by questions which bring *itself* in question" (*PI* §133).

LEGACY OF THE STAGYRITE

Wittgenstein once told Malcolm that "he really thought that in the *Tractatus* he had provided a perfected account of a view that is the *only* alternative to the viewpoint of his later work" (*Memoir*, 69). Of course, this perfected account within the *Tractatus* was rejected before the *Tractatus* ended, but it is a useful hypothesis that the account derived from Aristotle, for it is hard to imagine a clearer antithesis than the Aristotelian mindset to Wittgenstein's minute and lifelong activity dismantling philosophical structures. This despite the bravado of his response, three years before his death, to Drury's question, "Did you ever read anything of Aristotle's?"—"Here I am a one-time professor of philosophy who has never read a word of Aristotle!" (Drury, "Conversations," 171). Both question and answer suggest the awareness of a certain marginalization of Aristotle by Wittgenstein. But a practicing philosopher could not be blithely innocent of such an enormous presence, and he wasn't, although he had likely acquired a working knowledge of the relevant Aristotelian views in logic and metaphysics without undertaking detailed study, motivated by his feeling that they were the *only* alternative to his own.

There are, however, several direct references. Aristotle figures in Wittgenstein's first publication, in 1913, his review of *The Science of Logic* by P. Coffey that appeared in the *Cambridge Review* of that year. "The author's Logic," says the twenty-four-year-old reviewer, "is that of the scholastic philosophers, and he makes all their mistakes—of course with the usual references to Aristotle. (Aristotle, whose name is so much taken in vain by our logicians, would turn in his grave if he knew that so many Logicians know no more about Logic today than he did 2,000 years ago.)" Wittgenstein then complains that Coffey has not taken the slightest notice of the great advances made by modern mathematical logicians. There is a certain tact and evenhandedness in making Aristotle both great for his time and yet responsible for mistakes two millennia later. There could hardly be more persuasive evidence of his enormous influence than how Coffey defines the science of logic in 1913. None of this, however, establishes that Wittgenstein had a practitioner's knowledge of Aristotle's logic, though it is clear that he could not have been ignorant of its main principles and tendencies.

In what has been published as *Last Writings on the Philosophy of Psychology*, written almost four decades later, we read: "Bad Influence of Aristotelian logic. The logic of language is immeasurably more complicated than it looks" (vol. II, p.44^e). A little cryptic, but important for at least two reasons; one, the remark expresses the heart of the old charge from the *Preface* to the *Tractatus*: philosophical problems arise because the logic of our language has been misunderstood. The corollaries surely are that Aristotle misunderstood it first, and western thought has perpetuated his misunderstanding. The second is the similarity of the criticism to that leveled at Augustine at the start of the *Philosophical Investigations*: in his picture of the essence of human language "we find the roots of the following idea: Every word has a meaning. This meaning is correlated with the word. It is the object for which the word stands. Augustine does not speak of there being any *difference* between kinds of word" (*PI*: §1, emphasis added).[32] So we are reminded of the "original sins," as it were, of two great Western thinkers on language.

The distorting, limiting effect of Aristotelian linguistic thought is expanded upon a little more in another place. "Aristotelian logic," Wittgenstein says, "brands a contradiction as a non-sentence, which is to be excluded from language. But this logic only deals with a very small part of our language. (It is as if the first geometrical system had been a trigonometry; and as if we now believed that trigonometry is the real basis of geometry, if not the whole of geometry)" (*Last Writings* I, §525). The marks of Wittgenstein's thought are multiplicity, infinite difference, abundance. In the *Philosophical Investigations* (§23) he compares "the multiplicity of the tools in language and of the ways they are used, the multiplicity of kinds of word and sentence" with the bareness and poverty of "what logicians have said about the structure of language"—and here follows a self-deprecating joke—"including the author of the *Tractatus Logico-Philosophicus*." A joke with a bite—the author of the *Tractatus* wrote as ridiculously about logic as any other logician. Yes! But, by detecting this, the reader who understood him was to derive pleasure.[33] The linking of this remark to Aristotle is found in the *Remarks on the Foundations of Mathematics*. "'Mathematical logic'," says Wittgenstein, putting the expression itself in disparaging quotes, "has *completely deformed the thinking of mathematicians and of philosophers*, by setting up a superficial interpretation of the forms of our everyday language as an analysis of the structures of facts. *Of course in this it has only continued to build on the Aristotelian logic*" (156[e]; emphasis added). The charge is threefold: the interpretation of everyday linguistic forms is superficial; this superficial interpretation has then been set up as an analysis of reality; and the thinking of philosophers has been not merely influenced or affected by this process, but completely deformed.[34] So it is more than mere speculation to say that at the heart of the way of thinking Wittgenstein found honestly disgusting was Aristotelianism.[35]

Henry Staten, in his *Wittgenstein and Derrida*, mentions a scholar of Aristotle who concludes that "the principle he is defending has to be the principle of identity, which can be stated in either a positive form (A is A) or a negative one (A is not not-A); the negative form is often called the principle of contradiction" (163n.12). Buried away in notes from Wittgenstein's lectures is a relevant claim of his: "I invented a notation to get rid of the identity sign as used in 'A=A', because nobody ever says a chair is a chair; and the difficulties connected with this use vanish" (Ambrose, *Lectures 1932–1935*, 98–99).

The general outlines of the present argument about Aristotle and Wittgenstein have been clear for some time. For instance, the noted Italian scholar of linguistics Tullio de Mauro in his *Ludwig Wittgenstein: His Place in the Development of Semantics*, after quoting a key passage from Aristotle's *On Interpretation* and tracing its echoes through centuries of Western linguistic thought, advances the following analysis: "...the early Wittgenstein worked from the total acceptance of traditional ideas. But, accepting them, he gave them a formal rigour in which they had never been cast, not even by Aristotle. In this way he laid bare their most secret links and exposed all the consequences logically deriving from them to the limits of absurdity, indeed—and here lies his merit—beyond absurdity" (8, 23). This "hyper-Aristotelianism" fits well with what we have already observed about "clarification with courage" in his handling of Weininger. Allan Janik sees Wittgenstein undertaking "a refutation of the Aristotelian notion that there are 'Laws of Thought' or the Fregean notion that there is a hierarchical order of axioms" (*Essays on Wittgenstein and Weininger*, 90). The picture already drawn by these scholars develops in two ways: the direct critical references to Aristotle provided here establish that the refutation of his linguistic thought is not the accidental accomplishment of someone who hadn't read a word of Aristotle. Second, our juxtaposition of his attack with his treatment of Socrates-Plato and Augustine (to whom we will now turn) reveals a concealed stage design for another style of thinking. According to Derrida, Descartes and Kant were beginning to accomplish "the Greek aim: philosophy as science" ("Violence and Metaphysics," 82). For this Wittgenstein seems to have had no taste at all: "I have certainly not read too little, *rather too much*. I see that whenever I read a philosophical book, it doesn't improve my thoughts at all, it makes them worse" (ms. 135, 1947, qtd. in Monk 496).

THE PERILS OF AUGUSTINE

> He is in truth the conclusion and completion of the Christian Classical, its last and greatest thinker, its intellectual practitioner and tribune....His own real mind, the synthesizer of Classical Culture, ecclesiastical and episcopal authority, and intimate mysticism, could not possibly have been handed on by those who, environed by different conditions, have to deal with different tasks.
> —E. Troeltsch on Augustine, cited by Spengler

> In the Platonists, he said, God and his Word are constantly implied.
> —Bishop Simplicianus to Augustine, *Confessions*

At the start of the *Philosophical Investigations*, in what is by far the longest quotation in the entire work, Wittgenstein gives Augustine the privilege of having the very first say—a great privilege from an author who quoted little and gave few sources. But from an author who at the end of his last publication had also said that the correct method in philosophy was to say nothing but what can be said and *respond only when someone else says something metaphysical*, the privilege might raise a certain alarm. Why Augustine, then? We know of Wittgenstein explaining to Malcolm that "he decided to begin his *Investigations* with a quotation from the latter's *Confessions*, not because he could not find the conception expressed in that quotation stated as well by other philosophers, but because the conception *must* be important if so great a mind held it" (*Memoir*, 71). Possible implication: linguistic bewitchment in great and influential minds is all the more in need of therapeutic attention. Like Kierkegaard and Tolstoy, Augustine stood at that confluence of philosophy and religion to which Wittgenstein was also drawn. But unlike the former, Augustine has been called "the most profound and influential exegete in the history of the Church" (Robertson in Handelman 111). He was influential in all of Christianity. As the begetter of important Christian doctrines concerning "original sin" and "grace," he is profoundly at odds with Judaism, a good test case to expose the shallow sweep-it-under-the-rug attitude symbolized by the term "Judaeo-Christian tradition." It is not clear at all if his criticisms of Augustine were part of a well-considered strategic choice on Wittgenstein's part. He may have felt comfortable with Augustine because—unlike the Greeks—Wittgenstein could read him in the original. Augustine had read the Greeks, and thus he synthesizes the pagans and Graeco-Christianity—"the conclusion and completion of the Christian Classical." In fact, according to Spengler, Augustine in his late work *Retractions* "dared to assert that the true religion had existed before the coming of Christianity in the form of the Classical" (II: 204). This is a view that Wittgenstein had read. In other ways, too, Augustine sought to detach Christian tradition from the Judaic and align it with the "classical."[36]

Although it is unlikely, most of this may have been of no concern to Wittgenstein. What can be said with confidence is that he had acquired the historical and theological background to understand the implications of his choice of Augustine that we have mentioned, and perhaps others that we have not. For someone who saw himself as working within Judaic tradition, "the most profound and influential exegete in the history of the Church" is a worthy opponent, an informed rather than a random or naive choice. The opening of Wittgenstein's book was important. He seriously weighed different possibilities. The general thought was that he "would like to start with what is given in philosophy, with the written and spoken sentences, almost with the books" (Man. 10, 10, qtd. in Hallett, *Companion*, 73). This is the attitude not of a system-builder but of a deconstructor, a commentator, a therapist who sees in the patient's discourse knots to be untied. Considering the striking polemical element in his thought, Wittgenstein would have to take care in choosing opponents; "what is given in philosophy" he whittles down to a few sentences on language learning in the autobiography of an early medieval professor of rhetoric who became a bishop after converting to Christianity. Augustine's *Confessions* he described as "the most serious book ever written," yet he believed it contained a serious mistake in its conception of language. Augustine's ideology at the beginning of the *Investigations* "surrounds the working of language with a haze which makes clear vision impossible," while Wittgenstein's own method of studying words in their primitive applications "disperses the fog" (*PI* §5). §52 stresses the importance of "understanding what it is that opposes such an examination of details in philosophy." In the *Blue Book*, the polemical description of philosophy as "a fight against the fascination which forms of language exert upon us" follows immediately after a presentation of two thinkers' misleading views about those forms of language—first Augustine, and then Socrates. So it can be concluded that Wittgenstein had Augustine in his critical sights, choosing him with care and deliberation. With his "businessman's" approach to philosophy Wittgenstein was making a choice that would bring him—and us—the maximum returns for our attention: to get something settled rather than continue trying to milk the he-goat. In another comment on his choice, Wittgenstein explained that "[w]hat Augustine says has importance for us because it is the conception of a naturally clearthinking man" (Man. 111, 15, qtd. in Hallett, *Companion*, 73). This is more than he says of any Greek; the critique of Augustine is of a subtler importance than that of the Greeks—even a naturally clear-thinking man, any intelligent person, can go wrong about language, let his understanding be bewitched.

Hallett suggests that Augustine criticizes his own earlier naïve view in *De Magistro*, dialogues with his son, therefore "too much should not be made of one isolated passage" (*Companion*, 73). It is, of course, too late to say this, because the question is not what we make of it but what Wittgenstein did. Augustine's *Confessions*, where the fatal passage occurs, is certainly the most widely read of Augustine's works. Wittgenstein in any case is addressing himself to the text, not to the man, whose integrity and intelligence he affirms with every mention of his name. His research methods were not those of a graduate student. If he criticized views that are elsewhere retracted, this should concern neither the holder of the views nor the reader of Wittgenstein; what counts is the contribution of the criticism to the point being made. In the *Blue Book* passage on time already discussed, Augustine's way of thinking about time is the problem, something quite different from the simplistic view of language at the head of the *Investigations*, though not unconnected to it. It is in fact the view of the "isolated passage," buttressed by what Augustine says elsewhere about time and *an internal or private language* also critiqued by Wittgenstein, that prevails in Augustine's linguistic thinking, his overall practice of interpretation.[37] Had Augustine, outside the one "isolated" passage in the *Confessions*, thought about language as Wittgenstein did, and had his influence been the same as it in fact has been—immeasurably larger than Wittgenstein's, of course—a totally different religio-philosophical history would have resulted in the West. The Greek metaphysics of being and presence being entirely absent, so to speak, the doctrinal posture of Christianity towards Judaism would not have been so inimical. *This* is why Wittgenstein suggested that *the idea must be important if so great a mind held it.* It would appear that Wittgenstein realized—perhaps very early—that the essential difference between Graeco-Christian and Biblical-Jewish approaches was not in theology or religious dogma but in linguistic philosophy—approaches to the sign. Think well on this, take care of this, and everything else will take care of itself. Precocious semitic good sense consists of nothing else. And if this suggestion is correct, then he was ahead of several other linguistic thinkers who have tended to confirm his conclusion since the mid-twentieth century.

Wittgenstein consistently surprised his friends with what he chose to read and whom he chose to defend. Oddly for someone who constantly polemicized against it, he defended metaphysics.[38] He supported all forms of religious expression showing the love of God.[39] So we are not surprised to find an absence of hostility towards one whom he seems to have taken as a comrade-in-thought, and whose earnest linkage of linguistic matters with ethics he found impressive and compatible. Consider how Augustine, struggling with the interrelatedness of sign, memory, word, and image, falls to asking in his *Confessions*:

> Who is to carry the research beyond this point? Who can understand the truth of the matter? O Lord, I am working hard in this field, and the field of my labours is my own self. I have become a problem to myself, like land which a farmer works only with difficulty and at the cost of much sweat. For I am not now investigating the tract of the heavens or measuring the distance of the stars, or trying to discover how the earth hangs in space. I am investigating myself, my memory, my mind. (X, 16)

There is an echo of this in Wittgenstein's own notebooks: "Working in philosophy—like work in architecture in many respects—is really more a working on oneself. On one's own interpretation. On one's way of seeing things. (And what one expects of them)" (*C&V*: 16ᵉ). We are put in mind also of his exhausted remark in *Zettel*: sometimes while doing philosophy one would just like to emit an inarticulate sound. But for all his respect and fellow feeling, and perhaps with no different a feeling than with which he debated friends like Russell and Drury, Wittgenstein had to deeply question Augustine's semantic ideas.[40] And so, although he gave up the Shakespearean line "I'll teach you differences" for his motto at the beginning of the *Investigations*, *difference* raises its head no later than the seventh line of the text: he begins his teaching about it with the complaint that Augustine "does not speak of there being any differences between kinds of word."

Some issues related to Augustine's positions, touching on privacy and naming, are taken up in another chapter, but here let us look at the very Greek concept of identity. It has a home in the opening lines of Aristotle's *On Interpretation*—"states of mind which are the *same* for everyone, as are things, and these states are the reflection of things which are the *same* for everyone" (16a 3ff.)—and in the *Logic*. We saw above how Wittgenstein dealt with the notation for Aristotle's principle of identity, the one thing he wanted to defend. Multiplicity, multivocity in language was the one thing that seems to have been repressed in Augustine. For both these authorities truth, as Handelman puts it, was a totally self-identical present being. Theologically, the Christian solution to the linguistic problem of meaning was the word becoming flesh—infinite play, multiple language games arrested in sacrament, the same for everyone.

In the *Tractatus* we read: "Roughly speaking, to say of two things that they are identical is nonsense, and to say of one thing that it is identical with itself is to say nothing at all." Wittgenstein goes on to say that "the identity sign...is not an essential constituent of conceptual notation," and that "in a conceptual notation pseudo-propositions like 'a = a'...etc. cannot even be written down" (*Tractatus* 5533–4). Finally, in 62322, he drives the last nail in the coffin of identity with the argument that it is impossible to assert the identity of meaning of two expressions: "For in order to be able to assert anything about their meaning, I must know their meaning, and I cannot know their meaning without knowing whether what they mean is the same or different."

The criticism of identity was never given up by Wittgenstein. In 1948, just three years before his death, he told Drury: "Hegel seems to me to be always wanting to say that things which look different are really the same. Whereas my interest is in showing that things which look the same are really different." To see what Wittgenstein seems to be saying in terms of thinkers half a century after him, Handelman's account is suggestive: "In Levinas, Derrida finds an attempt to 'dislocate the Greek logos,' and thus to dislocate our identity and the principle of identity in general, which is a summons to depart from Greece, to liberate thought from the 'oppression' of the Same and the One, an 'ontological, or transcendental oppression,' which Derrida claims is the source of all oppression in the world" (Handelman, *Moses*, 171).

Be that as it may, let me conclude this account of the role of Augustine in the rhetorical aims of the *Investigations* by recalling the nobility of Wittgenstein's attitude towards his opponents, as instructive of ethics as any argument in the philosophy itself. An attitude contrasting in its exuberance is provided in *The Anti-Christ*, a work Wittgenstein read and was quite struck by (McGuinness 225): "One has only to read one of the Christian agitators, Saint Augustine for example, to realize, to *smell*, what dirty fellows had therewith come out on top. One would be deceiving oneself utterly if one presupposed a lack of intelligence of any sort on the part of the leaders of the Christian movement— oh they are shrewd, shrewd to the point of holiness, these Church Fathers!"

CHAPTER IV

Wittgenstein's Religion

I am not a religious man but I can't help seeing every problem from a religious point of view.

—Wittgenstein to Drury

It is impossible for me to say in my book one word about all that music has meant in my life. How then can I hope to be understood.

—Wittgenstein to Drury

Little has been certain about Wittgenstein's religion, and little is likely to be by the end of this brief chapter. What is generally accepted consists of negative information. No one understood Wittgenstein's views of religion; he did not as an adult associate himself with any confession; according to Grayling, Wittgenstein kept details of his religious ideas, which were unorthodox, a secret (*Wittgenstein*, 2). Yet it has been often assumed, on account of his infant baptism, and later evidence, that he was a Roman Catholic. Catholic rites were administered to him at death. Although there is actually plentiful material that has not been considered, I have no particular explanation to provide of Wittgenstein's religious beliefs. However, by examining his behavior—his conversations recorded by intimate friends, his writings, his choice of readings and reactions to them, some apparently significant omissions and repressions—it may be possible, if not to lessen the mystery, at least to suggest a reading of his religious attitude that elucidates the philosophical work. His writing is without doubt an expression of his religion—not secular, either in the current sense of non-religious, or in the traditional sense of belonging to the age as opposed to the eternal. In line with the Krausian dictum that the whole man must move together, I suggest that what is provided in the published works is the whittled-down, minimum correct understanding of linguistic matters needed for what we could call intellectual health, therapy essential to avoiding both idolatry and narcissism. The reader remains as free after the therapy as before: "Philosophy can in no way interfere with the actual use of language"; nor with anyone's ethics: "It leaves everything as it is" (*PI*: §124). Further clues are provided, but, as he indicated, only for those looking for hints, and agreement on what these are may be very difficult to achieve. Within the sphere of philosophy, what Wittgenstein said can be understood; but the point of his saying it must be sought where it seldom has been, in his religion, or more precisely, in his ethics. We might think of the religious point as the unwritten part of his work, and the more important part, as suggested in the letter to Ludwig von Ficker arguing for the publication of the *Tractatus*.[1]

Apart from having to fight shallow assumptions, there are other difficulties in investigating Wittgenstein's religion. The suggestion that he wished to keep the truth secret is both a challenge to uncover it and a temptation to go quite wrong in the attempt. The "secular humanist" audience that Wittgenstein necessarily wrote for and berated has not really changed much in the last half-century, which means that it is either not interested in the point of what he said or not equipped to follow his lead. "My type of thinking is not wanted in this present age," he told Drury. "I have to swim so strongly against the tide. Perhaps in a hundred years people will really want what I am writing" (94)—a Nietzschean premonition. What might a scientific person make, for instance, of a comment about psychoanalysis stressing not whether it was true or false, but that it was irreligious? How might an analytic philosopher be led to see that the private language argument was formulated for an ethical end? But the possibility remains that Wittgenstein, by his own standards quite appropriately, *is* being understood by small numbers of readers, and will be by even more in the coming decades. "In philosophizing we may not *terminate* a disease of thought. It must run its natural course, and *slow* cure is all important" (*Zettel* #382). There are to be no sudden conversions, perhaps, in the individual or in the mass; and no differently from Wittgenstein's works, the role of commentary on them is to diagnose the disease of thought, letting each patient then proceed to an unhurried cure.

Wittgenstein hinted that he wanted to be an honest religious thinker. This is a tall order in our age, perhaps in any age. The difficulty of course is the legacy of partisan politics in religion, leading to an attempt at separation of church and state in the post-Enlightenment era. The two societies Wittgenstein knew best, Austria and England, were not examples of such separation. He must have seen, during his war service, Catholic priests ritually blessing the armaments and armies of the dual monarchy. In the ancient Roman mold, the English monarch, Defender of the Faith, was also the champion of colonial conquest and empire. With his Krausian view of religious language, he could not simply write of the glory of God, for instance, as he noted Bach still could; the superficial use of such terms had so muddied language that this road could no longer be taken (Drury 94).

Wittgenstein compared the task of being an honest religious thinker to walking a tightrope—an image of virtue also used by Hasidic rabbis.[2] By way of being an honest thinker about logic, he had already found his route to the task: *to be an honest religious thinker, be an honest linguistic thinker*—and this means: debunking all dishonest linguistic thinkers. Thus confining himself, he would not have to travel the muddied roads of religious language, nor would he have to spell out what kind of ethics he had in mind, for ethics could not be talked about. Whether or not we want to call it an element of the "fundamental ideas" that came to him early, as he told Drury, this was the master plan of his life work. He was confident about it: "He did not think of the central conceptions of his philosophy as *possibly* in error" (Malcolm 60).

In general, looking into Wittgenstein's life gives the impression of important things happening to him (or in him) early and in isolation—not through the influence of other people. We have estimated his fundamental ideas coming early, before the *Tractatus* had been completed. What is not clear is the nature of these fundamental ideas and what their relation to other—less fundamental—levels of his work might have been. We cannot expect these questions to be answered definitely. But it is clear that Wittgenstein's personal life and work were seamlessly combined. Some events of a religious nature had happened and others had been realized that were waiting to find expression, if not in aeronautics, in art, perhaps, or in philosophical writing. Wittgenstein's remarks, what we know of the chronology of incidents, and the outlines of the thought together suggest an unfolding, a playing out of a set of insights that arrived early and were never in need of questioning.[3] They were held up only by an "enormous difficulty of expression" (*Notebooks 1914–1916*, 40^e). The early part of this chapter will provide a sketch of Wittgenstein's religious life. Later this will be fleshed out with details of his thinking on such subjects as the Bible, idolatry, prophecy, science, and so on.

From the biographical sources used here, which have not often been consulted in the effort to understand his philosophy, Wittgenstein's was clearly a life absorbed in religion. Rather than philosophy having a logic of its own, leaving religion a separate and personal matter, his philosophy grew in a richly religious soil, out of the desire, even the duty, to do something that was helpful to others—and was courageous.

At the high school in Linz where for a year Adolf Hitler was a fellow pupil,

Wittgenstein obtained high grades in Religion. In his twenty-first year, around 1910, his first recorded religious experience took place. Watching a play by Ludwig Anzengruber (*Die Kreuzelschreiber*), he heard a character say that nothing bad could happen to *him* no matter what went on in the world—an expression of the possibility of independence from fate and circumstance. Until this point, he said, his religious attitude had been contemptuous, but he was much struck by these lines in the play and began to see the possibilities of religion. It was not until two years later that he took up systematic reading for the first time in philosophy (see Pinsent's diary qtd. in McGuinness 104). But after the theatre experience evidence all points to a full-blown religious life that was conventional in its simple intensity, yet hard to describe conventionally. There are no serious external observances, and no mention of saints or saviors that would signify attachment to an established church. Attendance at church services with friends, admiration for medieval cathedrals, listening to Bach on the organ with an all-Jewish band of friends in a synagogue during war leave: such activities are recorded, but they could certainly also be engaged in by a non-religious person. (The organ mentioned by Engelmann suggests a Reform synagogue, or temple, in Olmütz/Olomouc). The choice of composers is also suggestive. Wittgenstein held Bach in esteem; he saw in him "humility and an enormous capacity for suffering, hence strength,"[4] and may well have been thinking of these as "Jewish" virtues. While well aware that Bach's music "is an expression of Lutheranism" (Drury 147), he considered it "more like language than Mozart's or Haydn's" (*C&V*: 34ᵉ). And he concurred, as we have seen, with what "Bach wrote on the title page of his *Orgelbuchlein*, 'To the glory of the most high God, and that my neighbour may be benefited thereby.' That is what I would have liked to say about my work" (Drury, "Conversations," 182). "Most sublime," says Engelmann, "were Fritz Zweig's renderings of Bach's organ music (which he played to us at the synagogue when it was not in use)" (64). This is one of those typical sentences that is worth some decoding in its own right. The band of music lovers in the synagogue (Fritz, his cousin Max Zweig, Heinrich Groag, Wittgenstein, Engelmann himself, and his brother, the pseudonymous cartoonist Peter Eng, as well as some less frequent members) were obviously of Jewish—perhaps even Zionist—sympathies: a group of Christians or secularists could hardly be expected to seek out a synagogue in its off-hours for their music making; and the group must have established some connection with the congregation to be extended this privilege. At the same time, since there is no mention of attending actual synagogue services, Wittgenstein hints at disdain towards organized religion; the choice

of music indicates a cultural liberalism. All this connects Wittgenstein to Zionism, a possibility made stronger when we see Engelmann pointedly noting: "In
our conversations we execrated Richard Wagner, that destroyer of music and
culture, who at the time was still considered the pope of music and above criticism" (64). There can be little doubt that the Bach lovers' group in the synagogue found Wagner's essay *Die Judentum in der Musik* particularly execrable,
whose anti-semitic themes were echoed by Weininger, also doubtless familiar
to this troupe of musicians.

Indeed, the rollicking cultural life of Olomouc could not escape the
shadow of dark events in the capital. The Fourteenth International Zionist
Congress had been scheduled for August 1925 in Vienna, triggering violent
anti-semitic activities that lasted for months; thousands of slanderous leaflets
were distributed, gangs of swastika-wearing youths terrorized the Jewish dis-
trict of Leopoldstadt, Jewish businesses downtown were frequently assaulted
(Timms 196). It was in this year that Engelmann appears to have made his
Zionist decision to move to Palestine. It drew an immediate approving reaction
from his friend, then serving as an elementary schoolteacher in the provinces:
"That you want to go to Palestine is the one piece of news that makes your letter cheering and hopeful for me. This may be the right thing to do and may
have a spiritual effect. *I might want to join you. Would you take me with you?*"
(Engelmann 55, emphasis added).

Early remarks recorded beginning within two years of the theatre experience indicate a great value placed on personal integrity, seen as dependent on
suffering and the power to endure it. An intense desire is attested to take on a
very difficult non-intellectual task (Wittgenstein's sister Hermine in Rhees,
213). Wittgenstein volunteered for war service and constantly sought the most
dangerous assignments, feeling that surviving the war would somehow prove
that he had been spared for some important task. Despair, like tragedy, was not
allowed to exist in his world: "From time to time I despair. This is the fault of
a wrong view of life" (war journal qtd. by Rhees, 215). The journal entries are
full of prayers and direct appeals to God: "So carry out your work in humility
and by God's will don't lose yourself!!" (qtd. in Rhees 216, my trans.). "God
help me." "Be at peace within yourself. But how do you find this peace within
yourself? *Only* if I live in a way pleasing to God. *Only* so can one bear life"
(Rhees 216, 218). Concentrated reflections on believing in God are found in
the *Notebooks 1914–1916*, which often overlap in content with the eventual text
of the *Tractatus*. The remarks, dated July 8, 1916, are separated in print, but I
run them together: "To believe in a God means to understand the question

about the meaning of life. To believe in a God means to see that the facts of the world are not the end of the matter. To believe in God means to see that life has a meaning" (74ᵉ). In these words, according to Rabbi Jack Spiro, "[t]he fundamental premise of Judaism in response to the question of meaning was stated generally by Ludwig Wittgenstein."[5] His philosophy in those years was embedded within, or derived from, the exploration of religious concepts. Yet, from the twenties on, quiet, undisturbed conviction he never achieved. Thirty years later, dealing with the difficulties of understanding oneself properly, he says: "And only if I were able to submerge myself in religion could these doubts be stilled. Because only religion would have the power to destroy vanity and penetrate all the nooks and crannies" (C&V: 48ᵉ). But his is a living body, he seems to say, too light to stay submerged in the waters of religion. How God judges a man, he wrote just a year before his death, cannot be imagined—"so if you want to stay within the religious sphere you must struggle" (C&V: 86ᵉ). Whether he could submerge himself or not, that religion could, in principle, destroy vanity (a goal of the highest priority), cure nervous instability (Malcolm 74), remove fear through prayer and thoughts of God, was never in doubt. A story from Wittgenstein's school teaching days will serve as an illustration. A school group returning from a trip to Vienna was overtaken by nightfall, and "...the children had to make a twelve-mile hike with Wittgenstein through the dark forest. Sensing that some of them were frightened, Wittgenstein quietly went from one to another, asking: 'Are you afraid? Well, then, you must think only about God.'" The narrator of this story, Bartley, comments: "The non-Christian 'Evangelist,' who began and ended each school day with the Pater Noster, did not attack the religion of his villagers any more than he attacked their dialect" (*Wittgenstein*, 2nd ed., 100). "Non-Christian 'Evangelist'" refers to an account around the same time of Wittgenstein's telling an Austrian villager, who had asked about his religion, that *although not a Christian*, he was an "evangelist." (90).[6]

Wittgenstein seems to have pondered over a new, refined religious life, or "the religion of the future." For it, organization would be suspect. Drury once confided he considered it important that there be ordained priests to carry on the traditional Latin liturgy. A priest in every village for this purpose would seem to be a wonderful idea, was Wittgenstein's response, but it hadn't worked out. In keeping with his earlier advice to Drury to make sure his religion was a matter only between him and God, Wittgenstein thought the religion of the future would be without any priests or ministers: "I think one of the things you and I have to learn is that we have to live without the consolation of belonging to a church."[7] And then, perhaps out of concern that he had taken away in one blow the intermediaries his friend might still have needed: "If you feel you must belong to some organization, why don't you join the Quakers?". Apparently caught between kindness and honesty, Wittgenstein came back the very next morning to tell Drury to forget his mention of the Quakers: "As if nowadays any one organization was better than another" (Drury, "Conversations," 129). In the Gospels he found huts, in Paul's epistles already a church; in one all men equal, in the other "something like a hierarchy; honours and official positions" (*C&V*: 30ᵉ). The abhorrence of pomp and circumstance went as far as the things of the mind: "Of one thing I am certain. The religion of the future will have to be extremely ascetic; and by that I don't mean just going without food and drink." Drury's reaction to this was that he sensed for the first time "the idea of an asceticism of the intellect" (Drury 129). Silence and abstention from "creation" and the writing of books (see Chapter III) would no doubt be part of this asceticism of the intellect.

During his school-teaching years in the Austrian countryside, at a time when he had the *Tractatus* behind him but was perhaps aware that it had not had the effect an author would have wished, Wittgenstein had an experience that has been little discussed but is potentially even more significant than his feeling of security in the theatre episode. There is apparently only one source of information about it, the Catholic teacher Ludwig Hänsel, once a fellow POW. They had remained close. His account states simply: "One night, during the time when he was a teacher, he had the feeling that he had been called but had refused" (Hänsel qtd. in Bartley, 2nd ed., 29). Bartley refers to a dream of himself as a priest that Wittgenstein associated with this incident, but his sources are not convincing. On the other hand, there is a letter to Paul Engelmann that appears to corroborate Hänsel's account of a call not answered: "I had a task, did not do it, and now the failure is wrecking my life. I ought to have done something positive with my life, to have become a star in the sky. Instead of which I remained stuck on earth, and now I am gradually fading out. My life has really become meaningless and so it consists only of futile episodes" (Engelmann 41). The period was indeed bad for Wittgenstein: deaths and suicides in the family, rejection of the *Tractatus* by several publishers, coping with constant disappointments in his new surroundings, perhaps despair over sexual problems that he also hinted about to Engelmann. So it would be understandable if the call came to him in a time of low self-esteem, as it were, when he could not rise to the occasion; but it is also understandable that he should soon berate himself bitterly for his inadequacy and search for some means of atonement.

The significance of this information to an understanding of the philosophy is that it may indicate an atonement motive in the subsequent writing. The prophet responding records in his book the circumstances of the call, his struggles to understand and comply with the task. The near-prophet who is unable to respond publicly must try the next best thing, to speak to a limited audience about God and ethics in a veiled way. Wittgenstein's later work, along with his feelings of dissembling and cowardice, could have issued from his continuing wish to atone for his failure to be a Jewish (i.e. religious) genius, without being able of course to admit it, except in very attenuated ways—through reiteration of Jewish descent and identification with Jewish tradition, hoping yet that these pointers would lead to his secret purpose being beamed to a select audience, if not broadcast as per the original summons.

The sequence of Wittgenstein's developing interests and readings in engineering, the foundations of mathematics, logic, and philosophy after 1910 is not clear, but by 1912, his second year at Cambridge, there are several sources about his thoughts and activities, including Russell's autobiography and his almost daily letters to Lady Ottoline Morrell, as well as the diary of David Pinsent, Wittgenstein's friend to whose memory the *Tractatus* was dedicated. From that diary we have already learned that Wittgenstein began his first planned readings in philosophy in the spring of 1912, and was not impressed by what he discovered. Around the same time, Russell, who was to write a book called *Why I Am Not a Christian*, wrote to Lady Ottoline: "He is far more terrible with Xtans than I am. He had liked F[armer], the undergraduate monk, and was horrified to learn that he is a monk. F. came to tea with him and Wittgenstein at once attacked him...Yesterday he returned to the charge, not arguing but only preaching honesty" (Russell qtd. in McGuinness 111). This was in March. In November of 1912, the monk Farmer, whom Pinsent describes as "a man Wittgenstein dislikes and believes to be dishonest minded," dropped in on the two friends. Months after the first meeting, Wittgenstein was still very antithetical, advising Farmer to read a good book on exact science, carrying on as if he was his Director of Studies, and letting him know exactly what he thought of him (Monk 65). It would be risky to draw firm conclusions from the case of Wittgenstein *contra* Farmer, since it is not clear whether the latter's monkhood, Christianity, Catholicism, dishonesty in intellectual matters or some combination of these was what angered Wittgenstein. It would be safe to say that Farmer's being *religious* wasn't the problem. From the suggestion that Wittgenstein was upset only on finding out that the man was a monk, which had apparently not been revealed earlier, we may deduce some antipa-

thy to celibacy and to an organized priesthood, perhaps also to dogmatic positions deriving from Christian doctrine that may have emerged in conversation—both of which are evidenced later, as we shall see.

Whatever the exact nature of the singular, isolated yet growing religious
concern in Wittgenstein, it was assuaged by reading *The Varieties of Religious
Experience*. In that same year of 1912, between the meetings with Farmer, he
began to read James's classic, and apparently continued to read and recommend it to others (including Drury) for many years. He wrote to Russell on
June 22, 1912: "Whenever I have time now I read James's 'Varieties of religious exp[erience].' This book does me a lot of good. I don't mean to say that
I will be a saint soon, but I am not sure that it does not improve me in a little
way in which I would like to improve *very much*: namely I think that it helps
me to get rid of the *Sorge* (in the sense in which Goethe used the word in the
2nd part of Faust)" (*Letters to Russell, Keynes and Moore*, 10). While he may
not have become a convert to pragmatism, his close reading of the book, from
what we know of how he read Weininger, Spengler and Freud for instance,
would have at least given him *information* about the whole range of human religious experience. By providing a variety of personal testimonies and analyses of prophetic experiences, James's work seems particularly to have given
Wittgenstein the chance to orient himself and calm down the tensions that
must arise in the individual who refuses to merge with an organization. His
striking catholicity towards the religion of others surely owes something to
James: "The way in which people have had to express their religious beliefs
differ enormously. *All genuine expressions of religion are wonderful, even those of
the most savage people*" (to Drury, 108, emphasis added). Yet Russell seemed to
think that James's book had put Wittgenstein on the road to intellectual ruin.
To Lady Ottoline in 1920: "I had felt in his book [the *Tractatus*] a flavour of
mysticism, but was astonished when I found that he has become a complete
mystic. He reads people like Kierkegaard and Angelus Silesius, and he seriously contemplates becoming a monk. It all started from William James's Varieties of Religious Experience, and grew (not unnaturally) during the winter
he spent alone in Norway before the war, when he was nearly mad" (*Letters to
Russell* et al., 82).

Russell typifies a twentieth-century intellectual's response to Wittgenstein.
In the following pages we shall see Wittgenstein's thinking on the Bible,
prophecy, idolatry, God, and other religious matters. By and large it is not part
of the picture of his mind held by scholars of philosophy, who see it composed
of other philosophers, such as Frege, Russell, and Moore. In the "canonical"

works, the *Tractatus* and the *Philosophical Investigations*, there are hardly any overt references to religion, since he was following a grand strategy of putting everything in place by being silent about it. Someone looking for hints—which really means someone equipped to study texts both he and the author consider relevant—may of course find clues. Our evidence for Wittgenstein's religious life derives not from the "canon" composed of the two main works but from talks with close friends for whom religion was meaningful, and from the extracanonical manuscripts where Wittgenstein also left suggestions, as a second line of communication, as it were, although he could not bring himself to be explicit.

By the end of the *Notebooks 1914–1916*, still in the thick of the war, it is likely that a certain conflict had developed in Wittgenstein over his desire to be an honest religious thinker. In his well-documented drive against self-deception and vanity, his refusal to divorce his logic from his sins, no doubt he was succeeding in maintaining an internal honesty about his work. But questions of self-presentation to the world he was unable to settle in a straightforward manner. Rush Rhees has given the most convincing account of his struggle, in connection with the "confession" of being more Jewish than was generally known that Wittgenstein made to friends and family in 1936, four years into the *Hitlerzeit* of his schoolmate from Linz. Much earlier, "[i]n his letters and in notes for himself he said he wished he might become a different man—that he could be rid of self-deception....Becoming clear about himself...that...he had been performing for himself in a character that was not genuine, was difficult: not because he wasn't clever enough to discern it, but because he hadn't the *will*—and could not recognize this" (Rhees, "Postscript," 191). This constant worry, apparently of several years' duration, Wittgenstein attempted to resolve with a confession of Jewishness. It helped, but the benefits were not long lasting; the very next year he was berating himself for being a coward. I would like to suggest that since he was guilty, as he well knew, *the confession* (his word, which we should really read as "affirmation") of "physical" Jewishness—which is all it was—*left untouched his intellectual Jewishness, the real issue*. Although this leaving-untouched would have continued to bother him, there were two possible mitigating factors. Concealing intellectual Jewishness would have been a first-class artistic challenge for Wittgenstein, like Tolstoy's turning his back on the reader.[8] He was well aware that he had the kind of mind that constantly made a virtue out of necessity (*C&V*: 76ᵉ). Furthermore, certainly in the times he wrote, an author who was not classified as "Jewish" could ensure his work the attention it merited, without the danger of prejudice. "Strike a coin from every mistake," he wrote (*C&V*: 69ᵉ). So we discover: on the one hand, disappointment with himself for cowardice, for not achieving his own standards of honesty, a disappointment and a complete dead end: "[w]hen you bump against the limits of your own honesty it is as though your thoughts get into a whirlpool, an infinite regress: You can *say* what you like, it takes you no further" (*C&V*: 8ᵉ); and on the other hand, striking a coin from this failing by continuing to write philosophy in a Jewish key, ironically, perhaps, better wrought and more effective because covert. In this scheme, the confession of "physical" Jewishness acts as a brilliantly effective red herring; the reaction of "conventional wisdom" is going to be: "A fine philosopher, but a bit bothered about Jewish ancestry, and one can understand: who wouldn't be?" For the average European of mildly anti-Semitic tendencies this would be completely natural, and would put paid to any serious consideration of Jewishness in the philosophy. Such a reader's prejudices would preclude a deeper understanding: to repeat an earlier quotation, "The honorable thing to do is to put a lock on the door which will be noticed only by those who can open it, not by the rest" (*C&V*: 8ᵉ). For anyone who did not see Jewish descent as a dishonorable liability, who knew something of persecution and the art of writing, who knew that Jewish self-perception must be integrated with Jewish behavior, furthering the intellectual mission of Israel, the confession of Jewish descent would lead immediately to the thought: "The man is saying he was actually more Jewish than people knew. Did he want to say just *that*, or was he telling us to look for something Jewish in his work?" What would be the point of such an affirmation or confession if it had no bearing on his life work?

WITTGENSTEIN AND THE BIBLE

There seems to have been surprising resistance to acknowledging Wittgenstein's knowledge of the Bible, particularly of the "Old Testament"; after paraphrasing what he says is Wittgenstein's detailed interpretation of his dream with its allusions to Exodus, Numbers, the rods of Moses and Aaron, the Ark of the Covenant, manna, and the tablets of the Law placed in the Ark, Bartley comments: "Wittgenstein discussed the connections I have just mentioned, but they appear to have come as suggestions for interpretations from some other party, possibly Hänsel, who, unlike Wittgenstein, was well acquainted with the Old Testament" (Bartley 2nd ed., 30). Monk has similarly asserted that "the religious associations of Palestine would always, for him, have had more to do with the New Testament than with the Old" (229). Religious Knowledge was the only subject in which Ludwig got the top grade in high school. At least three years before the time of which Bartley speaks, Wittgenstein had asked for the Bible (*"in einem kleinen aber noch leserlichen Format"*) to be sent to him at the front by Engelmann (in 1917).

We have attestations to Wittgenstein's reading of the Vulgate (*in toto*, see Engelmann, *Letters*, 111), Luther, Rosenzweig-Buber, King James and Smith-Goodspeed American versions of the Bible. Not knowing Hebrew or Greek, he seems to have deliberately compared versions in languages he did know. "My landlord has a modern American translation of the Bible," he once wrote to Malcolm; "I dislike the translation of the N.T. (by a man, E.J. Goodspeed), but the translation of the O.T. (by a group of people) makes a lot of things clearer to me & and seems to me *well* worth reading. Perhaps you'll see it someday." Note the emphasis on the "O.T." and the gentle suggestion of Bible study to Malcolm, the man who he hoped would be the "one person who will understand my book when it is published" (*Memoir* 44, 51). Among "the texts [that] arose in W[ittgenstein]'s discussions" with Bouwsma was Isaiah 45:9— "For as the heavens are higher than the earth, so are my ways higher than your ways, and my thoughts than your thoughts."[9]

Wittgenstein had studied Scripture. But one might ask: what do we know of his attitude towards it? One of the sources on this point is conversations with Drury. About this source, it is relevant to note Wittgenstein's telling Bouwsma that Drury was one of "[t]hose students of his whom he is now fairly certain he did some good." This puts him in a select group from which even Wittgenstein's "recognized disciples" in philosophy are excluded. Engelmann, Drury and Bouwsma seem to have been the three people who were most attentive and curious about religion in their contact with Wittgenstein. Drury was the recipient of several "hints" which he has at least passed down to us.

They talked a good bit about Kierkegaard, Wittgenstein once pointedly telling Drury: "Mind you I don't believe what Kierkegaard believed."[10] This may refer to what Kierkegaard believed as a Christian. On one occasion, in 1929, Drury said that for him "the Old Testament was no more than a collection of Hebrew folk-lore"; Wittgenstein agreed rather reflectively: "For me too the Old Testament is a collection of Hebrew folk-lore—yes, I would use that expression." In 1951, however, weeks before his death, he was not so acquiescent. Drury said: "There are some passages in the Old Testament that I find very offensive. For instance, the story where some children mock Elisha for his baldness: 'Go up, thou bald head.' And God sends bears out of the forest to eat them." Wittgenstein replied *"very sternly"*: "You mustn't pick and choose just what you want in that way," and adding: "Just remember what the Old Testament meant to a man like Kierkegaard. After all, children have been eaten by bears." Wittgenstein here is not only asserting the continued importance of the Old Testament, using the example of Kierkegaard that will carry conviction with Drury; he is also taking part in theodicy with reference to the God of the "Old Testament."[11] After Drury defends himself with more examples, he is told off like a dim-witted younger brother: "That has nothing to do with what I am talking about. You don't understand, you are quite out of your depth." "I did not know," says Drury, "how to reply to this. It seemed to me that the conversation was distasteful to him..." They went to the railway station for what was to be their last farewell, but Wittgenstein "suddenly referred to our dispute over the Old Testament: 'I must write you a letter about that'" (Drury, "Conversations," 183, emphasis added). He was to die before writing it, perhaps depriving us of a better account of how he read the Bible than we can now piece together.

WITTGENSTEIN AS A BIBLICAL THINKER

The adjective "biblical" bears a certain tense ambiguity shared by its substantive "Bible" and paralleled in the term "Judaeo-Christian," as in "the Judaeo-Christian tradition." An English dictionary from Wittgenstein's time defines "Bible" simply as "the sacred writings of the Christian Church, consisting of the Old and New Testaments." The word in early English use was actually confined to the Hebrew books and sometimes still is, as in "neither in the Bible nor in the Testament." But this precious distinction could not maintain itself against the ideological need to assimilate and appropriate the Bible of the Jews as the Old Testament of the Christian Bible, a binding that Nietzsche called "perhaps the greatest piece of temerity and "sin against the spirit" that literary Europe has on its conscience" (*Beyond Good and Evil*, aphorism 52). That this binding and appropriation should have taken place is entirely in keeping of course with the fact—as stated by Abraham Joshua Heschel—that "the basic premises of Western philosophy are derived from the Greek rather than the Hebraic thinking" (*God in Search of Man*, 24). Christianity was unimaginable without its Greek components, while the Hebrew aspects had to be altered or suppressed. Christianity emphasized faith in Christ and love of God, with requisite, some would say dogmatic, belief in the "immaculate conception," the divinity of Jesus, and his resurrection. Whereas the rabbis saw man as free and perfectible, the Christian emphasis was on the taint of original sin, acquired in the "fall of man," an incident in *Genesis* understood in the Hebrew tradition simply as a failure on Adam's part to acknowledge his guilt before his Creator, a failure of responsibility rather than the origin of innate human sinfulness. So, from Moses to the later prophets Judaism emphasized responsibility and ethics, with a monotheism undiluted by a triune God, and these emphases continue to be the Judaic part of the so-called Judaeo-Christian tradition. Although this chapter tries to explore them, it is not clear what Wittgenstein's thoughts on the divergences between Judaism and Christianity would have been. Walter Kaufmann, in his *Critique of Religion and Philosophy*, reminds us that "[n]ot all religions are religions of salvation: the Hebrew prophets, for example, did not believe in any afterlife, and their religion was not a religion of salvation.[12] The religion of the Old Testament was a religion without dogmas. Later Judaism...[is] also a religion without dogmas..." (181). Indeed, the religion of the Old Testament was not a religion at all; there was no self-consciousness about it.[13] Seeing Judaism as a confrontation with the Bible, Heschel says that "a philosophy of Judaism must be a confrontation with the thought of the Bible" (*God*, 25). Since we have already seen Wittgenstein confronting the thought of the Greeks, we want to see how he confronts the Bible, both in its Hebrew and its Christian versions. No religious polemicist, he was relatively explicit about the New Testament, while his thinking on Hebrew scripture has to be reconstructed by indirect methods. A remark from 1939–40 provides a clue to his view of scripture. Offering an image, one of the similes he took some pride in crafting, he appears at once involved and dispassionate: "The Old Testament seen as the body without its head; the New Testament: its head; the Epistles of the Apostles: the crown on the head." Comparing the image to the reality: "When I think of the Jewish Bible, the Old Testament on its own, I feel like saying the head is (still) missing from this body. These problems have not been solved. These hopes have not been fulfilled. But I do not necessarily have to think of a head as having a crown" (*C&V*: 35ᵉ). His feeling about the Jewish Bible few would dispute; Israel's covenant is unfulfilled, the nation of Israel was still in exile at the time of writing, Messiah has not come. From this remark as well as a previous quotation about Paul, it is also clear that Wittgenstein does not regard the Epistles highly, or as essential to Christianity. It is not clear whether he means that even *with* the New Testament the Jewish Bible is headless, or that it is headless *tout court*, or something else again, but in the head-crown combination the problem seems to lie; for if the earlier book was *incapable of bearing or supporting a head* at all, Christianity grafted itself on to the wrong body, and its claims are false. But if the Jewish

Bible only lacked a head, and Christianity provided it, why should anyone not become an adherent of Christianity? Why would Wittgenstein tell the Austrian peasant that *although not a Christian*, he was an evangelist? In his terminology the New Testament seems to mean Gospels alone; thinking them to be the right head for the Jewish body should qualify one as a Christian, albeit a dissenting or heretical one. Or did Wittgenstein perhaps believe that the Jewish body, despite the arrival of Christianity, "still" awaited a head? Certainly, he defended the Jewish Bible against Drury's piecemeal criticisms—"You mustn't pick and choose just what you want in that way" (which is suggestive of the rabbinic principle that the Torah is one) and reminded him of how much the Old Testament meant to a man like Kierkegaard, the deepest thinker of the nineteenth century—a point likely to carry some weight with Drury (183). Kierkegaard's attitude is contrasted with Schopenhauer's, to whom Wittgenstein is so often compared. Heschel points to Schopenhauer's hostility to the Bible and Judaism (*God*, 380n.), and Nathan Rotenstreich tells us that *the Nazis viewed him as a model thinker.*[14]

Kaufmann reminds us that the very idea of propositional truth was lacking in Scripture. Instead, "[t]he most persistent intellectual energy and the most prodigious analytic effort were devoted to the loving care of a tradition, to the continual contrivance of beautiful and profound interpretations, and to questions of morality and ritual" (*Critique*, 270). Biblical thinking diverges from other types of thinking, preeminently from philosophy and science. Wittgenstein's antipathy for the scientific and mathematical mindset will be examined later in this chapter. For the moment, let us consider his seemingly extreme position on existential propositions as drawn out of him by an amusingly literal-minded Bertrand Russell: "He maintained, for example, at one time that all existential propositions are meaningless. This was in a lecture room, and I invited him to consider the proposition: 'There is no hippopotamus in this room at present.' When he refused to believe this, I looked under all the desks without finding one; but he remained unconvinced" (*Mind* 60 no. 239, 1951, qtd. in McGuinness 89, an incident of 1911). This attitude is radical because it says simply that there is no propositional truth, that propositional language is not "about" the world. Language may be assented to in terms of the later concept of "language game." When he and Russell met—eight years later—to go over the *Tractatus* manuscript after World War I, the latter "refused to accept Wittgenstein's view that any assertion about the world as a whole was meaningless." Again the literalist Russell made three blobs of ink on a sheet of white paper, and Wittgenstein acknowledged that they were there, "but he would not admit that anything at all could be said about the world as a whole" (Monk, and Russell qtd., 182). With this goes any possibility of theoretical truths in philosophy. Neither did the doctrines of religion have any theoretical content.[15] Skepticism towards even empirical propositional truth is seen in the late writings published as *On Certainty*—see his answer in the very first remark on Moore's proof that he had two hands, "Here is one hand, and here is the other!": "If you do know that *here is one hand*, we'll grant you all the rest." To grant Russell that there was no hippopotamus in the room would also be to breach the dam against propositional truth, to accept "all the rest." This is formative of the intellectual asceticism that so struck Drury—trust in propositions as providing the pseudo-satisfaction of an intellectual rocking horse, eventually an idolatrous leaning that must detract from the things we must be silent about. Speech is indeed not relevant to religion: "I can quite well imagine a religion in which there are no doctrines, and hence nothing is said. Obviously the essence of religion can have nothing to do with the fact that speech occurs—or rather, if speech does occur, this itself is a component of religious behavior and not a theory. Therefore nothing turns on whether the words are true, false or nonsensical" (Waismann's "Notes on Talks with Wittgenstein," qtd. in Hallett 426–27). In analytical philosophy, perhaps in all philosophy, *everything* turns on whether the words are true, false, or nonsensical. For Wittgenstein, furthermore, "the propositions of logic are tautologies. Therefore the propositions of logic say nothing" (*Tractatus* 61–11).[16]

Among notes Wittgenstein made of his reading are some lines on the Bible from *Education of the Human Race* by the close friend and supporter of Moses Mendelssohn, Gotthold Ephraim Lessing, whom he much admired and recommended to his friends. Lessing's *Nathan der Weise*, about the reconciliation of the three religions of the book, Wittgenstein found "superb." (*Die Juden*, a 1729 play of Lessing's, sought to prove that a Jew can be of noble character). "I have been reading Lessing (on the Bible)," he notes, "...the verbal clothing and the style...absolutely full of tautologies, but of a style to exercise one's wits by seeming sometimes to say something different while really saying the same thing and at other times seeming to say the same thing *while at bottom meaning, or capable of meaning, something different*" (*C&V*: 8ᵉ, emphasis added). Perhaps the most effective use of tautology in the entire Bible is God's response to Moses when asked for His name: "I am (shall be) what I am (shall be)," avoiding any possibility of the magical, controlling use of names by Moses, like the practices of other priests.

Lessing's image of the clothing of language is already in the *Tractatus*:

"Language disguises thought. So much so, that from the outward forms of the clothing it is impossible to infer the form of the thought beneath it, because the outward form of the clothing is not designed to reveal the form of the body, but for entirely different purposes" (4002). *This* understanding of the logic of language Wittgenstein seems to have associated (through Lessing) with biblical style, and with his own style. The image recurs in the *Investigations*: "We remain unconscious of the prodigious diversity of all the everyday language games because the clothing of our language makes everything alike" (p. 224ᵉ). The theme bears comparison with a fundamental idea in a mystical tradition of interpreting the Hebrew Bible, found in the *Zohar*:

> Thus had the Torah not clothed itself in garments of this world, the world could not endure it. The stories of the Torah are thus only her outer garments, and whoever looks upon that garment as being the Torah itself, woe to that man-such a man will have no portion in the next world....Observe this. The garments worn by a man are the most visible part of him, and senseless people looking at the man do not seem to see more in him than the garments. But in truth the pride of the garments is the body of the man, and the pride of the body is the soul. Similarly the Torah has a body made up of the precepts of the Torah, called *gufe torah* [bodies, main principles of the Torah], and that in garments made up of worldly narrations. The senseless people only see the garment, the mere narrations; those who are somewhat wiser penetrate as far as the body. But the really wise, the servants of the most high King, those who stood on Mount Sinai, penetrate right through to the soul, the root principle of all, namely, to the real Torah (qtd. in Bakan, *Freud*, 247).

Whether or not by using the figure of language as clothing Wittgenstein meant to associate himself with a mystical approach to the biblical text, he was quite set against any rational justification of religious beliefs or feelings. This came up again and again in different situations. When Drury mentioned his desire to be ordained as an Anglican priest, one of Wittgenstein's immediate concerns was that his new friend would try and give philosophical justifications for Christian beliefs, under the impression that they needed proof. "You have intelligence," he told Drury: "it is not the best thing about you, but it is something you mustn't ignore.—The symbolisms of Catholicism are wonderful beyond words. But any attempt to make it into a philosophical system is offensive" (Drury, "Conversations," 117). Wittgenstein seems completely open to the symbolic text of Catholicism without systematization or theoretical rigidity (dogma), as wonderful beyond words, somewhat as rabbis look upon the Torah text, holy and eternal. If one thinks of theoretical rigidity as a metalanguage, then in Wittgenstein's terms the ordinary language of religion, as it were, the symbolic text that invites response and commentary, "is all right"; nothing more is needed. Malcolm tells us that Wittgenstein was impatient with "proofs" of the existence of God or attempts to give religion a rational foundation: "When I once quoted to him a remark of Kierkegaard's to this effect: "How can it be that Christ does not exist, since I know that He has saved me?" Wittgenstein exclaimed: 'You see! It isn't a question of *proving* anything!'" (71). Also on Catholicism, he told Drury that one dogma alone of the Roman Church would make it impossible for him to be a Catholic: namely, the existence of God can be proved by natural reason (123). Two years before his death he put down a lucid epigram on these themes: "If Christianity is the truth then all the philosophy that is written about it is false" (*C&V*: 83ᵉ). Rational philosophy does not strengthen a faith but runs counter to it; the two are mutually exclusive.[17]

Without oversimplification, the question of religious belief and language can be placed in a continuum with science and superstition. In scientific language and techniques we expect reason and proof, always with their attendant philosophical complications (for philosophers, at any rate). Hence the *Tractatus* makes science a separate category, though this was not quite the endorsement the Vienna Circle and other positivists took it to be. *Superstition* Wittgenstein called a sort of false science, issuing from fear. This leaves religious belief as a *trust* (*C&V*: 72ᵉ), and indeed, if we were not bewitched by false views of language, trust in human life would be enlarged, as other aspects of Wittgenstein's linguistic thought suggest. His biblical thinking, at any rate, suggests a return to the very old by way of the very new: twentieth-century thought working towards the immediacy of God to man and man to God. But this rediscovery bears a Krausian stamp; only he is an artist, said Kraus, who can make a riddle out of the solution.

IDOLATRY

> All that philosophy can do is to destroy idols. And that means not making any new ones—say out of "the absence of idols."
>
> —Wittgenstein, "Philosophy"

Most themes in Wittgenstein's philosophy are missing from his comments on religion, and his discussions of religion do not proceed from the lines of his philosophy. When there is to be no ostensible connection between the two, this is to be expected—when the philosophy is the overt, visible mechanism pointing to an effect that is concealed and at a remove. Idolatry is the exception. Not only does Wittgenstein explicitly conceive of his philosophy as having the power to destroy idols—and this is most important: *without replacing them with new ones*—implicitly many of his themes, both religious and philosophical, are efforts in the same direction. From a Jewish point of view,

> any intercession between God and Humankind is rank idolatry. For Christianity intercession, through either Jesus or the saints, is the only means by which a human could approach God. The distance between humankind and God is so great that for a human being to address God directly constitutes an affront to the divine majesty. More precisely, intermediaries between humankind and God are the necessary effect of the hierarchical system inherent in the corporational organization of the *Corpus Christi*, which the Church represents (Faur, *Shadow*, 74).

With intermediaries come hierarchy; recall Wittgenstein's attribution of the beginnings of hierarchy in his remarks on Paul and the Epistles; and if in the Judaic view any intercession between God and Humankind is rank idolatry, his exhortation to Drury—"Make sure your religion is a matter between you and God only" (Drury 117) acquires a Judaic character. For on the part of both Jewish and Muslim thinkers, it is Christianity that is under suspicion of idolatry—"with its belief in the Trinity, its doctrine of the Incarnation, its use of statues of the crucified Jesus and of the Madonna, and its worship of saints," instruments of intercession all (Unterman, *Jews*, 226). While idolatry is the obvious danger directly pointed out to friends in talking about religion, Wittgenstein targets it in less obvious ways in the philosophical writings. The entire intellectual apparatus of the western world, with its ideology of representation, mathesis, and systematization, its investments in logic, structure and theory, the pride taken in the achievements apparently enabled by these, may be seen as no better, in effect, than a pagan idolatry to which many sacrifices have been made—not because we *have* these things, it must be emphasized, or because we have created them; that is not idolatry: rather because we become *attached* to them, derive our divinities from them, hand over our freedoms to them in our worship of our own not thoroughly examined creations. And this is the power of language:

> The power language has to make everything look the same, which is most glaringly evident in the *dictionary* and which makes the personification of *time* possible: no less remarkable than would have been making divinities of the logical constants. (*C&V*: 22ᵉ)

Language is the generalizing vehicle, claiming to make reference and representation possible everywhere. Accepting its claims leads immediately to "the bewitchment of our understanding by means of our language" (die *Verhexung unsres Verstandes durch die Mitteln unserer Sprache, PI* §109). An example: "I might say the title *The Mysterious Universe* includes a kind of *idol worship*, the idol being Science and the Scientist" (*LC*: 27, emphasis added). For this condition, whether it is entered into unknowingly or deliberately, and against which philosophy is a battle, the responsibility lies not with language but with those who, in the phrase in the preface to the *Tractatus*, misunderstand its logic: the users and framers of language—more narrowly, those who attempt to theorize over it, or who express their understanding of its logic. More than a decade after the *Tractatus* was complete, well into his second phase of philosophical work, Wittgenstein re-emphasized that it was the narrower group, the Platos and the Augustines and their modern descendants, who compounded the problem: "Instinctively we use language rightly; but to the intellect this use is a problem" (*Lectures* 1930–32, D. Lee, ed., qtd. in Gier 49). Since our entire understanding is bewitched, once a mistaken understanding of the logic of language, with its assumed referential, representational capacities, has taken root, there is no limit as to which particular product of bewitchment we decide to regard as an idol especially worthy of worship; the choice may vary with the intellectual investments of an age. Forms of intellectual idolatry begin with language being taken to provide pictures of the world. In Wittgenstein the critique of the picture begins (and indeed need not have gone beyond) the so-called "Picture Theory of Meaning" of the *Tractatus*. But the lesson had to be recapitulated and repeated in the *Investigations*:

> (*Tractatus Logico-Philosophicus*, 4.5): "The general form of propositions is: This is how things are." ——That is the kind of proposition that one repeats to oneself countless times. One thinks that one is tracing the outline of the thing's nature over and over again, and one is merely tracing round the frame through which we look at it. (*PI* §114).

This time the lesson has to be driven home: "A *picture* held us captive. And we could not get outside it, for it lay in our language and language seemed to repeat it to us inexorably" (*PI* §115). There is a compassionate therapeutic logic in this retelling of our having become captive to the picture. The image is the beginning of idolatry, and philosophy, "as we use the word, is a fight against the fascination which forms of expression exert upon us" (*Blue Book*: 27)—the problem, and the dissolution of the problem in reflective philosophy. The *picture* connects *idea* and *idol* etymologically in the Greek: *eídolon* "image, phantom, idol," from *eidos* "that which is seen," akin to *idein* "to see" (Webster's New Collegiate).

This is a good point to attempt giving a meaning to Wittgenstein's direct remark to Drury, already quoted: "Your religious ideas have always seemed to me more Greek than Biblical. Whereas my thoughts are one hundred percent Hebraic" (175). One may construe the "one hundred percent Hebraic" as thinking that looks critically at all other thought and exposes all that it has found to be idolatrous, while substituting nothing that could in turn become the object of idolatry. There is thus no essential "Hebraic thought"; there is Greek thought, perhaps Graeco-German or German thought, Western thought. But that thinking is Hebraic which, with reference to the Hebrew Bible, seeks to speed up the decay of all idols *qua* idols; it could also be called biblical thinking, as Heschel calls it; but Heschel was overtly Jewish. There can be no confusion over his sense of the term; Wittgenstein, wishing to avoid the ambiguity of Jewish vs. Christian use of "biblical," referred to his thinking as Hebraic—one hundred percent!

Insofar as thinking is "Hebraic," it is of course not "racial," "psychological" or even "cultural," but merely involved in a more direct intertextuality with the Bible, which only accidentally happens to be in the Hebrew language. Of course we have a bad record of making the linguistic terms (Indo-European, German, Anglo-Saxon, Aryan, Hebrew) into racial ones, and so "thought connected with the Hebrew language Bible" can quickly become "the thinking of those who speak Hebrew" and thus something ridiculous like "Hebrew (or Jewish) racial thinking."

While language seems to be metonymic for race, religion is not; on account of the religion people "speak," as it were, we do not speak of the Muslim race or the Christian race or the Buddhist race, only, alas, of the Jewish race, although the rate of conversion into the Jewish religion from "outgroups" might be no less than for the others. "Outgroup" is a moot word for Jews, since the Bible is not their story alone, but includes history before and after their formation as a community. "The other" is immanent in the Bible; the Bible is not the triumphal account typical of national epics, but deals with the human future. Biblical thinking is (also) prophetic thinking.[18]

PROPHECY

It may come as a surprise that Wittgenstein hinted at having a prophet's self-image. He certainly struck several people as a prophetic personality, for instance, Bouwsma and Mrs. Pascal ("His single-mindedness, resoluteness, and will-power make him stand out as a prophet, a kind of general in battle, not just a philosopher," Pascal 59) among the people already cited. The British philosopher G.J.Warnock had the intuition that the *Tractatus* resembled a sacred text in style and composition. But a Polish doctor whom Wittgenstein befriended during his war service, and to whom he imparted his ideas, was told in one of their animated conversations: "You will become a great disciple but not a prophet." The doctor, Max Bieler, adds this comment: "I could say of him that he had many of the traits of a prophet but absolutely not the traits of a disciple." (McGuinness 235. Wittgenstein refers to prophecy, though not apparently in the strictly religious sense, in *PI* §461 and *On Certainty* #492).

In a letter to Moore in 1936, Wittgenstein remarks that he looks like an old prophet in one of the enclosed photographs. Apart from his direct acquaintance with prophecy from reading the Bible, he wrote of "the obscure language of prophecy, comprehensible to very few indeed" in 1931 (*C&V*), indicating that he had reflected on the subject. Wittgenstein is not only saying that prophecy is comprehensible to a very few, but that he personally *knows* it to be so. Otherwise it would only be hearsay, for philosophy only states what we know. There are extensive discussions of prophecy in Pascal's *Pensées*, in Spengler, and to a lesser extent in James's *The Varieties of Religious Experience*, which he once read in isolation in Norway as early as 1912—"when he was nearly mad," according to Russell's letter. Wittgenstein's well known remarks in his lecture on ethics may also indicate a prophetic identification: "My whole tendency and I believe the tendency of all men who ever tried to write or talk Ethics or Religion was to run against the boundaries of language. This running up against the walls of our cage is perfectly, absolutely hopeless." Foremost of all men who ever tried to talk religion and ethics are the prophets of Israel, and they invariably pointed beyond the bounds of language to the God of Israel.

Wittgenstein himself used the word "prophecy" several times, in the following locations: once in the *Philosophical Investigations* (§461), once in *Culture and Value* (9ᵉ, already quoted; twice if one counts the "*bon sens précoce*" of the Semitic races, 6ᵉ), several times on p.165 of the *Lectures 1932–1935* edited by Ambrose, once in *On Certainty* #492; he speaks of *oracle* and "how it is, when a man says that God has spoken to him or through his mouth" in volume I of the *Remarks on the Philosophy of Psychology* (p.145). It is hard to distinguish between the instances where the discussion pertains to prophecy in the religious sense and not to foretelling or forecasting, but the connecting thread seems to be prophecy in language, the language of prophecy. Emphasis on the obscurity of prophecy comes earliest, and here Wittgenstein is preceded among others by Maimonides in his *Guide*:

> Hence God, May He be exalted, caused His book to open with the *Account of the Beginning*....And because of the greatness and the importance of the subject and because our capacity falls short of apprehending the greatest of subjects as it really is, we are told about those profound matters—which divine wisdom has deemed necessary to convey to us—in parables and riddles and in very obscure words. (I: 9)

Wittgenstein, in his *Culture and Value* remark, links prophecy with epic description of a whole culture in the work of its greatest figures, and with foreseeing. Since he also wrote of holy men as the only Jewish geniuses, we may read him as crediting biblical figures with prophecy and foresight. The puzzle was about *the obscure language of prophecy, comprehensible to very few indeed.* Two tendencies seem clear in Wittgenstein's approach to this, one in the *PI*: "As if the mere prophecy, no matter whether true or false, foreshadowed the future" (§461). The second concerns the prophet's first person account, his own credibility, which he is entitled to evaluate as much as anyone else. The passage from the *Remarks on the Philosophy of Psychology* vol. I is worth quoting in full:

> But consider this: After all I sometimes take someone else's word,—so I would surely at least sometimes have to take my own word too, that I have such and such a conviction. But when I report my observation in a quasi-automatic fashion, then this report has nothing at all to do with my conviction. On the other hand I might have confidence in myself, or in my observing self, just as another person does. So I might say "I say 'It's raining', so it will presumably be true" Or: "The observer in me says 'It's raining', and I'm inclined to believe him." For isn't this—or something like this—how it is when a man says that God has spoken to him or through his mouth? (Pp. 144^e-145^e)

To *PI* §461 Hallett appends a remark from ms. 108: "For insofar as reality is describable, expectation describes it, and insofar as reality is foreseeable, expectation foresees it" (*Companion*, 489).

The general effect of these observations seems to be to lend credibility to the process of holy geniuses honestly speaking for God and describing certain expectations, although obscurely, it being for others ("very few indeed") to read these descriptions for everybody else. Moses was led to claim: "Hereby shall ye know that the Lord has sent me to do all these works, and that I have not done them of my own mind" (*Numbers* 16: 28). One might advance the claim about Wittgenstein personally that having been called to prophesy, he failed to answer, as already noted, but later spent time analyzing the process by which he might have succeeded.[19] He seems to have arrived at an understanding of the analogy between the force of the word of God itself ("By the word of the Lord the heavens were made, / And all their host by the breath of his mouth./For he spoke, and it came to be, / He commanded, and it stood forth" Ps.33: 6ff.), and the word of the human prophet: "As if the mere prophecy, no matter whether true or false, foreshadowed the future" (*PI* §461). Only the word of the human prophet needs a human response.

Drury records speaking to Wittgenstein about the sense of awe in the Bible which he did not feel when Plato talked about the gods. He quotes from the book of Malachi: "But who may abide the day of his coming, and who shall stand when he appeareth?" (3: 2). Wittgenstein, standing still and looking at him very intently, remarked of these words with their messianic ring: "I think you have just said something very important. Much more important than you realize" ("Conversations," 175). The preceding lines in the book of Malachi, the messenger, are: "And the messenger of the covenant, / Whom ye delight in, / Behold, he cometh, / Saith the LORD of hosts."

Bouwsma was so struck by the prophetic aspects of Wittgenstein's personality that he once prepared a note for a class on the nature of a prophet. This is part of what he wrote:

What is a prophet like? Wittgenstein is the nearest to a prophet I have ever known. He is a man who is like a tower, who stands high and unattached, leaning on no one. He has his own feet. He fears no man. "Nothing can hurt me!" But other men fear him. And why?...They fear his judgment. And so I feared Wittgenstein, felt responsible to him....I was in dread of his coming and of being with him....

In any case the acquaintance with Wittgenstein has given me some inkling as to what the power of the prophet was among his people. "Thus saith the Lord" is the token of that being high above all fear and all blandishment, fearless and feared, judge and conscience. Thus saith the Lord!

It is an awful thing to work under the gaze and questioning of such piercing eyes, and such discernment, knowing rubbish and gold! And one who speaks the word: "This is rubbish!" (xv-xvi)

WITTGENSTEIN'S GOD

Ein Wesen, das mit Gott in Verbindung steht, ist stark.
—Wittgenstein, *Denkbewegungen*

In the course of piecing together Wittgenstein's religious ideas we have already heard him say that to believe in God means to see life has a meaning, that he must live in a way pleasing to God, that he must work in humility, like Bach, and by God's will not lose himself. We have seen him practicing theodicy with reference to the God of the Old Testament. Much of this account is derived from early journal entries and conversations with friends. These are not often studied by philosophers, who may be surprised to learn that Wittgenstein believed in God at all or that he prayed fervently all his life, and who may anyhow want to deny that these facts and views have to do with "the philosophy" at all.

Wittgenstein's attitude towards God was characterized by a certain skepticism about conventional pieties: "Once he said: 'You cannot love God, for you do not know him,' and went on elaborating the theme" (Fania Pascal in Rhees 30). For the Christian, religion is impossible without loving God, but for the Jew, accustomed to the intellectual injunction to cherish the Torah more than God, this does not come as a rude argument. Wittgenstein was skeptical to the point of impatience about proofs of the existence of God, as we have seen him telling Drury: "It is a dogma of the Roman Church that the existence of God can be proved by natural reason. Now this dogma would make it impossible for me to be a Roman Catholic. If I thought of God as another being like myself, outside myself, only infinitely more powerful, then I would regard it as my duty to defy him" (Drury, "Conversations," 123). There are two theological arguments being made here, one the obvious protest against mixing faith and reason that was a continuing theme in conversations with Drury; the other is a stand against the popular anthropomorphism that can so easily lead to idolatrous ideas. As Rabbi Alan Unterman says, "To talk of God as a Father or a King, as angry or happy, as creating a world and being disappointed with his creation, etc...encourages the formation of a picture-image of God incompatible with other Jewish teachings about His nature. The talmudic rabbis would often preface their more extreme anthropomorphisms with the phrase 'as if it were possible' (i.e. to talk about God in these terms)" (20). Maimonides was quite emphatic on the purely figurative nature of any talk of God having arms and feet and such. Wittgenstein seems to be signalling his adherence to a transcendentalist view of God, seeing "all human language about God as merely man's attempt to grasp the incomprehensible....Philosophically minded Jewish theology has invariably opted for a transcendentalist position..." (Unterman 20). Perhaps not accidentally, Wittgenstein's theological excursus was preceded by the remark, "For a truly religious man nothing is tragic," after which he and Drury walked on in silence for a while. Since he had also noted that tragedy was unJewish, perhaps his train of thought led him to remark on another thing that was Catholic but in his view unJewish.

The skepticism continues in the direction of pretentious claims about understanding God or His actions. "I have been reading in a German author, a contemporary of Kant's, Hamann, where he says, commenting on the story of the fall in Genesis: 'How like God to wait until the cool of the evening before confronting Adam with his transgression.' Now I wouldn't for the life of me dare to say, 'how like God.' I wouldn't claim to know how God should act" (Drury 122). Likewise, a year before his death, he wrote: "How God judges a man is something we cannot imagine at all. If he really takes strength of temptation and the frailty of nature into account, whom can he condemn?" (C&V: 86ᵉ).

If one cannot love God, if the existence of God cannot be proven, and if we cannot imagine how God judges us, what can we do regarding God? Here we have some guidance from Wittgenstein: "Certainly it is correct to say: Conscience is the voice of God" (*Notebooks 1914–16* 75ᵉ). Good conscience is linked to austerity, probably to the intellectual asceticism that Drury had noted: "The good conscience is the happiness that the life of knowledge preserves. / The life of knowledge is the life that is happy in spite of the misery of the world. / The only life that is happy is the life that can renounce the amenities of the world" (*Notebooks 1914–16* 81ᵉ).

Apart from conscience, religious belief involves trust, in the spirit of *Proverbs* 3:5: "Trust in the Lord with all thy heart, and lean not upon thine own understanding". Trust is said to be etymologically related to truth (according to the OED, an obsolete sense of truth as a transitive verb is *trust*). As we saw above, distinguishing religious belief from superstition, Wittgenstein wrote: "Religious belief & superstition are completely different. One comes from *fear* & is a sort of false science. The other is a trust" (Man. 168,2, qtd. in Hallett, *Companion*, 426). This theme has been taken up by the philosopher Hilary Putnam with reference to some other remarks of Wittgenstein's in *On Certainty*. Putnam is talking about relativism and metaphysical foundations of language:

> I think that we get a better understanding of this situation if we see relativism not as a cure or a relief from the malady of "lacking a metaphysical foundation," but rather

see relativism *and* the desire for a metaphysical foundation as manifestations of the same disease. The thing to say to the relativist is that some things are true and some things are warranted and some things are reasonable, but of course we can only *say* so if we have an appropriate language. And we do have the language, and we can and do say so, even though that language does not itself rest on any metaphysical guarantee like Reason.

What does it rest on? Wittgenstein gives a shockingly simple answer: trust.

'§508: What can I rely on?

§509: I really want to say that a language game is only possible if one trusts something. (I did not say "can trust something")'

(*Renewing Philosophy*, 177).

If this human language on which our entire mental life rests is only possible on trust, how much more necessary must trust be with regard to God. If we extend our trust (unknowingly, perhaps) to our fellow beings in playing language games with them, when we know that we do this, what can keep us from extending our trust to the Creator?

However, the trust extended, unlike in the Christian view, cannot be through any intermediaries whatsoever: remember Wittgenstein's advice to Drury: "Oh, don't depend on circumstances. Make sure your religion is a matter between you and God only" (117). The Christian view, if Blaise Pascal can be held to represent it, is: "We know God only through Jesus Christ. Without this mediator all communication with God is broken off. Through Jesus we know God" (*Pensées*, Penguin ed., 85–6, = no. 189). Pascal goes on about original sin and prophecies, for him all part of the proof of God. We note that this goes against Wittgenstein's remark about the dogma of the Roman Church that the existence of God can be proved by natural reason, which made it impossible for him to be a Catholic (Drury 123). Note also that this further contradicts, for example, the remark about the trenchant parallelism between Pascal and Wittgenstein suggested by von Wright in his biographical sketch, for "...Pascal is trying to persuade his interlocutor not merely to believe, but is so doing to become a full member of the Catholic Church, the body of Christ outside which he saw no salvation" (Krailsheimer, *Introduction* to Penguin ed. of *Pensées*, 26). Of this Drury is well aware; see his anticipation of the point: "For Pascal there was only one true religion, Christianity; only one true form of Christianity, Catholicism; only one true expression of Catholicism, Port Royal. Now, although Wittgenstein would have respected this narrowness for its very intensity, such exclusiveness was foreign to his way of thinking" (108). Of course in the Judaic view, any intercession between God and humankind is rank idolatry

(Faur). The religion of the future for Wittgenstein was to be without priests and ministers, without even the consolation of belonging to a church.

Typically, the direct relation of God to each individual is given a grammatical formulation by Wittgenstein towards the end of his life, in the last remark of the collection *Zettel*: "'You can't hear God speak to someone else, you can hear him only if you are being addressed.'—That is a grammatical remark" (#717). This is reminiscent of the traditional Jewish understanding of the revelation at Sinai: God speaking individually to every member of His chosen. According to José Faur, the third person is viewed in Hebrew rhetoric as excluded from I-and-Thou conversations.

APROPOS CHRISTIANITY

> Either Jews or Christians must be wicked.
> —Pascal, *Pensées*

In exploring Wittgenstein's religion we have inevitably had to touch upon Christianity, the religion of his mother in which he was baptized and raised (his father converted to Protestantism, an act of protest in Catholic Austria, perhaps analogous to converting to Islam in Protestant America). The reader need hardly be reminded of the widespread assumption that Roman Catholicism was Wittgenstein's faith. But we have seen in his own statement that just one dogma of the Roman Church would have precluded him from being a Catholic. Now we will see his statements on Jesus, John and Paul, incidental remarks on Christianity, and his attitude to the many conversions to Roman Catholicism that swirled around him in his lifetime.

Referring to I Cor. 12 ("No man can say that Jesus is the Lord, but by the Holy Ghost"), Wittgenstein wrote in 1937: "And it is true: I cannot call him *Lord*; because that says nothing to me. I could call him 'the paragon,' 'God' even—or rather, I can understand it when he is called thus; but I cannot utter the word 'Lord' with meaning. *Because I do not believe that he will come to judge me*; because *that* says nothing to me. And it could say something to me, only if I lived *completely* differently" (*C&V*: 33ᵉ; original emphasis). Wittgenstein did not live the life of a Christian believer, though he imagined doing so. Only had he actually lived such a life, he thought, could he ever have been able to call Jesus Lord. An interesting application of the idea that the life one lives—the actions one undertakes—determine one's religion.

After Jesus, perhaps the next most imposing figure in the Christian religion is Paul. Wittgenstein valued the gospels over the writings of Paul: "In the Gospels—as it seems to me—everything is *less pretentious*, humbler, simpler. There you find huts; in Paul a church. There all men are equal and God himself is a man; in Paul there is something like a hierarchy; honours and official positions.—That, as it were, is what my NOSE tells me" (*C&V*: 30ᵉ). Furthermore, he picked on the Pauline doctrine of grace or predestination as an example of a kind of religion that, for him, was "ugly nonsense, irreligiousness. Hence it is not suitable for me, since the only use I could make of the picture I am offered would be a wrong one." There seems to be a parallel here to the attitude of Nietzsche: "In a formula: *Deus, qualem Paulus creavit, dei negatio*" (God, as Paul created him, is a denial of God) (*The Anti-Christ*, trans. Hollingdale, 163). But Wittgenstein continues without general condemnation: "If it is a good and godly picture, then it is so for someone at a quite different level, who must use it in his life in a way completely different from anything that would be possible for me" (*C&V*: 32ᵉ). The rejection is for himself alone, leaving open the possibility that Pauline Christianity might be eminently suitable for someone else. In this spirit he once told Drury that the only value of Albert Schweitzer's *The Quest for the Historical Jesus* was that "it shews how many, many different ways people can interpret the Gospel story" (121).

One of the most precise expositions of his attitude was made by Wittgenstein to Oets Bouwsma, the Dutch-American professor of philosophy with whom he stayed on a visit to America and who pressed him closely on some matters of religion, as did Drury, and at an earlier time Engelmann. Bouwsma's remarks make clear the linguistic method Wittgenstein was inclined to apply dispassionately to the most divisive religious questions, demonstrating a consistency between his "philosophy" and his religious thought. Bouwsma reports Wittgenstein's telling him that he "could make nothing of the dogma of the Incarnation. And the Gospel of John puzzles him. He does not 'understand' it." Then he went on to specify carefully that he did *not* mean that it was not understandable. The question becomes one of how others understand the Gospel of John, of *their use of the sentences* involved. Bouwsma's account continues: "And here one thing is clear. Whatever this use is, it is different from the use of ordinary sentences describing the world. But this difference must be recognized by both those who have a use for them and by those who do not. Those who have no use for them are not to disparage all use of them simply because they cannot deal with them as they deal with: 'Pussy says meow.' But likewise those who have use for them are not to resort to proofs and evidence as they too might with 'Pussy says meow'" (57).

Along with matters central to Christian doctrine and dogma, Wittgenstein often touched on the symbols of Christian culture with a mixture of passion and detachment. He chided Drury on hanging a crucifix in his room, not because he was offended by it but because Drury should not get too familiar with religious things. Seeing a draughtsman designing a cross in an architect's office, he declared that he couldn't for the life of him design a cross in this age: "I would rather go to Hell than try and design a cross." This was said apparently in 1936, and followed by regret at what he had said (Drury 149). Much earlier, to Engelmann, he had declared that von Ficker's journal *Der Brenner* "is nonsense (a Christian journal is intellectual make-believe)—" (letter 41, from Norway, 1921). Yet he also said to Drury: "There is a sense in which you and I are both Christians" (130). Perhaps guardedness as well as a desire to identify with the other can be seen in such a remark. In what sense? That Christianity is a Jewish sect? In the 1930's, from a man to whom he had confessed his Jewish descent, he would have been happy perhaps to have received the response, "in a sense we're both Jews." Wittgenstein was clear that his philosophy was applicable whatever one's religion happened to be: "Its advantage is that if you believe, say, Spinoza or Kant, this interferes with what you believe in religion; but if you believe me, nothing of the sort." Wittgenstein's version of Jewishness, if that's what it was, had unlimited applicability.

Wittgenstein's complex and restrained attitude towards Christianity can also be discerned from his reactions to the conversions frequent in his circle. On hearing that one of his pupils had become a Roman Catholic, he said: "I seem to be surrounded now by Roman Catholic converts! I don't know whether they pray for me. I hope they do" (to Drury, 162); in another similar situation he wrote back to a convert: "If someone tells me he has bought the outfit of a tight-rope walker I am not impressed until I see what is done with it" (*ibid.*, 103); Malcolm says in his *Memoir*: "Of Smythies and Anscombe, both of whom had become Roman Catholics, he once said to me: 'I could not possibly bring myself to believe all the things that they believe.'" Malcolm adds, quite rightly, that "in this remark he was not disparaging their belief. It was rather an observation about his own capacity" (73). Nevertheless, we have a man who believes wholeheartedly in God, is committed to living an ethical life, but lacks the "capacity" to commit himself to Roman Catholicism. When Drury revealed his intention of becoming ordained as an Anglican priest, Wittgenstein responded: "Don't think I ridicule this for one minute, but I can't approve; no, I can't approve. I would be afraid that one day that collar would choke you" (116); in the same conversation he remarked: "Russell and the parsons between them have done infinite harm, infinite harm."

Although as we saw Wittgenstein was known to be a vehement anti-Christian in his twenties, in the conversations with Drury and in *Culture and Value* he does express appreciation of certain aspects of Christianity, as do many recognized Jewish thinkers. Unfortunately, there is no known case of anyone's becoming a Jew or a philo-Semite as a result of the impact of Wittgenstein's thought. It is tempting to speculate that this is why he felt no one had understood him, although doubtless the remark about the purchase of the tightrope-walking outfit would apply to someone who had, too.

Among the reasons that Wittgenstein has been taken to have been a Christian is that, as he reported, Tolstoy's abridged Gospels was a book that saved his life during his war service. But it hardly follows that he was thenceforth a Christian; if one's life is saved by surgery, one does not necessarily become a surgeon. Wittgenstein may simply have been in infinite torment at the time; there is a related suggestion in *Culture and Value*: "The Christian religion is only for the man who needs infinite help, solely, that is, for the man who experiences infinite torment" (46ᵉ). Without intending to, Monk, who depicts Wittgenstein as a believing Christian evangelist, also provides a detail supporting the possibility suggested here: "During the first few months of the war, the spiritual sustenance that Wittgenstein derived from reading Tolstoy's *Gospels* 'kept him alive,' in the sense that it allowed him, as he put it, to lighten his external appearance, '*so as to leave undisturbed my inner being*'" (116, emphasis added). In other words, the book gave timely and temporary help, but did not result in anything deeper.

In *Denkbewegungen*, diaries from the 1930's published in 1997, there are several remarks that go to the core of Christian belief. For example: "You can't call Christ Redeemer without calling him God. For a man cannot redeem you" ("Du kannst Christus nicht den Erlöser nennen, ohne ihn Gott zu nennen. Denn ein Mensch kann Dich nicht erlösen" I, 69.) Later, again: "Actual Christian faith—not *faith*—I do not understand at all" ("Den eigentlichen *Christenglauben*—nicht den *Glauben*—verstehe ich noch gar nicht" I, 86; on the next page he records that he has no faith in redemption through the death of Christ; the translations here are mine).

In these diaries, published after the present work had taken shape, there is one clear and compelling remark that bears out the impossibility of a commitment to Christianity on Wittgenstein's part: "Das Christentum sagt eigentlich:

laß alle Klugheit fahren" (Klagge and Nordmann, eds., 138; translated as "Christianity is really saying: let go of all intelligence," 139). Rather than a moment of sudden insight, this has all the makings of a lifelong realization, one of those fundamental ideas that he told Drury came to him "a long time ago."

It is worth recording that Blake was one of Wittgenstein's favorite poets. On one occasion, in 1946, he told Drury that Blake's *Proverbs of Hell* contained many profound thoughts. "And then suddenly he quoted [the last two lines of *The Everlasting Gospel*]," (Drury, "Conversations," 165):

> I am sure this Jesus will not do
> Either for Englishman or Jew.

TALMUDIC-RABBINIC TRAITS IN WITTGENSTEIN

> ...my critical eye is an X-ray eye & can penetrate from 2 to 4000 pages. That's in fact how I get all my learning.
>
> —Wittgenstein, letter to Malcolm

We must remember that not only have several people remarked on Wittgenstein's ability to seize ideas and develop them in his own way from the barest details, but also that he observed this ability in himself. So on the one hand it is not necessary to prove that Wittgenstein made direct and intensive study of the Talmud to argue that he was stimulated by it or internalized some of its modes of argument. On the other hand, of course, by any overt expression of interest in such key Jewish texts, Wittgenstein would risk the raising of eyebrows in times of lethal antisemitism and blowing the concealing cover that he apparently wished to maintain. From his close reading of Spengler he obtained enough references to pursue a talmudic title or two, such as Salomon Funk's little book *Die Entstehung des Talmuds*, 1910. (We know that he did follow up by reading some of Spengler's references). Pascal's *Pensées* too provides numerous references to specific tractates of the Talmud. If he did read Maimonides, as I have suggested, the *Guide* would be another point of entry to talmudic literature.

The following will indicate the range of Spengler's treatment:

Terms used or defined by Spengler: Amhaarez, Amoraim, Essenes, Falasha, Haggada, Halakhah, Gemara, Kabbalah, Medrashim (*sic*), Mishnah (remarks on origin, development, completion, as commentary), Nephesh, Qaraites, Resh Galutha (Exilarch),

Ruach, Sadduccees, Sopherim, Synedrion (*sic*), Talmud, "throne-chariot of Ezekiel's Vision" = Merkabah mysticism, Torah, Zaddikism, Yiddish, Yesirah, Zionism, Zohar (Sohar)

Places of Jewish significance: Javneh, Sura, Pumbeditha

Rabbis: Gamaliel, Akiba, Bar Kochba, Maimonides, Joseph Qaro

Literary, philosophical, scientific figures: Philo, Josephus, Judah Ha Levi, Spinoza, Uriel Acosta (*sic*), Baal Shem Tov, Heinrich Hertz, Franz Boas (his research on race cited)

Relevant scholarly works of basic Jewish interest: Fromer, *Der Talmud*; Eduard Meyer, *Geschichte des Altertums*; M. J. Ben Gorion, *Die Sagen der Juden* (M.J. Ben Gurion is the *nom de plume* of Micha Josef Berdychevsky, who had written a book in 1896 on the unity of ethics and aesthetics). S. Funk, *Die Entstehung des Talmuds*.

Salomon Funk's work on the origin of the Talmud that Spengler cites is most interesting in the present connection. It appeared in 1910, about the time of Wittgenstein's religious experience in the theatre (McGuinness 94). A mere 123 pages in length, it was the work of an Hungarian rabbi who had led a congregation in Vienna. No bigger than a pack of cigarettes, it presented a balanced view of the Talmud to non-Jewish readers, and appeared in the popular Goeschen series (see Nadel, *Joyce and the Jews*, 119–20).

The *Philosophical Investigations* is remarkably unsystematic in contrast to the *Tractatus* with its dissolved system, and in this itself it may be compared to the talmudic mode. "The more genuinely and characteristically Jewish an idea or doctrine is," observes Gershom Scholem, "the more deliberately unsystematic it is. Its principle of construction is not that of a logical system" (*Major Trends*, 158, qtd. in Baron 487). Mauthner, whom Wittgenstein read and mentioned in the *Tractatus*, noted that "The Jew has—whether to his advantage or not—a certain aversion towards systems and the solemnity of robes of state; he takes things easily" (qtd. in Baron 487). Even Nietzsche, some examples of the congruence of whose thought with Wittgenstein's we have already seen, confessed: "I mistrust all systematizers...the will to a system is a lack of integrity." In the mystical tradition of Kabbala, too, there were technical terms for "jumping" or "skipping" from one conception to another in the manner— seemingly without parallel in philosophy—of the *Philosophical Investigations*.

In addition to using Maimonidean images such as a locked room to which the uninitiated do not have the key, and the unravelling of knots, Wittgenstein appears to have alluded to the exegetical distinction between *peshat* (plain, literal meaning) and *derash* (interpreted, figurative meaning) with reference to the *Tractatus*. After extensive and probing conversations with Wittgenstein about his book, the young Cambridge logician and philosopher Frank Ramsey wrote back from Austria to his mother: "Some of his sentences are intentionally ambiguous having an ordinary meaning and a more difficult meaning which he also believes."[20]

The concept of a written text being incomplete, always standing in need of oral interpretation, is a fundamentally Jewish one (Written Law vs. the Oral Law), and therefore it is significant that Wittgenstein repeatedly used this imagery with reference to the *Tractatus*. In a letter to Russell, after expressing surprise that some logical thoughts he had communicated should have had no effect at all on their recipient, he wrote: "...I'm now afraid that it might be very difficult for me to reach any understanding with you. And the small remaining hope that my manuscript might mean something to you has completely vanished. As you can imagine, I'm in no position to write a commentary on my book. I could only give you one orally." Around the same time he wrote to Keynes suggesting that Russell wouldn't be able to understand his book "without a very thorough explanation *which can't be written.*"

On the written as opposed to the oral in Jewish tradition, Spengler had this to say:

> More important still is the assumption, traceable in every Magian religion, of a secret revelation, or a secret meaning of the Scriptures, preserved not by being written down, but in the memory of adepts and propagated orally. According to Jewish notions, Moses received at Sinai not only the written, but *also a secret oral Torah...*, which it was forbidden to commit to writing. 'God foresaw,' says the Talmud, 'that one day a time would come when the heathen would possess themselves of the Torah and would say to Israel: "We, too, are the sons of God." Then will the Lord say: "Only he who knows my secrets is my son." And what are the secrets of God? The oral teachings.'
>
> (Spengler II: 246)

This allows us to claim with some confidence that at least by the time he read Spengler Wittgenstein was acquainted with this Talmudic thought.

The unwritten, the humanly unwritable, is connected to writing for those who already understand and to the idea of a limit to human thought that Wittgenstein mentions in the *Tractatus* at 6372: "Die Alten sind allerdings insofern klarer, als sie einen klaren Abschluß annerkennen, während es bei dem neuen System scheinen soll, als sei *alles* erklärt." The expression "Die Alten" (the elders, ancients) may in fact stand for the ancient rabbis. This idea of a limit is in any case to be found exactly expressed in Maimonides. "Their purpose [i.e. 'these texts set down by the prophets and the *Sages*'] in its entirety, rather is to make it known that the intellects of human beings have a limit at which they stop" (*Guide*, I, 32). Maimonides sees the limit placed on the human intellect as a way of showing regard for the honor of God. A sphere is left to which man can nonetheless aspire without speaking or writing about it. In view of the traditional Jewish teaching of human freedom based on a reciprocal relationship with God, this is potentially a sphere of activity shared with God.

We know from Wittgenstein's own words that he regarded the only use of philosophy as being against philosophers and against the philosophers in us (ms. 219, 11, qtd. in Hallett 382). This is part of his use of a dialectics reminiscent of the Talmud. The English philosopher John Austin humorously but precisely said of the dialectic method that it consisted of "the bit where you say it, and the bit where you take it back." In fact, towards the end of his life when an officer of the Rockefeller Foundation was trying to lure Wittgenstein to the United States with offers of money and the publication of his manuscripts, Wittgenstein spoke dismissively of his own philosophy: "But see, I write one sentence, and then I write another—just the opposite. And which shall stand?" (Bouwsma 73). Dialectic anti-philosophy was the practice also of Judah ha-Levi. Rabbi Alan Unterman says of him: "He...uses philosophical argument to show the incoherencies and inconsistencies in philosophy itself, and to undermine its status as a threat to traditional Judaism" (60). In Derrida's *Glas*, cast in the talmudic mold, one finds a succinct formulation, "La dialectique de la langue est dialectophage" (the dialectic of language is devouring of language/dialectic). Nahum Glatzer, editor and biographer of Franz Rosenzweig, tells us that Rosenzweig "fought against the abstract philosopher *in himself*..." In *The Star of Redemption* we read: "Philosophy started only when reasoning wedded itself to being. But it is precisely to philosophy, and precisely at this point, that we deny our allegiance. We seek what is everlasting, what does not first require reasoning in order to be" (20). Indeed, as Susan Handelman has suggested, the rabbinic tradition is skeptical of reason itself. One slim instance can be provided (from the *Lectures and Conversations*) where Wittgenstein seems to admit that he too was advancing a similar skepticism: "We would take sides, and that goes so far that there would really be great differences between us, which might come out in Mr. Lewy [a student] saying: 'Wittgenstein is trying to undermine reason,' *and this wouldn't be false*" (64; emphasis added).

Talmudic dialectic or *pilpul*, serving the cause of mental liberation, has been finely distinguished from the conceptions of dialectic in Western philosophy, used rather to propound theory. Heschel has pointed out that "Jewish thinking and living can only be adequately understood in terms of *a dialectic pattern*, containing opposite and contrasted properties" (*God*, 341, emphasis added).

Rabbinic tradition is also built around interpretation of legal and biblical texts. The manifold, even infinite nature of interpretive activity is a given. As Heschel observed, "Judaism is based upon a minimum of revelation and a maximum of interpretation....The source of authority is not the word as given in the text but Israel's understanding of the text" (*God*, 274). We have seen how much in this spirit was Wittgenstein's appreciation of the many meanings of scripture. Like the rabbis, his sense of interpretation was activist: "To interpret is to think, to do something"(*PI* p. 212); "When I interpret, I step from one level of thought to another" (*Zettel* #234). With this "catholicity" of interpretation went Wittgenstein's love for diversity and difference, extending to all religions. "The way in which people have had to express their religious beliefs differ enormously," he told Drury, as we have seen; "All genuine expressions of religion are wonderful, even those of the most savage peoples"; "...he was fond of quoting the proverb, 'It takes *many* sorts to make a world,' adding, 'that is a very beautiful and kindly saying'" (162, 108).

Historically minded philosophers and other academics have not been very understanding of Wittgenstein's impulse to be apart from history. As cited already in Chapter I, he wrote in the *Notebooks 1914–1916*: "What has history to do with me? Mine is the first and only world." In the *Mishnah* (*Sanhedrin* 4.5) we read "...but though God has stamped every man with the die of the first man, yet not one of them is identical with his fellow. Therefore everyone must say, 'For my sake was the world created.'" This passage occurs in the *Traditional Prayer Book* (p. 876). The Jewish philosopher Micha Josef Berdychevsky (also Berdychewski) is paraphrased by Nathan Rotenstreich (*Jews and German Philosophy*, 315) as saying: "There exists only one world which is my own." I note again that Berdichevsky or Ben Gorion, one of Spengler's references, had published a book in German in 1896 on the unity of ethics and aesthetics. According to Franz Rosenzweig in 1914, "the curse of historicity" was something the Jewish faith was free of (Glatzer, *Rosenzweig*, xxi). Rosenzweig connects this with "the old Jewish defiance," "the eternal reservation against visible, all-too-visible world history" (170).

FACE, CLOTHING, DREAMS: KABBALISTIC ECHOES?

> Of this world, consummate and pacified, it is said: "may he make his countenance to shine upon you" [see *Num.* 6:25]
> —Franz Rosenzweig, *The Star of Redemption*

In the *Philosophical Investigations* it is asserted that meaning—the ultimate quest in the human being's mental and emotional life—is a physiognomy (§568). Gier in his *Wittgenstein and Phenomenology* calls this a cryptic statement (160). A fascination with—more correctly a deep-rooted interest in—faces and physiognomies runs through Wittgenstein's writings, published and unpublished, as well as through the recorded conversations. Except for one or two expressions of puzzlement over this, it has hardly been taken seriously. In one case, Wittgenstein's philosophy has been called a "physiognomic phenomenalism" (Finch in Gier 95). His concern with faces ranged from large scale and deep religious symbolism to the most practical day to day concerns. At the cosmic level, Elizabeth Anscombe, one of the people closest to Wittgenstein, observes that "[t]here is a strong impression made by the end of the *Tractatus*, as if Wittgenstein saw the world looking at him with a face" (qtd. by Henry L. Finch, *Wittgenstein: The Later Philosophy*). Down to earth, associating faces with *one's others*, he chastised his friend Drury in a letter with *not paying enough attention to people's faces*: "[d]on't think about yourself, but think about others, e.g. your patients," 110; for another incident, see 141). Paying attention to people's faces is simply a practical way of making oneself "other-oriented."

As a symbol, the face or countenance is deeply and variously rooted in Jewish tradition. It indeed occupies a place linking the heights of encountering the divine with common responsibilities. The linkage is expressed thus by Levinas, who makes extensive use of the symbol himself: "The dimension of the divine opens forth from the human face....Hence metaphysics is enacted where the social relation is enacted—in our relations with men....*The Other is not the incarnation of God, but precisely by his face, in which he is disincarnate, is the manifestation of the height in which God is revealed.* It is our relations with men...that give to theological concepts the sole signification they admit of."[21] The face of the Other manifests the height in which God is revealed. In Kabbala, in the *Zohar*, according to Unterman, the ten *sefirot*, "matrices which have emanated from the Godhead and by which reality is formed and controlled.... are the faces of the divine King, the garments of God, divine names, the basic features of all language, etc." (101). According to Moshe Idel, two of these *sefirot, Yesod* and *Malkhut*, are referred to by one Kabbalist as *'Arikh 'Anpin* and *Ze'ir 'Anpin*. Idel understands this type of symbolism as "an integration of the *talmudic* portrayal of the cherubim as 'great face' and 'little face' within a context mentioning *the face or faces of God and the supernal faces*" (*Kabbalah: New Perspectives*, 134; reference to Talmud, *Sukkah* 5b; emphasis added).[22] The face of God is the symbolic goal of the searching man. David the psalmist sings: "In Thy behalf my heart hath said: / 'Seek ye My face';/ Thy face, LORD, will I seek./ Hide not Thy face from me" (27: 8–9). Maimonides devoted a whole chapter of his *Guide* to the symbolism of the face, collating some two dozen or more occurrences of the word in multiple usages in the Bible. The great medieval poet Judah ha-Levi, translated among others by Franz Rosenzweig, with whose translation (with Martin Buber) of the Hebrew Scriptures into German Wittgenstein was familiar, put it this way: "To see the face of my King is my sole desire" (Heschel 29). Conversely, times of Jewish misfortune are commonly symbolized as God hiding his face, a usage deriving, according to Maimonides, from Deut. 31: 17 (II: 626).

An even earlier and more fundamental usage is of course in Moses' face-to-face encounter with God. The Hebrew phrase for face-to-face is *panim 'el panim*. Faur, following Maimonides, understands God speaking to Moses face to face as presentness to presentness without an intermediary. But this is not to be understood as the face of God *being seen* by a human. As the poet Edmond Jabès put it, "All faces are His, therefore He has no face." The emphasis is on the directness—without the intermediary of an angel—of the experience. The phrase is explained by reference to Deut. 4: 12, where it does not occur, but a voice is heard. Unique and internal, the *panim* or face cannot be grasped in terms of anything else.[23] "Unlike Western thought," writes Faur, "in which 'face' is associated with 'exteriority' and is therefore visually exposed, in Hebrew *panim* 'face' means 'interiority.' The face is perceived through the (inner) psychological expressions such as anger and sadness; it is dynamic and subject to constant change. In order to perceive the 'face,' one requires active interpretation rather than passive 'looking'" (129). A face is to be *read* as a physiognomy; the face is writing, not presence. The faces that we see represent God in the other.

These traditional ideas have been developed, mainly in the direction of responsibility symbolized by the face of the other, by writers like Rosenzweig, Heschel, Derrida, and Levinas. On this point the last is perhaps the most articulate. The face theme is recognized as so important that a collection of writings on him is entitled *Face to Face with Levinas*.[24] The editors of *Re-Reading*

Levinas note in their introduction: "Levinas finds the face of the Other (*autrui*) a point of irreducible alterity which resists the philosophical logos. The self finds itself put in question by and obliged to respond to the Other. The obligation to respond amounts to a responsibility that cannot be evaded, but that has been ignored or dissimulated within the philosophical tradition" (Bernasconi & Critchley xi). Irreducible alterity and the obligation to respond to it resist and chastise the logos, the Greek-derived philosophical tradition. One of the writers in this collection refers to the epiphany of the face as the experience *par excellence* in Levinas and "the condition of the possibility of language" (Greisch 68). Meaning is a physiognomy, as Wittgenstein put it.

The idea of face, countenance or physiognomy, terms often used interchangeably, is associated in the dictionary with inner character as revealed outwardly. It occurs for the first time in Wittgenstein early enough to be among his fundamental ideas, as he spoke of them to Drury—in 1916, five years before the appearance of the *Tractatus*, during his war service. "One conception," he notes: "As I can infer my spirit (character, will) from my physiognomy, so I can infer the spirit (will) of each thing from its physiognomy. But can I *infer* my spirit from my physiognomy?" (*Notebooks 1914–1916*: 84ᵉ). Soon after his return to writing philosophy, in 1932, he notes that the face is the soul of the body; the *Zohar* has a parallel: "The mold of the heart is shown in the face" (qtd. in Baron 114). Both the conversational and the written Wittgensteinian sources are loaded with references to the face theme.

We have already noted one or two of these in Drury. Let us survey the rest (some words are emphasized below for clarity). In 1929 he observes that "[i]t is the case that we forget the meaning of certain *facial expressions* and misinterpret their reproduction" (119). He remarks to Drury one day about the degeneration that can be observed in the human spirit by comparing differences between *the faces* of Beethoven, Schubert, and Chopin vs. those of Russell, Freud and Einstein that he had seen in a bookstore window (127). *The faces* of Lenin, Pius IX and Kierkegaard are remarked on (141, 145). Another close friend and biographer, Malcolm, reports: "It was important to him that there should be some "*friendly faces*" in his classes. He often remarked that he liked a certain "*face*" and he wanted that *face* to be there even if the person said nothing. During World War II, when he lectured on Saturdays, an *American negro soldier* was a member of the class. Wittgenstein remarked more than once what *a friendly and good-natured face* the man had, and how sorry he was when he ceased to come" (28–29; *Zettel* §506 discusses the meaning of friendly eyes, mouths, etc.). Malcolm also quotes some notes he made of Wittgenstein lecturing: "Doubt, belief, certainty—like feelings, emotions, pain, etc.—have *characteristic facial expressions*. Knowledge does not have a characteristic facial expression. There is a *tone* of doubt, and a tone of conviction, but no tone of knowledge" (92).

As for the published writings, perhaps the best indication of the prevalence of the face theme can be given by the number of indexical references to it.[25] Thus, *Culture and Value* has thirteen in 87 pages; my copy of *Zettel* has no index, but I counted seven occurrences between pages 87 and 93; the *Blue and Brown Books* have sixteen in 185 pages; the index of the *Philosophical Investigations* lists nine, but there are actually at least eleven in 232 pages; the *Remarks on the Philosophy of Psychology* I, close to a hundred out of 1137 remarks; the *Remarks on the Philosophy of Psychology* II, 44 out of 737; the *Last Writings on the Philosophy of Psychology*, eighty out of 979 remarks. This digression into statistics is meant only to show the continuous attention Wittgenstein gave to this theme, and therefore that it is important, not extraneous; however, just one quotation from the very end of the *Last Writings* will suffice to show the congruence of what Wittgenstein was driving at with the central point of the traditional view which we have already seen: "You look at a face and say 'I wonder what's going on behind that face?'—But you don't have to say that. The external does not have to be seen as a facade behind which the mental powers are at work" (127^e). The unity of this thought with what is argued in this study about privacy, ethics, trust, the inner, and the outer (for instance, pp. 108–9 *re* trust and Putnam, and 147 ff.) can hardly be missed. If one does not have to wonder as to what is going on behind a face, this leads to a strengthening of trust just as the collapse of the barrier between publicness and privacy does, on the basis of the private language argument. In fact, these are aspects of the same argument: the "language of the face" is direct and observable, it is as futile to keep it private, secret or hidden as any other language.

Another symbol or figure that occurs in Wittgenstein is that of clothing. We have seen that it runs through the *Tractatus* and the *Philosophical Investigations*. As the *Tractatus* has it, "Language disguises thought. So much so, that from the *outward form of the clothing* it is impossible to infer the form of the thought beneath it, because *the outward form of the clothing* is not designed to reveal the form of the body, but for entirely different purposes" (4002, emphasis added). This passage is built on the trope *language is a body with different layers, including a superficial one which is like clothing on this body*. According to Abraham Abulafia, who flourished in the twelfth century, the word for "this form which the kabbalists call 'clothing'" is *malbush*. Layering is of course suggestive of the four hermeneutic levels of textual interpretation, from the most superficial or apparent to the deepest or inner. Joseph Karo says that "in man's waking life the soul is clothed by the body" (Jacobs 106). The nexus person : text : clothing : body : Torah is basic in the *Zohar*: "...the Torah has a body made up of the precepts of the Torah, called *gufe torah*, and the body is enveloped in garments made up of worldly narrations. The senseless people see only the garment...those who are somewhat wiser penetrate as far as the body. But the really wise, the servants of the most high King, those who stood on Mount Sinai, penetrate right through to the soul, the root principle of all, namely, to the real Torah." [26]

The *Philosophical Investigations* suggests our dream-like unconsciousness (or lack of wisdom) regarding the "prodigious diversity of the everyday language-games because the clothing of our language makes everything alike" (p.224).

Dreams, too, were an early and continuing interest of Wittgenstein's. He analyzed some of his own dreams, as reported by Bartley, and discussed Freud's ideas at length (e.g. in the *Lectures and Conversations...*). Whether his thinking on dreams was tinged with mysticism can only be considered on the basis of scattered data. For brevity's sake, I will recall just one case. In a pre-*Tractatus* letter to Engelmann, he observed: "We are asleep. (I have said this before to Mr. Groag, and it is true.) *Our* life is like a dream. But in our better hours we wake up just enough to realize that we are dreaming. Most of the time, though, we are fast asleep. I cannot waken myself. I am trying hard, my dream body moves, but my real one *does not stir*. This, alas, is how it is!" (7). In a modern book on kabbalistic psychology, Edward Hoffman says: "In a very real sense, as the Kabbalah informs us, we go about our daily routines as though half asleep, never fully waking up to the realities around us" (*The Way of Splendor*, 129). If this connection is rightly made, it would once again be evidence of Wittgenstein's early and continuing use of Jewish sources and modes of thought.

In earlier unpublished work I explored Wittgenstein's interest in names and naming as possibly linked to Jewish tradition. Here I will mention the work of another scholar, Bruce Erlich, and his brief paper "The Aesthetics of True Naming: On the Judaic Tradition of Wittgenstein, Lukacs, and Walter Benjamin." He says in conclusion: "I...only...note this visitation of identifiably Jewish mystical themes, reemerging in modern Europe unexpectedly and often without knowledge of those who uttered them, mere decades before obliteration," and makes reference to Scholem's works. In my opinion Wittgenstein was not one of those in whom these themes appeared "without knowledge."

WITTGENSTEIN ON SCIENCE

> There is a latent metaphysics underlying all the natural sciences and even the ex-
> pressions of everyday speech; this must be exposed and done away with. Then,
> "common place materialism and common place theology vanish like ghosts." But
> this vanishing is painful and makes an ethical demand.
>
> —M. O'C. Drury

Wittgenstein's attitude to science is a rather revealing aspect of his mentality
in religion. It is clearly and precisely expressed, leaving little doubt about its
importance. Appearing early, it is confirmed throughout his life. In the early
Notebooks, for instance, and included in the *Tractatus* (6371) appears the conviction that at bottom "the whole *Weltanschauung* of the moderns involves the
illusion that the so-called laws of nature are explanations of natural phenomena." This may be the founding illusion of science, its *raison d'être*, and was
dangerous for a philosopher or a religious person to come under. Wittgenstein
also wanted to combat any idea that science was liberating. Talking to Rush
Rhees, he said: "In fact, nothing is more *conservative* than science. Science lays
down railway tracks. And for scientists it is important that their work should
move along those tracks." Rhees adds that at other times Wittgenstein spoke of
"railway tracks" as the image behind the way some people thought and spoke
of "scientific laws" or "natural necessity" (Rhees 223).

These and other remarks brought together here are not an attack on science, but on the view of science and scientific method that people adopt.
Writing in 1947, Wittgenstein sees a two-fold effect: "Science: enrichment and
impoverishment. *One* particular method elbows all the others aside. They all
seem paltry by comparison, preliminary stages at best" (*C&V*: 60e). Had other
methods, such as his own, been able to flourish despite science, we might
enjoy enrichment without the stifling conformity of thought. But this not
having turned out to be the case, he was pessimistic: "It isn't absurd, e.g., to
believe that the age of science and technology is the beginning of the end for
humanity; that the idea of great progress is a delusion, along with the idea
that the truth will ultimately be known; that there is nothing good or desirable
about scientific knowledge and that mankind, in seeking it, is falling into a
trap. It is by no means obvious that this is not how things are" (*C&V*: 56e).
This is a Faustian image of humankind's dealing with the diabolic in science.
The trap is not one we fall into inevitably; but without the corrective of
Wittgensteinian ethical philosophy "...perhaps science and industry, having
caused infinite misery in the process, will unite the world—I mean condense

it into a *single* unit, though one in which peace is the last thing that will find a home" (*C&V*: 63ᵉ).

For these reasons Wittgenstein concluded that the solution of scientific problems held no allure for him. His interests were elsewhere—aptly enough, concerned with freedom: "...What I mean is: we couldn't say now 'If they discover so and so, then I'll say I am free'" (from Notes taken by Y. Smythies of a lecture on Freedom of the Will, delivered in Cambridge. Probably 1944–46). In *Zettel* he asks; "'Why do you demand explanations? If they are given you, you will once more be facing a terminus. They cannot get you any further than you are at present'" (#315). Here is an exchange with himself that dovetails nicely with the comment by Rabbi Leo Baeck already noted: "Every answer given arouses new questions. The progress of science is matched by an increase in the hidden and mysterious" (*Judaism and Science*, qtd. in Baron 436).

RELIGION, ETHICS AND THE PRIVATE LANGUAGE ARGUMENT

The literature on privacy is frustratingly naïve about the philosophy of language. Even a collection with the title *Philosophical Dimensions of Privacy*, edited by a philosopher (Schoeman) and published by Cambridge University Press in 1984, has no contribution on the linguistics of privacy and no mention of philosophers of language well-known in the Anglo-Saxon world such as Austin, Searle or Wittgenstein, not to speak of Jacques Derrida. This may not be accidental. Reference to some of these writers would threaten to explode the foundations of privacy claims. On these foundations, language itself is held to be, if not private, at least privatizable. *The idea of privatizable language*—a whole language or a segment of one that only one person can understand, manipulate, preserve, or choose to forget—*and the idea of a coherent ego* are mutually supportive. If I can control language by myself, I must be an independent actor. In whatever area I can negotiate, I am equipped to avoid discourse. In the societies of which we are speaking, these areas of avoidance or repression have typically included questions of race and sex, which have surfaced in the American consciousness in the somewhat distorted form of the "political correctness" debate. Out of personal avoidance comes the possibility of political repression.

The linguistic fallacies involved here can be illuminated by an exposition of the significance of Wittgenstein's private language argument for ethics. As Terry Eagleton in his book *Against the Grain* points out, "The person who uses the same *privately invented* sign each time an experience comes up, has grasped the point that signs, to be signs at all, must be in Derrida's term 'iterable,' but not the point that it is just this iterability which fissures their self-identity—that since there is no 'pure' repetition, the question of what counts as difference or identity is a social question to be contended over within discourse and forms of life, not a problem resolvable by 'experience'" (Eagleton 102, emphasis added). The relevant point for the ideology of privacy is that the linguistic means of representation of thought or action one might seek to keep private has no self-identity by itself, confined to the actor's mind. It only assumes a temporary identity in discourse, temporary because it has to be continually renegotiated with the other who makes discourse possible. Contending with the other carries with it the threat, which can also be taken as a pleasure, of constant subversion, even without subversive intent on the other's part, of the private meaning one might wish to control. This shows in fact the untenability of any private meaning: not only can it always be publicly and successfully challenged, but the "same" actor, differing from himself or herself, can challenge it in circumstances that would have to be described as located between the private and the public. (The American presidency claims a kind of public privacy, known as *executive privilege*, usually invoked in the face of scandal). The only way to preserve the illusion of privacy is to avoid the challenge, a rather undemocratic attitude.

Let us now connect the question of privacy with Wittgenstein's deliberations on the possibility of a private language, defined as a language whose knowledge and use is confined to one person, and known to philosophers as *the private language argument*. Hundreds of papers have been written about it, but to the best of my knowledge its ethical implications have never been clarified. The argument itself is similar in effect to Eagleton's exposition of Derrida on the sign. Why is a private language not possible? For one thing, because it would be totally dependent on the individual's memory, it is fallible. An individual attempting to speak to himself or herself in such a language would soon be asking: "Is this thing that I'm calling an X today the same thing that I decided to call an X last week? In fact, what is 'today' today? I wish I could talk to someone about it all!" In brief, our notions of privacy, propriety, and rights are socially learned and used, dependent on corroboration by others, which, as we have already seen, can never be exact. There can't be a private custom, for instance. And since word usage is *custom*, there can't be private word usage. As Wittgenstein put it, "one would like to say: whatever is going to seem right to me is right. And that only means that here we can't talk about 'right'" (*PI* §258;

note that, although Wittgenstein spares us this additional barb here, we can't talk about "wrong" either. This is one of the main reasons why Wittgenstein emphasized that ethics could not be talked about: language is just too heterodox, ethics must be left to God and the individual conscience). A passage illustrating Wittgenstein's limpid presentation is useful here:

> Now someone tells me that he knows what pain is only from his own case [this is Eagleton's privately invented sign]!—Suppose everyone had a box with something in it: we call it a "beetle". No one can look into anyone else's box, and everyone says he knows what a beetle is only by looking at his beetle.—Here it would be quite possible for everyone to have something different in his box. We might even imagine such a thing constantly changing.—But suppose the word "beetle" had a use in these people's language?—If so it would not be used as the name of a thing. The thing in the box has no place in the language-game at all; not even as a *something*: for the box might even be empty.—No, one can "divide through" by the thing in the box; it cancels out, what ever it is. That is to say: if we construe the grammar of the expression of sensation on the model of "object and name" the object drops out of consideration as irrelevant. (*Philosophical Investigations* §293).

"The object drops out of consideration as irrelevant" is Wittgenstein's nonjargonistic way of saying that the signifier has been liberated. For we conceive not only of the grammar of sensation, but of all language, in the Greek-Aristotelian mode of name and object, or signifier and signified, favoring the latter, and trying to avoid looking too closely at the signifier or name. A feminist literary critic has acutely noted the dream of Western social science and philosophy to use language so that there can be no mistakes, achieved through a reliance upon a signified-based theory of meaning (Meese 184n citing Arnold Krupat, "Post-Structuralism and Oral Literature"). Wittgenstein had tried to awaken us from this dream very early in the twentieth century. Yet the literature on privacy has studiously avoided looking at the signifiers that both enable and disrupt its discourse.

What are the implications for ethics if the possibility of a private language is denied? Imagine believers in linguistic privacy. When conceiving of or committing any action, they are convinced also, unthinkingly, of the private iterability of its sign and referent. Only they know and can interpret what their private actions mean. This assumed hermetic closure from public scrutiny leads automatically to the conviction that the outside world has no control over the conception, execution and ethical import of any action committed in linguistic privacy. In other words, the linguistic ideology of privacy provides the ground, the unconscious justification, for unethical actions, those one wants to hide or is ashamed of. Remembering, of course, that there are many more aspects of Wittgenstein's language critique that buttressed its effects and lessons, one could go so far as to hold the privacy ideology responsible for the hypocrisy, lack of generosity, and narcissism of any culture that accepts it (and most do). To expose the fallacy of linguistic privacy is to begin to expound aright the logic of language, thus removing a great and unnoticed temptation to unethical actions, or sin, to use the traditional expression. This was central to Wittgenstein's exclusively ethical interest in philosophy. He was quite clear about the importance of getting the logic of language straight, and put it this way in the preface to the only book he published: "The book deals with the problems of philosophy, and shows, I believe, that the reason why these problems are posed is that the logic of our language is misunderstood" (Preface to the *Tractatus*, 3). Clarity about the logic of language in Wittgenstein's sense would lead to openness, regard for the other who makes discourse possible, a sense of community, and an investigative attitude towards language and texts, as opposed to individualism, an increasing desire for privacy (from openness to seclusion), and a literalist-dogmatic attitude towards texts, exemplified in American law and politics by the quest for the "original intent" of the framers of the Constitution.

Apart from the private language argument, there is another aspect of Wittgenstein's linguistic thought that has direct bearing on the privacy literature. Just as the signified-based theory of meaning has inevitably been invoked in putting forward arguments for linguistic privacy, the view of language as a rule-governed activity also appears in its defense. In the "Theory" part of his book *The Right to Privacy: Gays, Lesbians and the Constitution*, in a chapter on "The Concept of Legal Privacy," Vincent J. Samar claims:

> Privacy is, in its primary form, activity that is self-regarding [a phrase of John Stuart Mill's given the following definition by Samar (68): An action is self-regarding (private) with respect to a group of other actors if and only if the consequences of the act impinge in the first instance on the basic interests of the actor and not on the interests of the specified class of actors]. To understand activity, one needs to understand the rules that govern the activity. Once one understands these rules, one realizes that the rules themselves entail limits. To participate in certain activities is to accept rules on one's behavior. To play chess, for example, is to accept the rules of chess....*Since all activities are understood as rule-governed behaviors*, privacy must therefore be understood in the context of rule-governed activities.
>
> (Samar 72, emphasis added)

Two initial observations on these formulations: firstly, one sees here the ghost of the Saussurean idea that the *langue* is rule-governed and *parole* consists of the application of these, what Pierre Bourdieu has aptly called the legalism of the Saussurean concept of language. On Samar's view, it would appear that before one picks one's nose in private, for instance, one must accept that a set of rules govern this activity, *as all other activities*. Secondly, an interesting paradox crops up: part of the concept of privacy is for me to be free to do what I want in solitude, but in order to earn that right I must accept someone else's code of rules about *everything* that I may do, since, as Samar claims, all activities are understood as rule-governed behaviors. The regulators as well as the recipients of privacy seem to be part of an authoritarian complicity.

Wittgenstein argued with great persistence against the rule-governed model of language. It is one of the chief themes of the *Philosophical Investigations*. He stressed the incoherence of the notion of rule, and the freedom we enjoy even in so "rule-governed" an activity as mathematics. He achieved what in effect was a deconstruction of the mathematician Hilbert's Platonic dream of an axiomatic system completely derivable from logic, the mathematical version of the dream of using language without mistakes. The threat of mistakes, which is responded to by "the bourgeois quest for certainty" is another way of describing the persistence of textual ambiguity. Mathematics, too, can be seen in terms of the continuously changing iterability of its signifiers. Late in his life, Wittgenstein made hundreds of remarks questioning certainty in many ways, which were published under the title *On Certainty*. Of course, within logic itself Kurt Gödel showed that axiomatic systems are either incomplete or inconsistent.[27]

The preceding discussion of Wittgenstein's thought on privacy is a convenient point at which to turn to the status of privacy in a non-secular light. By his considerations of privacy Wittgenstein sought to alert the modern secular philosopher to the traditional view of biblical religion that God sees all things, and that it is fruitless to seek privacy from Him, and by implication from our fellow creatures. This attitude is already adumbrated in the research of Barrington Moore, who contrasts it with what he found in Greek civilization. "Secrecy from God," he says, "was equated with wickedness" (172). However, in one of the passages from Isaiah partly cited by Moore, the prophet accuses his audience: "And thou hast been secure in thy wickedness, /Thou hast said: 'None seeth me'; /Thy wisdom and thy knowledge, /It hath perverted thee; /And thou hast said in thy heart: /'I am, and there is none else beside me'"

(Isaiah 47: 10). *There is no mention here of hiding from God.* The charge is rather of a guilty solitude assuaged by the thought that one is unseen by one's fellow creature. Significantly, Isaiah's explanation for this behavior is not the inherent wickedness of the person addressed, but his or her wisdom *and knowledge*—"thy wisdom and thy knowledge, it hath perverted thee"—a wisdom that could also be called ideology. Was Isaiah, like Wittgenstein, suggesting that a misunderstanding of the logic of our language leads to this particular variety of wickedness? Another point of interest here is Isaiah's emphasis on the extreme individualism he has noticed: "I am, and there is none else beside me." Incidentally, in the next verse, where Isaiah says that evil shall come upon this person, there is still no mention of God, leaving open the possibility that he sees the punishment as self-provoked *karma* brought about by bad philosophy of language, perhaps.

There are of course passages in the Bible that warn against hiding from God. Psalm 139 acknowledges God's omniscience and the futility of flight from Him:

> O LORD, Thou hast searched me, and known me.
> Thou knowest my downsitting and my uprising,
> Thou understandest my thought afar off....
> And art acquainted with all my ways.
> For there is not a word in my tongue,
> But, lo, O LORD, Thou knowest it altogether....
> Whither shall I go from Thy spirit'?
> Or whither shall I flee from Thy presence'?

In his *Nine Talmudic Readings*, Levinas has taken up this psalm. "Always the hand of God grabs me and guides me," he says. "It is impossible to escape from God, not to be present before his sleepless gaze." Citing the lines "If I say, 'Surely darkness will conceal me, night will provide me with cover,' darkness is not dark for you; night is as light as the day; darkness and light are the same,'" Levinas comments: "In other words, man's humanity would be the end of interiority, the end of the subject. Everything is open. I am everywhere looked through, touched by the hand. Thus one can understand why Jonah could not escape his mission" (167). Man's humanity as the end of interiority is an old theme in Jewish tradition, not a chance comment from Levinas. Bringing the human interior and exterior into harmony, thus ending both the possibility of hypocrisy and the desire for privacy, is a constant goal of Jewish ethical reflection. "None may enter the academy," the Talmud says, "who is not inwardly as outwardly" (*Berakot* 28b: Gamaliel II). There is also a relevant remark referring especially to scholars: "A scholar who is not inside as he is outside is no scholar" (Raba in *Yoma* 72b). Wittgenstein reflected on the matter directly in this way: "Someone who in this way...penitently opens his heart to God in confession lays it open for other men too. In doing this he loses the dignity that goes with his personal prestige....We could also say: Hate between men comes from cutting ourselves off from each other. Because we don't want any one else to look inside us, since it's not a pretty sight in there. Of course, you must continue to feel ashamed of what's inside you, but not ashamed of yourself before your fellow-men" (*C&V*: 46ᵉ).

We see therefore that questioning privacy can be undertaken through current textual thinking, or through Wittgenstein on rule-following and linguistic privacy, and it can be traced back to the very roots of Judaic tradition. The voguishness of privacy for some three centuries is associated with the cult of the individual and the privatization of property, while the concept happened to fit well with mainstream "commonsense" philosophy of language, the kind based on the signified. But the more it is stressed that God sees all things, indeed understands each word on our tongues, as Psalm 139 says, the less we see the point of secrecy toward our fellow. Since whether or not sexual intercourse is practiced openly or not is a diagnostic crux for anthropologists and others investigating privacy, there is a revealing account in the Talmud about Jewish–Gentile differences on sexuality:

> Said Rabbi Katina: When the Israelites came for the three feasts to the Temple in Jerusalem, the courtyard of the Temple was opened before them, and they were shown the Cherubim holding each other in intimate embrace, and it was said to them: Behold, the mutual love between us and God is as the love of a man and a woman. Said Resh Lakish: When the barbarians entered the Temple, they saw the Cherubim in intimate mutual embrace. They dragged them outside the square, and said: Behold! Israel, whose blessing is a blessing and whose curse a curse, occupies herself with such things?! And then they reviled them.
>
> —Talmud, *Yoma* 54

CHAPTER V

Wittgenstein and the
Clarification of Postmodernism

In the future, ideals will not be communicated by attempts to describe them, which inevitably distort, but by the models of an appropriate conduct in life.

—Paul Engelmann

Intellectual vanity, whether in himself or in others, was something that Wittgenstein detested. I believe he considered it more important to be free from all trace of vanity than to achieve a great reputation in philosophy.

—Maurice Drury

Haven't you heard? Post-modernism is dead, killed by its own hubris.

—Whitewash, on eWorld, 8/13/95

SIMPLE YET POSTMODERN?

Wittgenstein appears to have realized the intimate, even inevitable connection between Judaism and linguistic thought. The constant theme of our misunderstanding the logic of our language connects seamlessly, if not obviously, with the ethical and the hinted-at religious. An example of the practical though very indirect and unobtrusive way this is indicated by Wittgenstein is the references to Moses in the *Philosophical Investigations*. These occur in two not very widely separated sections, §79 and §87. §79, beginning with the possible meanings of someone saying "Moses did not exist," goes on to demonstrate with a whole slew of biblical details—including Pharaoh's daughter and Israelites led through the desert—that a name need not have a fixed meaning good for all uses, and concludes that even a scientific term may have fluctuating definitions.[1] The movement from semantics to philosophy of science deftly draws an analogy to religious belief or faith—namely that the language of science is just as provisional as language in which religious personages are named. The unasked question for an academic-rational culture: if it is so willing to invest in the language of science, why not in the activity that names Moses? Skepticism in one area is no more or no less justified than in the other—this is one of Wittgenstein's great insecurity-producing challenges.

When the question of the meaning of Moses' name is taken up again in §87, it becomes embroiled with the most ordinary words of language, such as *red*, *dark* and *sweet*, leading to the interlocutor's quandary: how can I understand any explanation, if words in the explanation need to be explained too? Am I faced with an infinite regress? Here again the unstated suggestion is that consideration of the puzzles of language will lead inevitably—in the course of the regress—to the puzzles of biblical religion and its personalities, Creation, Babel, Sinai, prophecy, each with its decidedly linguistic component. Conversely too, of course, focusing on biblical accounts leads to linguistic questions, but in our age the reverse is the more likely trajectory. Although Jews may be more inclined to see this because it is so much in tune with Jewish tradition, the point is of universal significance. Unlike thinking based on dogma, thinking based on language affects all who speak, and it is ignored at their risk. As Moses Mendelssohn argued in eighteenth-century Berlin, "[t]he doctrines of Judaism were those of the universal religion of reason, available to all men through reflection, and not dependent on revelation" (Unterman 75). In other words, a minimum of revelation, a maximum of interpretation, or reflection. Reflecting on the choice of the name Moses as an example here may illustrate the meaning of going beyond what Wittgenstein is saying to the point of his saying it, something he said would be very difficult. Why Moses? This seems to be a typical hint. Why not Napoleon? Jesus? King Charles? No choice is free of connotations. In the case of Moses, chief prophet of the Jews, author— and chief figure—of the Torah, first teacher and lawgiver of what became known as the Judaeo-Christian tradition, who beheld the burning bush, answered the call of God (which Wittgenstein had not), received revelation, asked God what His name was, and received the famous reply. The choice of his name as an example is no accidental choice and could hardly have been made unawares by Wittgenstein. According to Hilmy, this example of the name "Moses" was first drafted in 1931.[2] This places it around the same time that Wittgenstein was writing about the issues of central Jewish interest described earlier.

At the end of the last chapter we saw the compatibility of ethical import between Derrida's thinking on *difference* and Wittgenstein's on private language. The general compatibility of the two has long been recognized by competent observers, such as Richard Rorty and Henry Staten. In the case of Wittgenstein this compatibility with Derrida and deconstruction extends through all his work, for as we have argued he was never a positivist or a structuralist, but always one seeking to make clear the ethical ramifications of a mistaken understanding of language.[3] As far as that is concerned, we have seen the line connecting Levinas, Derrida and Wittgenstein with Jewish tradition, drawing only Wittgenstein's part of the connecting line, the rest of it having been drawn already. The caveat is necessary here that, unlike Wittgenstein, Derrida has not associated himself explicitly with Jewish tradition, but has been associated by others responding to his allusions and what they take to be his hints.[4] Our reading, developing his own statements, places Wittgenstein in a Jewish constellation and argues further that many in this constellation have been aware of *différance* and the need to challenge with *différance* the stranglehold of Greek-derived metaphysics. "Don't look for the meaning, look for the use" is a succinct formula for the constant demonstration of linguistic difference, in itself sufficient to terminate the quest for atomistic meaning ("here the word, there the meaning," as the *PI* has it), sufficient to lead on to liberating deconstructive discoveries, according to the individual's capacities.

Is Wittgenstein's writing then just an earlier form of deconstruction? He did note how "I destroy! I destroy" seemed to fit the mood of his work, and indeed there is in the history of deconstruction a link to the word *destroy* by way of Heidegger. Although important differences lie in the *Zeitgeist* of Wittgenstein's inter-war period and of Derrida's from the 1960's on, only a few years of *Hitlerzeit* separate Wittgenstein's extreme worry (1938) about his people in Vienna and his trip there to see to their welfare, from Derrida and his siblings experiencing French Vichy antisemitism in Algeria (1941–42). We recall that Ludwig in his youth too had learnt from his older brother that they could not pass for Aryans to join a health club of their choice. For both families, as for millions of others, medieval times had returned, reducing the Enlightenment to a hypocritical sham (on the Nazi takeover in Germany, Wittgenstein said: "The dark ages are coming again. I wouldn't be surprised, Drury, if you and I were to live to see such horrors as people being burnt alive as witches" [152]). Wittgenstein, who, writing the Preface to the *Philosophical Investigations* in 1945, pointedly used the phrase "in the darkness of this time", wrote during some of the worst times for Jewry, while the postwar period, despite the memory of the Holocaust, is often counted among the best, in terms of freedom of movement, of expression, the founding and prosperity of Israel, and its victories against its enemies.[5]

A difference between Wittgenstein on the one hand and Derrida and Levinas on the other will already be obvious—the former suggests on the present reading the concealed and scattered modes of the *converso*, while the other two can forthrightly identify themselves as intellectuals who are Jewish, Levinas even more directly as a Jewish intellectual. The *converso* is deprived of any belonging until, if his ruse succeeds, he is read in the light of the tradition he is pointing to. As a rootless *Vogelfrei*,[6] Wittgenstein suffered the double frustration of not being able to identify with any band of writers or school of philosophers, yet finding himself variously and wrongly identified by his readers. One marker of individuality that he crafted was his style, truly distinct from the often loquacious postmodern posturing, yet unmerged with the rational equableness of high modernism. Here, in his clarity and simplicity of style, Wittgenstein is remote from almost any postmodern. Of the *Philosophical Investigations*, von Wright has written: "The style is simple and perspicuous, the construction of sentences firm and free, the rhythm flows easily. The form is sometimes that of dialogue, with questions and replies; sometimes, as in the *Tractatus*, it condenses to aphorisms. There is a striking absence of all literary ornamentation, and of technical jargon or terminology. The union of measured moderation with richest imagination, the simultaneous impression of natural continuation and surprising turns, leads one to think of some other great productions of the genius of Vienna" ("Biographical Sketch," 21). Von Wright has music in mind, and suggests that the qualities of Wittgenstein's style are reminiscent of Schubert. His writing procedure parallels Beethoven's, whose final versions of major works were *simplified* from what we see in his notebooks—just as the limpid lines of the *Philosophical Investigations* have behind them many a labored paragraph in the manuscripts.[7] Simplicity is not accidental in Wittgenstein's writing, as can be judged from this remark made when he was contemplating the *Investigations* project: "If this book is written as it should be, everything I say must be easy to understand, indeed trivial; but it will be hard to understand *why* I say it."[8] This is a rather dramatically different rhetorical option from that taken by any avowed postmodernist.

From another source we know that Wittgenstein was friendly with a son of G.E. Moore who played in a jazz band, and prevailed upon the junior Moore to explain the musical innovations of that genre. It is not hard to imagine here a search on Wittgenstein's part—interested as he was in the perfect style for his needs—for some kind of synaesthetic stimulus or transference from jazz to his philosophical expression. Certainly, in 1949 Wittgenstein approvingly recalled

Broad's observation that the *Tractatus* was *highly syncopated* (see p. 28 above); syncopation in music (elision in grammar) is a basic characteristic of jazz. As jazz is a breaking free from or a "send up" of *classical* or European music, using much the same instruments, so Wittgenstein's thought can be seen as a dissent from classical philosophy, having created its own rhythms and syncopations, yet, like jazz, defying the conventional periodizations of intellectual history.

APOPHASIS, RELIGION AND MUSIC

Indeed music had a presence in Wittgenstein's life that he could not express directly in his writing, and an instructive analogy is likely to exist with the place of religion in his life. Paul Engelmann records how enraptured Wittgenstein was by "Mozart's Journey to Prague," a story by Mörike with "passages describing musical effects in words: 'Coming as from remotest starry worlds, the sounds fall from the mouth of silver trombones, icy cold, cutting through marrow and soul; fall through the blueness of the night,' he would recite with a shudder of awe" (86). Notice that the awe is generated by a poetic *description* of the poetry of music, not by the slightest attempt at a theoretical or critical *explanation* of the effects. Attempting the latter is analogous to trying to speak directly about ethics.

There are extensive discussions of both music and religion outside the published texts, while in them these subjects are repressed. In the case of music its appearance in the texts might have had an artistic effect or purpose, but the ethico-religious goal of Wittgenstein's work would not have been furthered. How are we then to read his remark to Drury, "It is impossible for me to say in my book one word about all that music has meant in my life. How then can I hope to be understood?" (Drury 94). Why is it impossible to say anything about music, and why is he bemoaning its impossibility? Because music is *wordless*; to *show* all that music has meant in one's life (here the distinction between showing and saying crops up) one might conceivably cause all the meaningful music to be played, but to augment the impression this makes nothing could be *said*. Hence the impossibility that Wittgenstein complains about of saying one word. Drury records him as saying in a lecture "that you couldn't speak of the meaning of a work of art, say a particular piece of music, as if the meaning was something that could be separated from the work itself" (155). Interestingly, this is connected with the hope of being understood, or rather the lack of hope. If you can't say one word about something, how can you expect comprehension? There is an immediate analogy to ethics, with the necessity of putting everything in place by being silent about it. The mention of music reminds us of the whole thinking of the *Preface* to the *Tractatus*—writing for one reader who already understands. Wittgenstein made another remark on the repression of explicit religious themes in his work: "I am not a religious man but I cannot help seeing every problem from a religious point of view" (Drury 94). He sees the religious angle in every problem, but he cannot express these insights as religious in his writing. He must deny that he is a religious man, yet can an unreligious man see all the religious angles?

Wittgenstein's attitude fits the earliest definition of apophasis in the English language: "Apophasis...a kind of an Irony, whereby we deny that we say or doe that which we especially say or doe" (J. Smith, *The mysterie of rhetorique unvail'd*, 1637, p.164, qtd. in the OED). While staying focused exclusively on the core of religiosity, he must not openly indicate *in the work* that this is the case—"I am not a religious man. I cannot appear to be a religious man in my writings. But I am a religious man, though I cannot reveal in my writings or even to my friends what kind of a religious man I am." Simply put, some such convolutions provide the clarifying connections between Wittgenstein's talk, writing and silences.

Music and religion both have to do with the limits of language, with saying and showing. Not writing about them is a self-imposed discipline incomprehensible to those who misunderstand the logic of language, and it imposes a tremendous artistic challenge on the writer: to do what we want to do without seeming to do it, to say what we want to say without seeming to say it, to limit our "communication" to those who already understand, hence accept a very high risk of failure to achieve anything at all.

However much a part of his life music might be, however analogous to religion, music still has its esthetic-entertainment aspect; it is not a moral duty to be musical, or to instruct others in music. The kind of prophetic personality that Wittgenstein saw himself as had no role in life other than to communicate—whatever the barriers to such communication might be, and however indirectly, including by means of his conduct of life—his religious message. In writing, in language, was the word of God given, not in music, within the realm of pleasure. Religion was duty. And one thing Wittgenstein was certain of, he once said, is that we were not here to have a good time (King in Rhees 90). This is not to deny that achieving personal integrity, responding as one is capable to a call from God, helping one's neighbor through one's work—

Wittgenstein's dearest ideals—may not have their pleasurable aspects. Music and religion were enormously meaningful and pleasurable in Wittgenstein's life, but traditional and esoteric convictions about communication prevented him from explicitly introducing music and religion into his work. Not that they could not literally be spoken of or written about directly; the attempt, however, results in the *Geschwätz* or idle chatter so despised by Wittgenstein and the like-minded Engelmann. Of the two, music was a lesser loss—he could explicitly complain about the constraint. But the greater the importance of what he couldn't talk about, the more the repression: he was led to deny being a religious person at all, yet paradoxically asserted towards the end of his life that his thought was one hundred percent Hebraic! *It was so without his proclaiming—as far as possible within the logic of repression of course—that it was so.* Only when unsuccessful is repression recognizable; the all-important claim of Hebraicness extruded to the surface, appearing as a mere stray remark in a conversation with a friend.

VERSIONS OF POSTMODERNISM

How does any of this relate to postmodernism? If we define postmodernism simply as the demonstration, made by Levinas, Derrida and scholars related to them, that the road to ethics goes through the philosophy of language, then Wittgenstein was traveling this road and setting up signposts for his readers in the heyday of modernism. As he observed in 1931, "[l]anguage sets everyone the same traps; it is an immense network of easily accessible wrong turnings....What I have to do then is erect signposts at all the junctions where there are wrong turnings so as to help people past the danger points" (*C&V*: 18ᵉ). This attitude is rather reminiscent of Maimonides' *Guide*. Indeed, Faur has pointed out that "[t]he root of the term *Tora* is *yara* 'to point' the way, a cognate of the Arabic *dalala* 'guidepost,' making up the first word of Maimonides's *Guide for the Perplexed*" (*Homo Mysticus* 168). The *helpful* nature of the *Philosophical Investigations* is not to be missed—few postmodernist writings can be imagined making the same claim of helpfulness about themselves. If the specifically Judaic nature of this demonstration concerning language be considered, then too we have read Wittgenstein as suggesting that the puzzles of language lead to the puzzles of biblical monotheistic religion, ethics being the common link in their solution. But the ways in which postmodernism may be conceived are numerous.

One of them is as the questioning of all metanarratives—of history, science, religion, philosophy, whatever. This questioning is usually compatible with valorizations of productive readings and reader responses—putting the reader on a par with the author in a movement of disciplined liberation. Not only does Wittgenstein read his "sources"—Weininger, Spengler and others—in this way, but by his reticence and refusal to be part of any metanarrative, he lays *himself* open to be so read. What we have undertaken here can be seen as proof of this, for we have tried to bring out how Wittgenstein's work is allied with the oldest, still flourishing critical, anti-authoritarian ethical tradition in the world, with a prophetic message for the nations, the Judaism that has also given birth to postmodernism.[9]

Others have highlighted dehellenization as an aspect of postmodernism compatible with the Judaic. The term refers to a thorough-going questioning of the hellenic domination of literary criticism and of the philosophical background literary criticism draws upon. The "Yale Critics," including Harold Bloom, Jacques Derrida, Geoffrey Hartman, and Paul de Man, have historically been in the forefront of this movement. Rather than accept the view of a traditional critic such as T.S. Eliot (also a prominent modernist) that the critic's task is only to elucidate master-texts of literature in subservience, Geoffrey Hartman asserted that "[c]riticism, in short, is not extraliterary, not outside of literature or art looking in: it is a defining and influential part of its subject...".[10] For criticism to cast itself as a defining and influential part of its subject is to claim the role of *midrash* in relation to the scriptural text. Geoffrey Hartman happens to be a contributor to an innovative volume of essays entitled *Midrash and Literature*.

Biblical Hebrew does not mark the script with vowel signs. In this sense it is unreadable as it stands, a vocalized script being ritually unacceptable. The standard or masoretic vocalization was therefore the result of readers' intervention. This seems to be symbolic of the interventionist model of *midrash* or commentary, apparently invoked by Derrida too when he speaks of the reader's interventions in the text. The traditional-historical lineage of this model has been described in this way: "Implied in the classical uses of the term [*midrash*] is the notion that the results of interpretations of the sacred texts are in some sense sacred. The early rabbis voiced this when they suggested that their writings constituted an oral Torah tradition that had been given to Moses at the revelation at Mount Sinai along with the text of the Israelite written Torah. The notion of a dual Torah signifies that the authority of the text and of the interpretation are correlative" (Tzvee Zahavy, "Midrash and Medieval

Commentary," 82). The rabbis consistently suggest *different* vocalizations to extract meanings and senses from the same concatenation of consonants.

DEHELLENIZATION

Criticism as *midrash* is an important departure from hellenism in the direction of judaization. This is the same direction Levinas's thought travels in, according to Derrida: "from the Greek site...toward a prophetic speech," a thought which "seeks to liberate itself from the Greek domination of the Same and the One...as if from oppression itself—an oppression certainly comparable to none other in the world, an ontological or transcendental oppression, but also the origin or alibi of all oppression in the world" (Derrida, "Violence and Metaphysics: An Essay on the Thought of Emmanuel Levinas," 82–83). As G. Douglas Atkins puts it, "Derrida's and Hartman's is an anti-Hellenic world" (773). In it "Reality" or "Being" becomes textual, existence becomes linguistic. The Wittgensteinian questioning of language, of names—like other questionings in the same tradition—leads to answers about history, about Moses, or ethics, and of course to further questions that eventually bring the individual face to face with himself, even with God. Instead of remaining bewitched by language, we see through it, cease to allow it to represent existence to us. For not being able to say the really important things we are compensated by a profound silence only in which our individuality, difference and nearness to God—and our aloneness from other human beings—can be realized.

It is not surprising that the Hebrew and the Hellenic diverge over the very linguistic element *word*, which, in the notions of *davar* and *logos* reverberates so intensely through the Jewish and Christian religious traditions. The Greek term, Atkins writes, "refers to the meaning, the ordered and reasonable content....*Davhar*, however, means not only 'word' but also 'deed'" (775). "Words", wrote Wittgenstein, "are also deeds" (*PI* §546; cf. *C&V*: 46ᵉ: "Words are deeds"). A claim could be made that this is a direct allusion by Wittgenstein to the Hebrew-Greek divergence over the notion of *word*, but in any case, while *logos* points to the meaning, Wittgenstein stressed the *use*, which is active, dynamic, and hence related to *deed*. Such etymological evidence opposing the Hebrew and the Greek alerts us to the necessity of carefully distinguishing between Judaism and Greco-Christianity even if we wish to retain the idea of a (or the) Judeo-Christian tradition.

The movement toward dehellenization in literary criticism was preceded by one in theology. For instance, Atkins details how Thomas J.J. Altizer, along with Dewart, Tillich and others, "specifically attacks the Christian 'bondage to a transcendent, a sovereign, and an impassive God,' which derives from the 'Greek metaphysical idea of God as an eternal and unmoving being'" (774). Nietzsche is an inspiration common to the Protestant Altizer, the Catholic John Dominic Crossan, and also to Jacques Derrida. As we develop a clearer idea of his direction and impetus, we can add Wittgenstein to this conjunction. The nearness between literary criticism and theology seen in the dehellenizing trend is strangely reminiscent of Wittgenstein's binding of "analytical" philosophy to religion, ethics and mysticism, something that seemed so alarming to his one-time co-worker Bertrand Russell.

Grouping together the dehellenizing theologians with the Judaic literary thinkers such as Hartman, Levinas and Derrida gives us at least one kind of postmodernism with a Hebraic character—radically textual, indirect about ethics yet centered on it, often directly invoking Jewish texts and motifs. It is to be contrasted with a stream composed of other writers who seem to some extent still allied to secular humanism—Michel Foucault, Jean Baudrillard, Jean Francois Lyotard. Although the first and the last are known to have been strongly influenced by Wittgenstein,[11] in general their Marxian-Nietzschean blends of atheistic thought have kept them from taking part in the Judaic-inspired process of clarification with which I connect Wittgenstein and the other postmodern thinkers.

THEORY AND POSTMODERNISM

Wittgenstein's attitude to theory, so important an aspect of intellectual enterprise in his time and since, can be seen as analogous to the postmodern antipathy to the metanarrative. The parallel for this term for Wittgenstein was *metalanguage*, essential for the metanarrative to be expressed. He was against the idea of a metalanguage. He simply did not see the justification for imagining a level of language that, compared to everyday language, was elevated, stable, controlled, pure: "When I talk about language (words, sentences, etc.) I must speak the language of every day. Is this language somehow too coarse and material for what we want to say? *Then how is another one to be constructed?*—And how strange that we should be able to do anything at all with the one we have!" (*PI* §120; original emphasis). Wittgenstein saw the way we misunderstand the logic of language as the immediate and inevitable result of a mistaken theory *which could not be corrected in the medium of language*: "...we do not *command a clear view* of the use of our words.—Our grammar is lacking in this sort of perspicuity" (*PI* §122; already in the *Tractatus*, 4002, decades earlier: "Everyday language is a part of the human organism and is no less complicated than it. It is humanly impossible to gather immediately from it what the logic of language is"). Instead of trying to force our grammar to go against one of its characteristics, Wittgenstein adopts the indirect methods of creating in-between cases and perspicuous representation and asks us to be suspicious of two explanations built in the same medium to cure the faults of one. Metalanguage is essential for the claim to theory; the simple slogan "ordinary language is all right" was directed against the move to both metalanguage and theory.[12] In §109 of the *Philosophical Investigations*, one of the crucial sections where Wittgenstein's conception of philosophy is outlined, is the clear declaration: "And we may not advance any kind of theory." This is also the point of saying that "we must do away with all *explanation* [theorizing], and description alone must take its place" (*PI* §109). The problems he is concerned with, not empirical ones, are solved "by looking into the workings of our language, and that in such a way as to make us recognize those workings: *in despite of* an urge to misunderstand them." The importance of the statement about not advancing any kind of theory is heightened when we note that it is placed in the section that includes the famous recasting of philosophy as the "battle against the bewitchment of our intelligence by means of our language."

To attempt a little *midrash* on this section, the transformation of philosophy into an internal gaze is paramount here. We must look into the workings of our language, despite what *must* be an urge to misunderstand them, the urge which has led us for millennia to be satisfied with the explanations deriving from hellenistic sources. How we see language leads to the very heart of our ethical intelligence or lack of it. A pointed letter of Wittgenstein's to Norman Malcolm brings this out. He tells his chosen disciple that harder than thinking about metalinguistic terms like *certainty*, *probability* and *perception*, is "to think, or *try* to think, really honestly about your life & and other peoples [*sic*] lives. And the trouble is that thinking about these things is *not thrilling*, but often downright nasty. And when it's nasty then it's *most* important" (Malcolm 39). Just as we want to avoid looking into our ethical insides when they are nasty, we have a propensity to avoid a correct understanding of the logic of our language because our understanding is destabilised when stripped of the comfort of plausible theories. The tendencies to avoid looking at our lives, our insides, honestly, or to misunderstand the logic of language, also encourage the substi-

tution of theoretical notions or *idols*. God, writes Atkins, "is not to be identified with the idols of the human mind, with nature, place, or structure of any
kind" (775). Nor, we might add, with theory, perhaps the most prestigious idol
of the human mind.[13] In his article on deconstruction and theory in the collection *States of "Theory,"* edited by David Carroll, Jacques Derrida makes clear
the non-theoretical nature of his own work: "Deconstruction...doesn't have
any status, any theoretical status. There is no manifesto for it, no manifesto as
such" (93). This is fully in keeping with Wittgenstein's attitude, though oddly
enough—an indication of how prescient aspects of his work have been little
used in later decades—the collection makes no reference to Wittgenstein on
theory. Derrida writes of "Western philosophy's very decision, since Plato, to
consider itself as science, as theory: that is, precisely as that which Levinas
wishes to put into question..." ("Violence and Metaphysics," 118). Wittgenstein, the World War I POW, and Levinas, prisoner in the next war, had both
arrived at the same equation of two idolatries, science as theory, and set about
exposing them.[14]

There is divisive controversy among postmodernist scholars as to the status of theory. Contesting the contentions of leftists that they do not have a theoretical axe to grind, only a "critical self-consciousness," Stanley Fish has
retorted: "If critical self-consciousness is anything, it is the self-description of
a persuasive agenda that dare not speak its name; for if it were to do so and acknowledge itself as a design, it could no longer claim the purity that supposedly marks it off from every other form of coercion and constraint" (qtd. in
Norris, *What's Wrong with Postmodernism?* 91). In this scheme the reader does
not become persuaded by overt means—the force of the theory—as is usually the case; either an already persuaded reader has been addressed, or the
reader is self-persuaded. This description fits Wittgenstein only partly: indeed
in him the persuasive agenda does not speak its name. However, it can hardly
be called a design, which I take to be a theoretical scheme, because of the
apophatic factor in the technique. Wittgenstein does not seek to confirm the
transmission of theoretical knowledge in the manner of a scientist. Neither is
his agenda akin to "every other form of coercion and constraint." For him
philosophy leaves the world as it is, and a much more desirable mark of philosophy's success than transmission of knowledge is the subsequent *behavior*,
in full freedom, of the reader. Some account of this was actually provided by
Wittgenstein. "It is characteristic of obsessions that they are not recognized
and at certain stages are not even recognizable. These are attacked as scientific
problems are, and are treated perfectly hopelessly, as if we had to find out

something new. The problems do not appear to concern questions about language but rather questions of fact of which we do not yet know enough. *It is for this reason that you are constantly tempted to think I am giving you some information, and that you expect from me a theory.* In using the words 'I think so-and-so' it looks as if I were discussing the problems of a science called metaphysics" (*Wittgenstein's Lectures 1932–35*, ed. Ambrose, 99). In other words, it seems that there can be something between aimless creative or descriptive writing on the one hand and writing with a persuasive agenda on the other. Wittgenstein appears closer to the latter camp; he remarked once on how much what he was doing was "persuading people to change their style of thinking." But he may actually be in a camp by himself and perhaps very few others. For the persuasion is achieved by a limited technique: discrediting the current style of thinking. Nothing is said about how or what the persuaded person is to think, or indeed in what style. This too is characteristic of Derridean deconstruction. Not a theory, and notoriously incapable of charting a new course, it signifies, in the words of a contributor to *Deconstruction and the Possibility of Justice*, "the collapse of the project to understand things within the medium of thought," and so it "cannot build new systems of understanding" (Brudner 1191), although there is reason, as has been indicated, to see it as pointing to an ancient tradition that has already encountered these limits and has responded with an ethical teaching not vitiated by a questionable linguistic philosophy.

And here one can hardly resist making a passing comment which cannot be developed for lack of space—that these commonalities between Wittgenstein and Derrida are shared by both with Buddhism, which tries strenuously to avoid a doctrine such as nothingness (*sunyata*) being taken for a philosophical theory.[15]

Should additional evidence that Wittgenstein appertains to the current scene be needed, consider the French critic Roland Barthes, who "is of particular importance to post-structuralist theory because he bridges the structuralist and post-structuralist movements."[16] According to one account, Barthes in his *Elements of Semiology* is credited with the following advance: "Given one metalanguage for one explanation, it follows that there may be another in turn, and a metalanguage may replace a 'first-order' language. Each order of language implicitly relies on a metalanguage by which it is explained, and ironically, therefore, deconstruction is placed precariously in the position of becoming (against its principles and design) a metalanguage itself. Thus, discourse upon discourse in regression; and all discourses are exposed to inter-rogation. This is one aspect of Barthes's post-structuralist thinking and is, fundamentally, deconstructive."[17] Barthes came to these thoughts after conventional "structuralist" thoughts. But, in the words of Russell's introduction, this is what Wittgenstein had already concluded as a young man in his first work almost fifty years earlier: "...that every language has...a structure concerning which, *in the language*, nothing can be said, but that there may be another language dealing with the structure of the first language, and having itself a new structure, and that to this hierarchy of languages there may be no limit. Mr. Wittgenstein would of course reply that his whole theory is applicable unchanged to the totality of such languages" (Russell, *Introduction to the Tractatus*, xxii). We see again that the anti-metalanguage, anti-theory posture of the "later" Wittgenstein is only an elaboration and restatement of thinking expressed very early in life, and both his statements, while made well before the development of postmodernism, are yet to be found at its heart. Mention may be made, finally, of a postmodernist perhaps even more prominent than Barthes, Jean-Francois Lyotard, author of *The Postmodern Condition*. In his influential and widely read *The Differend: Phrases in Dispute*, exceptionally in postmodern writing, Wittgenstein is the most cited contemporary philosopher. It is arguable if in this work the author has been able to do anything beyond what any intelligent reader of Wittgenstein can do on his or her own. But what is nevertheless of interest to us is that another contemporary philosopher prominently cited by Lyotard happens to be one we are about to look at again—Levinas. Seven of his works are drawn upon, including his *Nine Talmudic Readings*, in which one can see the Jewish basis of his postmodern ethical thought. The prominence in the work of Lyotard of the known Jew Levinas and the unknown Jew Wittgenstein is a small but clear indication of the interweaving of postmodernism with Jewishness even in the thought of non-Jews.

LEVINAS, DERRIDA, ETHICS

The thinking of Wittgenstein and Levinas on ethics has this in common, that no system or set of prescriptions at all is built up. One would like to believe that this is the result of both having arrived at a similar understanding of the logic of language, shown in Wittgenstein's statement about language's bewitching powers, and in this from Levinas: "Language is perhaps to be defined as the very power to break the continuity of being or of history" (*Totality and Infinity*, 195). Just as Wittgenstein's writing, after giving all manner of hints, allusions and analyses, wishes—in the style of some therapist or Zen master—to leave the reader on his own and the world as it is, Levinas will not be drawn into even the least specific of directives. Nor will he provide a theory. Derrida's enthusiastic apology for Levinas on these points is incisive and clear:

> It is true that Ethics, in Levinas's sense, is an Ethics without law and without concept, which maintains its non-violent purity only before being determined as concepts and laws. This is not an objection: let us not forget that Levinas does not seek to propose laws or moral rules, does not seek to determine a morality, but rather the essence of the ethical relation in general. But as this determination does not offer itself as a *theory* of ethics, in question, then, is an Ethics of Ethics. In this case, it is perhaps serious that this Ethics of Ethics can occasion neither a determined ethics nor determined laws without forgetting itself. Moreover, is this Ethics of Ethics beyond all laws? Is it not the Law of laws? A coherence which breaks down the coherence of the discourse against coherence—the infinite concept, hidden within the protest against the concept." ("Violence and Metaphysics", 111)

By eschewing any direct discussion of ethics, and by orienting his philosophy away from changing the world, Wittgenstein had already made himself a powerful precursor of Levinas. His remarks in conversation on ethics were of the same simple or "unsophisticated" kind noted by Monk in connection with mathematical logic (n.12 above). Of what Derrida calls "the essence of the ethical relation in general", Wittgenstein's version can be gathered from this remark: "...only if you try to be helpful to other people will you in the end find your way to God" (to Drury, 129). In twenty words, eighteen of them monosyllabic and the others of two syllables, the essence of the religious attitude. What one's own determination of being helpful to others might be is left completely open. Just following orders, prescriptions or laws is no good even if they are "ethical." The very individuality and difference, one's own interpretations, are what develop us into unique relationships with God. Diversity and freedom in ethical behavior, as in textual interpretation, is the condition of our development. A Levinas scholar, Jean Greisch, quotes him as saying: "My task does not consist in constructing ethics, I am simply trying to find its meaning." "It is precisely this refusal to give oneself over to a foundational enterprise," Greisch comments, "that Levinas has in common with Wittgenstein" ("The Face and Reading," in *Re-Reading Levinas*, 71).

INNER AND OUTER: ETHICS AND JUSTICE

In the account so far of the stances on ethics of Wittgenstein and Levinas, there is a danger of a distinction between the inner and the outer world of the person becoming legitimized, of inwardness setting itself up as a "private" domain for the interpretation of public texts, an inwardness to which no one else can have access, an inwardness whose legitimacy is not questioned. This danger is averted by remembering the discussion at the end of the last chapter of private language in Wittgenstein's sense. There we saw how the inner-outer distinction is tied in with hellenistic linguistic ideology and ethics. The erasing of this false distinction has politically liberating and ethically illuminating effects. This is one of Wittgenstein's great contributions that has so far remained undeveloped in postmodernism, though Levinas shares the same basic insight: that even "private" conceptions of the ethical are made in the public language one shares with one's other. As Derrida puts it, "...*Levinas recognizes that there is no thought before language and outside of it*" ("Violence and Metaphysics," 110). Ethical concepts and judgments are therefore formed in language, and in a public language. There is no possibility of their being private, and this goes for the *acts* too to which the concepts and judgments refer. Our very conceptions of the ethical are formed in a public medium. Therefore there can be no privacy to the results of those conceptions—to the particular actions that we deem ethical or otherwise. Since the ethicality of actions cannot be determined by the "private" individual committing them, it is futile to believe them to be private. The determination of ethicality must be left to one's other, just as the determination of meaning or grammaticality in language is negotiated. Such "alternative" ways of dealing with ethical offenses may in fact be practiced in "aboriginal" or "primitive" societies, where there is no attempt to legislate an elaborate or rigid criminal code. The codes of "advanced" societies can be understood as a public response to control the devious and shady "private" realm, conceived in binary opposition to the public. If one were convinced that one's "good" or "evil" actions were equally visible to all—and of course to God— one would no longer attempt to conform to preconceived notions of good and evil, but develop each action out of individual responsibility, i.e. develop one's freedom: publicness, privacy, "good" and "evil" be damned, as it were. This without forgetting a direct and individual relationship with God, something that cannot normally be ignored or sidestepped by a Jew, but can within various atheistic or nihilistic systems. Interiority, or privacy, or "the inner" is one of the bewitchments born out of a wrong understanding of the logic of language—what is implied when Levinas says that "man's humanity would be the end of interiority, the end of the subject" (*Nine Talmudic Readings*, 167).

Our reading of Wittgenstein on the ethics of privacy is partly confirmed by his own later statement: "The 'inner' is a delusion. That is: the whole complex of ideas alluded to by this word is like a painted curtain drawn in front of the scene of the actual word use" (*Last Writings on the Philosophy of Psychology* II: 84ᵉ). The collapsing of the "two spheres," the inner and the outer, into one that has as yet no name is also indicated by this remark from the source just mentioned: "One could even say: The uncertainty about the inner is an uncertainty about something outer" (88). In the later writings, contemporaneous with the composition of the *Philosophical Investigations*, the connection between openness to God and openness to men is also made clear: "Someone who...penitently opens his heart to God in confession lays it open for other men too. In this he loses the dignity that goes with his personal prestige and becomes like a child. That means without official position, dignity or disparity from others. A man can bare himself before others only out of a particular kind of love. A love which acknowledges, as it were, that we are all wicked children. We could also say: Hate between men comes from our cutting ourselves off from each other. Because we don't want anyone else to look inside us, since it's not a pretty sight in there" (*C&V*: 46ᵉ).

An assumption of linguistic privacy, the possibility of a private language, leads all but inevitably to fear and hatred of the other and the attempt to cut oneself of from God. But God asks: "Can any hide himself in secret places that I shall not see him?" (Jer. 23: 24). Maimonides, even in medieval times, had to remind his reader of this text in Jeremiah before he could observe: "...when perfect men understand this, they achieve such humility, such awe and fear of God...that their secret conduct with their wives and in latrines is like their public conduct with other people....They also s[ay]: *Who is modest? Whoever behaves by night as he behaves by day*" (*Guide* II chap. 52, p.629; the last quotation is from the Talmud).

The connection between privacy and ethical dysfunction (to coin a voguish phrase) is biblical. The thought—thoughts—of Wittgenstein and Levinas can be seen in context with this three-fold point: both thinkers are abolishing privacy or interiority, rendering it theoretically unnecessary; for this abolition they are claiming an ethical consequence; this consequence, with its old and clear basis in the Bible itself, had already been developed in traditional accounts like Maimonides' *Guide*. Such a three-fold understanding further clarifies the Jewish inspirations of postmodernism, especially as it relates to ethics.

But the Wittgensteinian-postmodern conjunction, composed crudely of "logic of language-privacy-ethics" as we have described it here, while it is linked historically to Judaism, is also *a means for confronting at their root problems that seem ready to overwhelm our societies.* Some of the areas this conjunction affects—apart from the broadest conception of ethics itself—are the conservative view of privacy, the underpinnings of the communications and information revolution, communitarianism, interfaith dialogue, and critiques of justice and justice systems. Although he saw it as leaving the world alone, not forcing itself on the world, there is no reason for the world not to *choose* to be altered by Wittgenstein's philosophy. *Ideologies of privacy, for instance, have long affected the law, family and society, the planning and design of our living environments.* These are all subject to gradual change with the application of the analysis we are discussing. While investing in privacy and individualism to break away from the European ills of nationalism and religious oppression, American society has failed to attain to a culture of community. Responsibility for the other, helping other people find their own way to ethics and God, has hardly been a prominent value. Now everyone may understand that individualism and privacy, while justifiable reactions to oppressive, hierarchical societies, need not be permanent ideals. *Linguistic philosophy* as outlined here suggests trust rather than secrecy as the mark of community. Covert or private conduct, sought to be hidden from one's fellow, and in our secular age even from God, as we have seen, is not natural or instinctive but a direct result of linguistic ideology. Education, which has thus far imparted the wrong inspirations from the wrong metaphysics, is the only possibility for transforming what we have inherited. Wittgenstein's great interest in education should be seen in this context. Not only did he devote six years of his life to teaching small children—during which time he must have learnt a tremendous amount about parents, teachers and children and the passing on of ideologies—he also constantly kept in mind the links between education, training and ethics in his later writings.[18] His work had a clarifying as well as a practical side to it. A philosophy glorifying God and leaving the world as it is had nevertheless to do with benefiting his neighbor, as in the admired dedication of Bach's *Orgelbuchlein*.

Jewish tradition in general is nothing without education. The Yiddish word for synagogue is *shul*, and the Hebrew is *bet hamidrash*, or house of *midrash* (interpretation). There is an understanding that God educates himself, studies Torah like other students. Interestingly, the Talmud emphasizes the communal nature of study: "Learning is really achieved only in company" (*Berakot* 63, qtd. in Leo Rosten, *The Joys of Yiddish*, 375). "Whatever the motives," Rosten comments, "however naive the reasoning, an entire culture was structured around reading, study, a reverence for words. And this, please note, for centuries and centuries during which the overwhelming majority of mankind was illiterate" (*Joys*, 511). Derrida too has taken a distinct interest in education, concentrating his energies on the teaching of philosophy in high schools. Changes in the light of postmodernism in this crucial area could be the subversive or transformative force that inaugurates big changes in our entire culture or the "nouvelle ère historique" that Derrida refers to in his essay "Force of Law: The 'Mystical Foundation of Authority'" (1031).[19]

This essay is again and again supportive and clarificatory of our themes exploring justice, ethics and rules as related to postmodernism. It has, first of all, a rare direct reference by Derrida to Wittgenstein—he would like to take in a Wittgensteinian direction the use of the word "mystical," which in the title phrase goes back to Pascal and before him to Montaigne (943). We may take this as a pointer to the community of interest between Derrida and Wittgenstein. But this is only one of several important facets of the paper. It shows too, for instance, the disciplinary conjunction in deconstruction and how it intervenes in the real world (931), taking us back to Wittgenstein's multidisciplinary influences described in chapter I of this book. The "absence of rules" in deconstruction is made clear (923), an absence anticipated in the *Philosophical Investigations* and discussed in Chatterjee, "Linguistics." Derrida, in discussing law and rule, takes the very Wittgensteinian point of view that "[e]ach case is other, each decision is different and requires an absolutely unique interpretation, which no existing, coded rule can or ought to guarantee absolutely" (961). He claims that "deconstruction is justice" (945), but that he is only able to address it indirectly: "...one cannot speak *directly* about justice, thematize or objectivize justice, say "this is just" and even less "I am just," without immediately betraying justice, if not law (droit)" (935). Almost three decades earlier he had written, as we just saw: "it is perhaps serious that this Ethics of Ethics can occasion neither a determined ethics nor determined laws without forgetting itself." This is clearly reminiscent of Wittgenstein's attitude: any attempt to speak about ethics results in *Geschwätz*. As to the indeterminacy of laws and rules, the underlying theme here, we will soon see a lawyer's opinion. But here is what Abraham Joshua Heschel, whom we have drawn on before, had to say: "Rules are generalizations. In actual living, we come upon countless problems for which no general solutions are available. There are many ways of applying a general rule to a concrete situation. There are evil applications of noble rules. Thus the choice of the right way of applying a general rule to a particular situation is "left to the heart," to the individual, in one's conscience" (*God*, 327). The phrase "left to the heart" is from the Talmud. It suits very well the thematics of choice and ethical freedom pursued by Wittgenstein not only in connection with ordinary language but also in his explorations of the foundations of mathematics.

Derrida's "'Force of Law': The 'Mystical Foundation of Authority'" has running through it the opposition of Jewish (divine violence) and Greek (mythical violence), e.g. 973n., 981, 1027; the mythological dimension of violence, linked to fascism and Nazism, is Grecoid, 1041; he stops barely short of saying that the basic political opposition is then Greco-Nazi *versus* Jew, or simply Nazi *versus* Jew, as others have suggested.[20] *Derrida further sees as* linguistic *not only the basic problem of violence but also its overcoming*: "once again it is very much a question of the violence of language, but also of the advent of non-violence through a certain language"—a hopefulness identical to Wittgenstein's about the momentous benefits of understanding the logic of language aright (1019). Finally, Derrida questions the notion that the essence of language is originally communicative; this, according to Benjamin's formulation cited by Derrida, leads to a fall into a language of mediate communication, where words, having become means, incite babbling (*Geschwätz*); that Wittgensteinian word again, this time from the writing of Benjamin (1023).

Derrida's writing on justice is not an isolated literary or philosophical exercise. It appears in a collection just short of a thousand pages, representing dozens of practicing lawyers and law professors who show themselves to be capable students and practitioners of deconstruction in regard to legal theory and practice. Not many of them refer to Wittgenstein in their contributions as Derrida himself does, but there is evidence that Wittgenstein is read quite widely in his own right among intellectual lawyers. Our discussion anyhow helps show that despite his being sidelined in the contemporary scene, Wittgenstein as read here becomes an effective participant-deconstructor in the same conjunction of law, politics, ethics and literary theory addressed by the collection *Deconstruction and the Possibility of Justice*. To glance briefly at one of the other contributions, Arthur J. Jacobson, a professor of law at Yeshiva University, in his article "The Idolatry of Rules: Writing Law According to Moses, with Reference to other Jurisprudences," undertakes an investigation into the complexities of posing and applying rules in Moses' law. The dynamic attitude towards them—involving language games, forms of life, family resemblances—protects from stultifying legal "systems" and "theories". As Jacobson notes in conclusion, "([p]ositivism and naturalism regard the incessant creation or recreation of rules out of the very action the rules are supposed to govern as a destabilizing invitation to anarchy. The dynamic jurisprudences regard the incessant creation or re-creation of rules as at once the striving of persons (toward salvation, liberation, or reciprocity, as the case may be) and a spur to action" (1132). Both Wittgenstein and Derrida have been accused of issuing destabilizing invitations to anarchy. But salvation, reciprocity and liberation are indeed the directions opened up to us on understanding aright the logic of our language.

WITTGENSTEIN AS CONTEMPORARY TEXT: SOME ADVANTAGES

Although Derrida and Wittgenstein converge so clearly on ethics, they are not fungible, partly for the stylistic reasons already mentioned. As we currently stand, in terms of educational structure, it takes a well-prepared and intellectually adventurous reader to benefit from Derrida's writing. Deconstruction is thus likely to remain the domain of interest of a limited number of graduate students and specialists, while the *Blue and Brown Books* and even the *Philosophical Investigations* can be read in a high school philosophy course, as part of undergraduate training in the philosophy of education, or in any setting for the average person interested in philosophy, ethics, religion, such as independent discussion groups or those sponsored by churches, synagogues, libraries, or bookstores. No Hegel and little initial background in Anglo-American philosophy is required; these writings do not contain specialized terms, abstractions or theoretical neologisms. The *Tractatus* is best approached much later, unless readers are familiar enough with logic. In general, Wittgenstein speaks of ordinary language accessibly in ordinary language; a beginner can be guided to an understanding of his critique of language through such passages alone, leaving aside for the moment discussion of areas like psychology and mathematics. Most of Wittgenstein's themes— the grip of language, word usage and meaning, language games, cultural contexts, privacy, the craving for generality, everyday psychology involving pains, headaches, memory, wishes, children, dogs, and such—are easily the most familiar and the most transparently treated in any serious philosopher of any age. The combination of an ethical interest running through all this must be strongly appealing to non-academics such as teachers, lawyers, people with religious interests, artists and actors, who together make up a substantial section of the reading public. The free-flowing style of all the later writings also provides many points of entry and exit to and from the text for readers of different temperaments; if they simply keep reading, one or the other kind of example or argument will speak to them. The understanding leaps over to other kinds—no need for the linear accumulation of principles and concepts necessary with the great systematic philosophers.

The idea of philosophy not as an activity culminating in theory or explanation but in ethical self-examination (ideally leading to spiritual understanding and happiness) is a timely one. It sets Wittgenstein easily apart from practically all schools of the Western tradition. Perhaps because of his refusal to found a school, he has remained unentangled in the politics of academic intellectuals. But his linguistic route is potentially fascinating to all disciplines within the academy dealing with language—communications, philosophy, education, comparative religion, linguistics, rhetoric, theatre, cultural studies, gender studies, literature, cultural anthropology, semiotics. The idea that in each of these disciplines its ideology of language has ethical consequences should be hard to ignore.

With or without the Jewish subtext provided in the present work, Wittgenstein enjoys a large compatibility with critical Eastern religions like Buddhism. This makes him of interest to many in the West, including marginal Jews, who have moved away from Judaism to Eastern philosophies, and also to a large non-Western audience, who may already espouse a linguistic ideology partly compatible with Wittgenstein's.[21] Nevertheless, the Judaic is best approached in its own terms.

For a man who believed his teaching could not be separated from his conduct of life, Wittgenstein derives personal credibility from his integrity (firm and complete rejection of one of the largest personal fortunes in Austria), practical talents (aeronautical engineering), a gifted and anguished family background, service as volunteer soldier (taken prisoner of war), elementary school teacher, gardener, hospital orderly and—Professor of Philosophy at Cambridge University: a résumé with unusual aspects few philosophers can match. No wonder that he has inspired a number of novels, films and plays.

With the political and commercial recognition of Israel by the world over recent years, a better atmosphere for reflective study of Jewish intellectual tradition—from which the study of Wittgenstein may benefit too—is likely in relation to other "book" religions. Just the absence of such an atmosphere could have been one of the prompters for Wittgenstein to "go under" or conceal his message from the reader in the Tolstoyan manner that he so admired.

In one of his compact and powerful similes, Wittgenstein said doing philosophy was like rearranging the books on a bookshelf. When one finishes reading them, they inspire a little thinking that leads to making new juxtapositions and groupings. That is all—writing a new book is not essential to philosophy, it's all been written and taught about before. José Faur quotes Maurice Blanchot: "The book begins with the Bible....The Bible not only offers us the highest model of a book....[it] also encompasses all books, no matter how alien they are to biblical revelation....the books that follow it are always contemporaneous with the Bible." "Accordingly," he says, "'writing' and the 'people of the Book' are mutually exclusive. The Hebrews became 'the people of the Book'... by accepting the full implications of the Book. Rather than play 'the insane game of writing,' they heeded the advice of King Solomon—the traditional author of Ecclesiastes—that 'of making many books there is no end'" (Eccles. 12: 12). The canonization of the Hebrew Scriptures (ca. 100 C.E.) is the formal acknowledgment of this advice" (*Golden Doves*, 132–33). If the Hebrew people, as a people, have renounced writing in deference to the Book of all books, and if one of them appears to write, as we said before, that "writing" must be looked at very carefully, it must be related to this traditional conception—Jewish writing as commentary. We have seen Wittgenstein speak to this quite clearly: "It is only when the nature of a Jewish work is confused with that of a non-Jewish work that there is any danger, especially when the author of the Jewish work falls into the confusion himself, as he so easily may. Doesn't he look as proud as though he had produced the milk himself?" (*C&V*: 19ᵉ). The creative delusion amounts to trying to ignore or supplant the Bible. The Hebrew tries only to respond to it.

Where then shall we place Wittgenstein on the bookshelf? We have advanced a particular view of postmodernism, stressing the movement leading from critique of language to an ethic of freedom and responsibility developed in Jewish tradition. We have associated Derrida, Levinas, Lyotard, and Wittgenstein with this picture, although of course the three French thinkers became active years after Wittgenstein's death. With their share of *hubris* they may have a role in the death of postmodernism, if indeed it is dead, but Wittgenstein, who took pains to fight hubris, can likely revive what in it is worth reviving.

But with every utterance of its name postmodernism rings in instability and the irrelevance of scholarly periodization; and this seems to be implied in

Wittgenstein's remark about rearranging books, for surely some books widely separated in time and space come together, others close to each other are separated—that is what doing philosophy is. The first urgent separation is of the *Tractatus* from the works of Frege, Russell and Moore—Wittgenstein was no analytical philosopher; he only talked to some and learnt how not to do philosophy. The *Philosophical Investigations* must likewise be separated from these three and from the works of most commentators. These latter have assuredly made contributions to the study of Wittgenstein, but their academic spirit and culture are not distinguished from what he so clearly found uncongenial in his lifetime. So we place him rather near the language-and-ethics-oriented crowd, the Krauses, the Kafkas, the Canettis, the Joyces. Kraus and Canetti have already been referred to here. Joyce's affinities to the other three are depicted in the study by Ira Nadel.[22]

On reading some Kafka at her behest, Wittgenstein said to Elizabeth Anscombe: "This man gives himself a great deal of trouble not writing about his trouble" (Monk 498). He recommended the usual dosage of Weininger to her, saying that he was a man who, whatever his faults, really did write about his trouble. It might be noted that the exchange of suggestions for reading did not involve one favorite novelist for another, but one Jewish writer for another. By his return suggestion Wittgenstein was characterizing Kafka as a writer who did not quite succeed in grappling with his Jewishness. It is as if he were telling Anscombe (as he had tried to tell several others): about the Jewish man's troubles, read this brilliant, confused, self-hating young scholar who committed suicide, he is more instructive on anti-semitism and race prejudice than Franz Kafka. Imagine a precocious, scholarly young black man, deeming true in what became a wildly popular book the white man's most invidious stereotypes of blacks, recommending suicide for any individuals who displayed such characteristics, and committing suicide himself soon after the book's appearance. This is an all-round tragedy, a triumph of racism. Both Weininger and the imagined black author must be seen as playing back to their societies what they had uncritically internalized, the societies delirious to see their prejudices confirmed, the suicides a token of realized mistakes. So Weininger's volume must stay on the shelf troublingly, uncomfortably near Wittgenstein's for the immediate future.

To Kafka others have detected a closeness that Wittgenstein himself did not. "His work can be construed as a continuous parable on the impossibility of genuine human communication, or as he put it to Max Brod in 1921, on 'the impossibility of not writing, the impossibility of writing in German, the impossibility of writing differently. One could almost add a fourth impossibility: the impossibility of writing'"—that is a comment of George Steiner's on Kafka (*Babel*, 65); "a continuous parable on the impossibility of genuine human communication" will strike the reader as a not inaccurate summary of Wittgenstein's opus, though of course without the elusive ethical consequences. As he put it himself, "My difficulty is only an—enormous—difficulty of expression" (*Notebooks 1914–1916*: 40^e). In another place he suggests that the impossibility of expressing the conditions of the agreement in language between a thought and reality is *the solution of the problem* (see Hallett 210).

The last group of Wittgenstein's companions on the bookshelf must be drawn from the "judaizing" theologians and literary critics: Schneidau, Levinas, Altizer, Derrida, Hartman, who have continued the process of dehellenization from around the time of Wittgenstein's death.[23]

ENVOI

In the diaries published in 1997, after this study was substantially complete, Wittgenstein records in 1937 what constitutes a call to Jews and a summation of his expectations. The text and translation are as follows:

Juden! ihr habt der Welt schon lange nichts mehr gegeben, wofür sie Euch dankt. Und das nicht, weil sie undankbar ist. Denn man fühlt nicht Dank für jede Gabe, bloss weil sie für uns nützlich ist.

Drum gebt ihr wieder etwas, wofür Euch nicht kalte Anerkennung, sondern warmer Dank gebührt.

Aber das Einzige, was sie von Euch braucht, ist Eure werfung unter das Schicksal.

Ihr könnt ihr Rosen geben, die blühen werden, nie verwelken.

(*Denkbewegungen*, 1997, I, 105)

"Jews! For a long time you have not given anything to the world for which it is grateful to you. And that is not because it is ungrateful. Because one does not feel grateful for each gift just because it is useful to us. Therefore, give it something which will not bring you cold recognition but warm thanks. But the only thing it needs from you is that you accept your destiny. You can give it roses that will bloom and never wilt" (trans. Ingeborg Carsten-Miller).

These remarks express some very clear thoughts: 1. Jews gave something to the world for which it was grateful. 2. Their gifts since then have been (merely) useful, so they have brought no gratitude. 3. Give the world something, which will bring not just cold recognition, but its warm thanks. 4. The only thing the world needs from you is that you accept your destiny. 5. You have the capacity to give something of eternal value.

These words are future-oriented, and assert that Israel has a destiny linked to the rest of humanity ("the world," or "the nations") that remains relevant, one might add, despite Jesus and Mohammad (Christianity and Islam) and other religions. Wittgenstein's view of this destiny, of eternal value to the world, is also Israel's view, its *raison d'être*. Obviously, one who understands this, and identifies with Jews, is not a self-hating anti-Semite but must do what he can to bring Israel's destiny about. Jews and non-Jews must collaborate in fulfilling this destiny. Rather than perversely trying to subvert it, we see Wittgenstein as furthering Israel's destiny by pointing to its ethical and intellectual tradition, and by opposing what it opposed.[23]

Epilogue to a Reading

...he had, at all times, a shrewd idea of what was going on around him in the wider world.

—Fania Pascal, "Wittgenstein: A Personal Memoir"

What makes a subject hard to understand—if it's significant and important—is not that before you understand it you need to be specially trained in abstruse matters, but the contrast between understanding the subject and what most people *want* to see. Because of this the very things which are the most obvious may become the hardest to understand. What has to be overcome is a difficulty having to do with the will, rather than with the intellect.

—Wittgenstein, *Culture and Value*

Of course it does often happen that, as one develops, a man's expression of his religion becomes much drier. I had a protestant aunt, and the only religious observance she kept was to observe every Good Friday in complete silence and complete abstinence.

—Wittgenstein to Drury

I have to live with people with whom I cannot make myself understood.—That is a thought that I actually do have often. At the same time with the feeling that it is actually my own fault.

—Wittgenstein, dream report, in Monk

I don't try to make you *believe* something you won't believe, but to make you *do* something you won't *do*.

—Wittgenstein, in Hilmy

The sickness of a time is cured by an alteration in the mode of life of human beings, and it was possible for the sickness of philosophical problems to get cured only through a changed mode of thought and life, not through a medicine invented by an individual.

—Wittgenstein, *Remarks on the Foundations of Mathematics*

The preceding chapters are a reading. A mass of detail, of information, is looked at and shaped into a certain meaning, one that has not been proffered before. Meanings and readings are evanescent; such life as can be sustained in them is the reader's contribution, made manifest in the reader's actions. For the reader, Derrida suggests, the author is already dead. I have been Wittgenstein's reader; in these few pages I dwell in the margin, partly alive, as my own reader.

This reading then should have one indisputable effect: to make Wittgenstein familiar to those who have not been close to him, and unfamiliar to those to whom he has been familiar. This double newness is the same effect a first book on a subject may have. Indeed, our reading bases itself on the view that the early and late work are one, emphasizes *the link between language and ethics* as the key to Wittgenstein's method. It is the first to factor in the crucial conversational and epistolary material, the first to look for and "take" the hints Wittgenstein said he had left, and most important, the first to step out of academic philosophy and look at Wittgenstein in the light of Jewish tradition. In these ways, therefore, there is a "firstness" about the reading.

But of all these, foremost is the idea that the compatibility of his thought with Judaism, rather than being coincidental, results from an artistic intent by which *Wittgenstein wished to lead his reader on slowly from the gentile to the Jewish world of thought as part of the deep solution to philosophical (or religious and ethical) problems.* This is why he spoke of wanting to persuade people to change their way of thinking, of being disgusted with one way of thinking; why he seemed so certain, ever since the *Preface* to the *Tractatus*, that he had solved all the problems of philosophy, and also realized how little that was against what remained to be done. If Wittgenstein was convinced of the rightness of his plan, and it is plain that he was, there was no need for him to give it the adjective, Jewish. In his usage, for instance, Jewish and "truly religious" were equivalent; no reason why "truly philosophical" and "Jewish thought" might not be too. No "arrogance" or "nationalistic pride" need be seen in anyone who puts things this way, for it is only an expression of certain biblical prophecies (here, that all nations shall come to Zion and learn how God is worshipped there), that Jewish teaching shall prevail, Israel shall indeed be "a light unto the nations." In this reversal of the Christian "missionary" concept of the spread of religious ideas (or rather, the original biblical idea before its reversal in Christian and later Muslim proselytization), those who listen (the Nations) and those who teach by their tradition and actions (the people of Israel) are both "Jewish" and/or "truly religious."

Self-confidence and practicality can coincide in a lack of explicitness, a minimalism forsaking the use of labels by nature otiose. It was not practical for Wittgenstein in the first half of the twentieth century to brandish the Jewishness of his work or thought; but nor was it necessary, given his confidence over having solved the intellectual-ethical problems inflicted by Greco-philosophy. As an ancient rabbinic saying advises, "if you see a generation that loves the Torah, spread the Torah abroad. Otherwise keep it to yourself." If one is confident the answer is right, one does not need immediate recognition by others; it will come; so much the better if his readers learn to see from their own intellectual experience, in time, the Jewishness of his work and the virtues of the tradition that illuminates it. They will be close to being the ideal readers who derive pleasure from already having had and understood the thoughts in the book.

Wittgenstein's life shows an interesting oscillation between the Jewish-imbued world of Vienna and Austro-Hungary in which he grew up, the Manchester and Cambridge of his undergraduate days, the Austro-Hungary of army life with direct exposure to Jewish life in *stetls* and into the post-World War I period, the return to Cambridge in the late 1920's. With the exception of his close personal friend, Piero Sraffa, nobody in Wittgenstein's professional coterie—Russell, Moore, later von Wright, Malcolm, Anscombe, Rhees, Drury—was Jewish, yet at earlier stages almost everybody was—Engelmann, Groag, Zweig, the Olomouc group. Somewhat like Freud, he was surrounded by Jews at the most personal level, yet the success of his work would rest on its continuation by Gentiles (Jung in Freud's case) in the profession. If this were indeed so, it would have been eminently advantageous if, consciously or unconsciously, by design or by accident, the Jewish connections of psychoanalysis, as of Wittgenstein's thought, were not at the fore, if these developments were seen simply as science or a critique of language respectively. If one is convinced that one's method is correct and in need of universal comprehension, why evoke hatred and bigotry and limit readership to members of a sect by burdening the method with a sectarian name? Indeed, even if invented and introduced by Jews, to the extent that some thought procedure needs to be universally comprehended, it is *not* Jewish or sectarian. To think otherwise leads to calling Einstein's work, in Nazi style, "Jew physics," and other such absurdities. Absent Christianity, even the Hebrew Bible is not a Jewish religious text but a message to the world via Israel.

Born perhaps of the womb of Jewish tradition, Wittgenstein's thought finally goes to work under its own name. While Christianity claims to be the "New Israel" (*novus Israel*), traditional Israel has never interrupted her mission.

Buddhism provides an analogy. If you leave aside the vexed question of the "chosen people," the Buddha (the "Light of Asia") and Israel (called upon to be "a light unto the nations") both have completely universal messages, even though Israel, as a nation of priests, is also called upon by its covenant to set an example, to be different. Psychoanalysis and Wittgensteinian thought may have operated as secular agents. This does not prevent, with the passage of time and the coming of an age of intellectual flexibility and tolerance, crediting these agents as Jewish in conception, just as we regard logic and metaphysics as significantly Greek. Both swings of the pendulum—from total denial to acceptance—of Jewish contributions are understandable, and eventually some dialectical synthesis may be reached. (Though it may exist, I am not implying any identity or overlap between Wittgenstein's work and psychoanalysis: recall his trenchant criticisms of Freud, combined with a certain admiration. Yet both men in their own ways have thought of their work as connected to Jewish tradition).

❦ ❦ ❦

My reader has the right to ask about the route to this rather extraordinary reading, yet not really extraordinary, only delayed and deferred by a particular concealment. What might have been its origin and progression? Once stated, the answer always runs the risk of appearing elementary; yet a mystery, including the mystery of Wittgenstein's intent, that is, expressed textual intent, as recoverable by textual evidence, not "psychological" or "actual" intent, is not solved until the steps in the solution are made transparent. The beginning of the search lay, as for any reader of Wittgenstein, in an interest in language and meaning, coupled in this case to a dissatisfaction with existing "structuralist" answers. The merging of ethical questions and linguistic answers was attractive to me as a reader acquainted with, and at the time quite drawn to the *sunyata* (no-thing-ness or "zero-ness") school of Buddhism. But how, exactly, were ethics and esthetics one? Were there two Wittgensteins, or only one? How could one possibly put everything in place by being silent about it? Answers to questions framed in this way eluded me for several years, during which I read, was taken by, and eventually rejected Chris Gudmunsen's *Wittgenstein and Buddhism* as a satisfactory explanation of Wittgenstein's work (though I remain convinced of the parallelisms drawn by the author, and of his very Spenglerian point that similar movements of thought in societies far apart in time and space can bring about similar reactions and that this necessary realization has largely eluded Western thought). *Wittgenstein seemed to want express a very specific relation to his own time and space; his writing was organic to the history that he was living through.* This made Buddhism, however theoretically appropriate, an irrelevant suggestion. Not claiming Wittgenstein to have been a Buddhist, Gudmunsen's book, while clarifying Wittgenstein's method and his philosophical conclusions, did not directly illuminate his religion, which had become my interest.

Later I read what was then available (in the late 1970's) on Wittgenstein's life and background—the writings of Malcolm, Janik and Toulmin, Paul Engelmann. And I also became acquainted with Jacques Derrida and other "deconstructionists," realizing early their close compatibility with Wittgenstein as regards both language *and* ethics, and seeing with interest that this movement too was being discovered as "Buddhist" and "Taoist."

The first of these readings convinced me of the importance of some kind of ethical religion in Wittgenstein's work that had not been clarified, certainly had been underestimated by a secular academic readership, in general a readership also not able to let into its ken the Eastern schools straddling the rump in thought between "religion" and "philosophy." (For one with an Eastern upbringing, the rump is less of a problem). Reading in deconstruction demonstrated more clearly than previously-drawn analogies to Schopenhauer, Kierkegaard, Tolstoy and other Western worthies, that Wittgenstein, though a great radical, was not alone, and if he had no predecessors in philosophy, as von Wright had claimed, he reassuringly had what one may call *post*decessors as distinguished from the *disciples* he did not want—with the catch that the deconstructionists appeared completely unaware of Wittgenstein, certainly of the radical reading of him which I was moving towards. So I conceived of a religious thinker, with no predecessor, akin to Buddhism but no Buddhist, whose thought seemed recapitulated in a whole French school within a decade or two of his death. At this point I happened to read Frederic Grunfeld's *Prophets without Honor: Freud, Kafka. Einstein and their World.* This work is impressive for its recalling to memory some of the same mental landscapes as *Wittgenstein's Vienna* from a sympathetic Jewish point of view. Predisposed by personal history and circumstance to an interest in the fate of European Jewry, to me Grunfeld's work brought home the enormity of the blow dealt to Jewish intellectuals and artists, alive as passionate and idealistic men and women rather than as the later—alas more familiar—naked and emaciated (at best) "victims of the Holocaust." I learnt too how much the Wittgensteins had in common with other German-speaking marginal and converted Jewish families—the Mahlers and Schoenbergs and Benjamins, and how little conversion meant against the weight of their inherited experience as part of the Jewish people. Coming from a land that had been dominated by Buddhism after starting out as "Hindu," where some Hindus had taken up Christianity in ancient times and later times, where some Buddhists had reconverted to Hinduism but had retained strongly Buddhist philosophical ideas (in the region of my birth, for instance), where Hindus had accepted Islam in millions when rulers of Muslim faith had held political domination for half a millennium (much as Slavs had converted to Islam in Bosnia Herzegovina), a land where there is a modern movement to "unconvert" former Hindus, for such a person as I, a switch at the baptismal font from the persecuted and despised Jewish faith for the manifold opportunities of twentieth-century civilization does not signal the evaporation of three thousand years of Jewish experience. Indeed, given the complex tensions obtaining in Christian Europe, conversion, as Robert Wistrich has observed, did not eliminate the Jewish convert's identity problem but rather intensified it (Wistrich, *Revolutionary Jews*, 101).

The situation was ripe for an hypothesis that Wittgenstein was somehow "being Jewish" as a writer. I knew little of what that might mean. But the decisive moment came to me soon, when, reading in *Culture and Value*, the remark about genius amongst Jews found only in the holy man, other Jews ("I, for instance") being merely talented, jumped out of the page (the reader may wish to review the discussion of this remark in Chapter III). So!—*Wittgenstein did belong to a tradition, and he knew it*! The excitement led me to drop all other thoughts and focus on the implications. I consulted rabbis, took courses in Jewish history, philosophy and mysticism, and interrogated Wittgenstein scholars about the "Jewish possibility." The last drew uniformly negative responses (as did thorough computerized searches of the Wittgenstein literature) except for tiny scattered exceptions—Rabbi Ignaz Maybaum writing a brief article in a Jewish magazine about Wittgenstein and Rosenzweig, Rabbi Jack Spiro noting that the Jewish idea of meaning had been expressed by Wittgenstein, someone suggesting in a literary journal that Wittgenstein's "theory" of language had something in common with Kafka's view). Not much, but enough to keep one working. Very soon after, another unexpectedly explicit clue, given that I had reconciled myself to the intellectual equivalent of reconstructing a whole being from bone fragments and strands of hair—the declaration that while Drury's ideas on religion were basically Greek, his were one hundred percent Hebraic! This was more than a clue, actually, it was, it seemed to me—to use an ill-suited figure—the smoking gun, Wittgenstein's declaration of the nature and purpose of his thought, giving meaning to all the evasion and silence and "confessing." It only remained to work out what he meant by saying his thought was Hebraic. Much easier said than done, of course.

More than a decade has gone by since that stage, marked by many happy meetings, discussions, delays, insights, suggestions, prayers, and continuous reading. In February 1988 I was asked to make my first public presentation of this project, as it then stood, to the Jewish Studies Workshop at the University of Chicago. Though my attainments in Judaic studies were questionable, I received some kind invitations to speak: on "Ludwig Wittgenstein and Jewish Education," on "The Jewish Mind" (the second topic was suggested to me, but my *chutzpah* in accepting it now appears dizzying). In 1989 I attended the Tenth World Congress of Jewish Studies in Jerusalem and made a presentation on "Wittgenstein as a Jewish Thinker." The collegial interest in my work was gratifying. I made friends. I showed some drafts to Robert Wistrich. He asked me to contribute an essay on Wittgenstein, whom he had himself studied quite thoroughly, to his forthcoming project *Austrians and Jews in the Twentieth Century*, which eventually appeared from St. Martin's Press in 1992. Jacques Derrida was kind enough to read that essay while on a lecture visit to Chicago and expressed his interest in the continuation of the project, as did the Talmudic scholar and distinguished Sephardi rabbi José Faur. Even if my reading was close to the truth, I was uncertain how to proceed. Perhaps Wittgenstein would have thought quite sufficient the publication of an article. But a friend whose judgment I trusted assured me that one who skillfully clothes something of this nature, also anticipates the pleasure of having it carefully stripped. This was convincing. I began to sketch a book-length treatment which would do three things: show that the traditional bisection of Wittgenstein was wrong and misleading; that the resulting single Wittgenstein—call him early or late, or both or neither—could be read with profit and pleasure as a Jewish writer; and that there was enough supporting evidence for this in the conversations, manuscripts, and memoirs by intimates, in addition to the "canonical" writings. After years of teaching and other duties, and the constant feeling that someone much better qualified and informed than I should actually be doing it, this project drew, if not to a close, close to the point of publication.

Some thoughts as to what this reading clarifies about Wittgenstein's work that had before been obscure, and what factors might have delayed such a reading until now, may be of interest.

Our study cannot but have appeared rambling and fragmented at various points to the reader, and to some this will be a deficiency. To them I owe a more or less orderly account of what this interpretation does that others do not, so that connections not at first apparent may become clearer. The claim is to have given a meaning to the sense of wholeness and unity of construction in Wittgenstein's writing that we noted at the very beginning in his own account: "Each of the sentences I write is trying to say the whole thing, i.e. the same thing over and over again; it is as though they were all simply views of one object seen from different angles" (*C&V*: 7ᵉ). If he is trying to transmit Jewish monotheistic teaching, this fits well with both the wholeness and the repetition—the name *Mishnah*, of a major component of Jewish law, means *repetition*, Maimonides' major work *Mishneh Torah* is "repetition of the Teaching." We explain the fact that Wittgenstein spoke of receiving and deploying hints, as well as what the hints might have been that he left us. Clearer too is the great effort to illuminate ethics while never treating it directly. Although more detail is always possible in this area, we see that the enormous importance of people's behavior in setting up practice and understanding, while explored with reference to ordinary language and custom in the *Investigations*, points powerfully to a long tradition of Jewish observance and practice. At a little distance from this, but enormously meaningful for our own intellectual epoch, we explain the critique of academic proceedings in general, exemplified by Wittgenstein's determined distance from them. We are able to understand now Wittgenstein's thinking on science and mathematics as areas redolent with idolatrous temptations to which all but a few have succumbed. We have cast light on how one may be concerned at the same moment with logic and one's sins, and we have shown definitely the wholeness of Wittgenstein's writing as transcending any phase, early or late. Wittgenstein's place in the current and future scene, his conception of the relation of religion to philosophy and his place, or nonplace, in Western culture may be easier to think about. We have tried to explain his religion. It remains to highlight the vanity of these claims by asserting how little is achieved, were they all true.

There have been some hostile exchanges in the Wittgenstein literature over his possible homosexual relationships, but the field is in general remarkably free of polemics. I too have had little reason to polemicize. Considering that there has been so much recent writing on Wittgenstein, especially on issues combining biography and interpretation, an obvious question arises: why are the long and detailed biographies that have recently appeared (McGuinness, Monk) silent on the possibilities proposed here? Why doesn't a Jewish reading exist already? Even as I was thankful for the opportunity to undertake the first one, this question has intrigued me. The answer can be that such a reading was attempted, but the reader, or readers, failing to amass enough appropriate evidence, did not or could not proceed—the present reading arrogates to itself the implication that it has simply "done better" and come into the light of day. But I have uncovered no evidence of previous unsuccessful attempts (although Bartley makes an undocumented assertion that Paul Engelmann "and others" *thought*, at least, that Wittgenstein's work was "typically Jewish," (56), the last not being a very clear phrase in any case). So such a reading may never have been attempted, forcing us to speculate: why not? Some strands of analysis making up the possible answer may be suggested:

1. The secular philosopher's or scholar's reluctance or inability to deal with religion, even though the tremendous import of religion in his life and work is staring the scholar of Wittgenstein in the face.

2. Lack of knowledge of or expertise in Jewish tradition, in the academy in general, certainly in comparison to widespread general familiarity with the Christian part of the "Judeo-Christian" tradition. Granted that scholars of Jewish background are well represented in the academy, any knowledge of Jewish tradition they may have is generally kept separate from their professional interests; some others may feel inhibited from appearing to "brag" about someone else's Jewishness, as one may well seem to in making the present argument about Wittgenstein. I am reminded of the response of one prominent and serious Israeli scholar of Wittgenstein with whom I conversed about these matters. He tried to pick holes in my thesis, while I defended it. Then he said, in response to one of my counterarguments, seemingly as a total *non sequitur*: "But we are a very small nation..." In the impetus of the argument I immediately replied: "But I'm not from a small nation." Only when I was in mid-reply did his remark come home to me: "We're a small nation—it's not seemly for us to go around claiming figures of world-wide eminence to be Jewish. It might even be dangerous..." Although I never verified it, I took his *non sequitur* to mean that he conceded I was probably right, but it was not really for him to make the argument that I had made.

3. Granted that there have been religion scholars interested in Wittgenstein, they have all been either practicing Christians or were imbued, if unconsciously, in Christian assumptions and tradition. Unlikely to real-

ize that conversions to Christianity of Jews in the last two centuries were often *pro forma*, strengthening an interior Jewish feeling rather than instilling a total allegiance to Jesus. Scholars of Christian background would not be predisposed to detect veiled or disguised expressions of Jewish thought. Jewish scholars of religion, on the other hand, are inclined to work with thinkers (for instance Buber, Rosenzweig, Baeck, Heschel, Fackenheim among the moderns) whose affiliation with Jewish tradition is unambiguous. The purview of these scholars, with few exceptions, does not include thinkers of extremely attenuated Jewishness, as they may have perceived Wittgenstein to be. The "press" he has received from Jewish writers is actually as a "self-hater," much imbued with Weiningerism (Schwarzschild, Lurie; the latter has argued in a paper in Hebrew, according to friends who have read it for me, that Wittgenstein's remarks on Jews and Jewishness are couched in the language of anti-Semitism deriving from Spengler and others, and that this is why he stopped making them after the 1930's, when such language became discredited; against this of course see the discussion above in Chapter III). Until 1985–86, J. C. Nyíri's paper was the only one of some 6,000 titles in the Wittgenstein bibliography to refer to any Jewish theme, but his concern with Wittgenstein's "conservatism" is very different from mine.

4.   Given the knowledge that Wittgenstein kept his religion secret, all possibilities should be considered: that Wittgenstein was (secretly) a feminist, Taoist, Buddhist, Jew, founder of a "previously unknown" cult, Shiite Muslim, Hindu (he liked Tagore), heretic Christian, crypto-Sufi, et al. But this was never done. Nobody considered a broad range of possibilities. Does that have to do with the ethnocentric, Euro-Greek, Greco-Christian complexion of "philosophy"? Yes; how could it not?

A more convincing case may yet be made for one of these possibilities just mentioned (or some other) than I have been able to make for Judaism. But to make a good argument, one has to know or imagine what one is looking for, rather like the old lady who went up to Dr. Johnson while he was being feted on the publication of his Dictionary and told him: "Dr. Johnson, I perceive that your dictionary contains vulgar words." "Madam," he is said to have replied, "I perceive that you have been looking for them!" A more appropriate example may be the recent claim by two researchers in human anatomy to have found a new muscle between the eye and the jawbone. They claimed that the study and teaching of anatomy is so routinized (e.g. dissections of the head are carried out from certain angles only) that despite the tremendous activity in the study of human anatomy, discoveries are precluded. In this case the researchers decided to dissect from the front, I believe, rather than from the conventional angle, to much ridicule from their colleagues, who went so far as to call them crazy. Of course I am in no position to endorse their finding, but both their claim and their description of colleagues' attitudes are perfectly plausible. Again recently, a lump of blue mineral "unknown to science," acquired in a Moroccan *suq*, was brought in to British geologists. The research funds, training facilities, personnel, and commercial applications of geology no doubt exceed those of philosophy. Estimates are that it will take a year or two for geology to deal with the mystery mineral. So it need not be a cause for consternation if an elusive but clarifying reading of an obscure philosopher were to appear outside the sequence of "systematic" scholarship about him.

A positive argument on the nature of Wittgenstein's religion must be able to cast healthy doubt on other possibilities. That involves taking them seriously. Fergus Kerr in his *Theology after Wittgenstein* thinks that Wittgenstein's remark about one hundred percent Hebraic thinking was probably a joke. Further comment is difficult, but let us try. Why should Wittgenstein, always intensely serious about religion, be joking just at the point where he mentions the Hebraic? Is it not more likely that Kerr either does not understand what such thinking might be, or that he dimly discerns a threat in the possibility, and therefore tries to disarm it as humorous?

5. As noted, two Jewish scholars actually have dealt specifically with Wittgenstein's existential—if not intellectual—Jewishness (Steven Schwarzschild and Yubal Lurie). Both of them see him as a Weiningerian "selfhater." Ashkenazim in general may not be attuned to the idea of "concealed" Jews; their tradition stresses, surely to some extent in emulation of early Christians, openness and martyrdom. Wittgenstein in any case was never formally a Jew; born concealed, as it were, because his ancestry was insufficient to make him "automatically" Jewish, there was no constraint whatsoever on his interior choices; when he made them he chose to keep them internal, somewhat in conformity with his dictum that the important things cannot—or need not—be said. He was also free to be as elusive and indirect as he wished in the

artistic conceiving of his work. What is unsaid can be *divined* by others. This is nothing but the common mystical formula that goes something like this: "he who understands will know what [this hint or this silence] means." What one knows or believes or wants to accept from past reading, one sees as part of the meaning of present and future reading. That surely is the basis of tradition. Wittgenstein would have counted on this both in himself and in his readers, Jewish or non-Jewish. Concealment is therefore not an act of cowardice, or merely a means of eluding censors, although it may have the latter advantage. It is an affirmation by the transmitter that whether open or concealed, the message is true and right; it is not diminished by concealment, nor does openness increase its validity. Wittgenstein's particular mode of concealment makes a further affirmation: however deep the concealment, however indirect and veiled the message, it will get through; indirectness and the depth of concealment become modes of the Jewish art of commentary or exposition: a non-writing that points towards the book of books. God himself conceals, and conceals himself. Here may lie the meaning of Wittgenstein's assertion that the *Tractatus* was a philosophical and a literary work at the same time—literary in the Tolstoyan mold, with no preaching or explanation from the author. The artistry is such that the "moral," needing no explanation, is contained in the denseness of the intellectual description.

The possibility of the present reading earlier in the history of Wittgenstein interpretation therefore could have fallen through these cracks in the layout of academic activity. Of the cracks, even a thin one would allow "extremely attenuated Jewishness" to fall through, a Jewishness reading so low on the meter, as it were, as to be below the threshold of normal observability. What was not observable became the non-existent. What was observable (e.g. being part of a coterie of assimilated Jewish friends in Olomouc-Vienna, expressing a wish to be taken to Palestine with one of them) was not noticed. Direct evidence (e.g. the "one hundred percent Hebraic" remark to Drury) was either ignored or treated as a joke (Kerr says: "The charge that Drury's religious ideas were too 'Greek,' while his own were purely 'Hebraic,' *which may in any case have been a joke*, could be *no more than a conventional view about the Hellenization of Christianity*" [emphasis added]; Wittgenstein's remark is taken at anything but face value—as humor, or, convolutedly, as a conventional *Christian* view. The possibility that he was simply telling a close friend that his thought was completely Hebraic achieves no resonance, and there can be only two reasons why: either ignorance, or theological distortion on the part of Christian-oriented readers, for fear of the truth. Kerr can see Wittgenstein joking about Hebraic thought, or he can see Hebraic thought in a Christian setting, but he cannot see Hebraic thought in its own right; for how numerous prominent Euro-German philosophers also could not, see Nathan Rotenstreich's *Jews and German Philosophy: The Polemics of Emancipation*). With these three strikes and other similar ones against it, Wittgenstein's intellectual Jewishness had little chance to emerge in the conversation of philosophy.

In the public world this Jewishness was either so deployed—manipulated—by Wittgenstein, or so attenuated, or simply lost in the shuffle of circumstances, that the *Encyclopedia Judaica*, an extensive reference work devoting full coverage to modern Jewish thought, published in the 1960's and '70's, does not mention him at all, while *it includes as a Jewish musician his brother Paul*, the pianist who had lost his right arm in combat and lived in New York. Ironically, of course, it was Ludwig, and not Paul, who had called private meetings with members of his family and friends to announce that he was more Jewish than was generally known. This is the same Paul who, as an adolescent, seemed more aware than his little brother Ludwig of the likelihood of racist prejudice against people of their descent. Their lives diverged during the thirties, and perhaps any variety of Jewishness would more likely be sympathetically recognized and noted in New York musical circles than among Cambridge philosophers. Be that as it may, it is clear that the paradoxes of apparent evasiveness and marginality are highly significant in Ludwig's case; attenuated Jewishness at the surface, on the outside, may turn dialectically into a powerful interior Jewish intellectual force, inversely proportionate: the lesser the surface presence of what one may call enthusiastic Jewishness, the greater intellectual clarity and commitment at depth, as Wittgenstein suggested with his "calm surface with molten lava underneath" simile. The very possibility of detachment from any state of being Jewish, of a mask of artistic concealment, can liberate intellectual and religious energies into a commitment much deeper than if one had to constantly cope with the most adverse circumstances. This is not by any means a generalization. It seems to apply to Wittgenstein, and may be extended in varying ways to a number of "marginal" figures such as Canetti, Kafka, Freud, Kraus, Mahler, Schoenberg, Derrida. It may well be that because the Jews of Spain, as a people, experienced forced conversion, life in a dominant Muslim-Christian culture, racism of the *pureza de sangre* ("purity of blood") variety not unlike the Nuremberg laws, torture, and mass expulsion, in a sort of preview of events that overtook Ashkenazim hundreds of years later, they, the Sephardim, understand the category of *converso* or *anusim* or "crypto-Jew" in its intellectual sense more clearly, while the category had to be re-invented in our century among the Ashkenazim, something that we just are beginning to understand: Jewishness has such immense psychic-intellectual dispersion that it can be reconstituted by an individual after generations of forced or pragmatic conversions and persecution of one's ancestors. Heredity is in fact not essential. As a corrective to the Christian idea of the immediate efficacy of conversion, for instance, instead of the "stern Protestant ethic" attributed by Janik and Toulmin to Ludwig's father Karl, one may ask if Karl's ethic—and his son's—did not rather derive from some pre-conversion Jewish family tradition such as the one whose existence among the Wittgensteins is already documented in the literature.

The secondary literature on Wittgenstein, if the present reading is correct, while meticulous, insightful, and still invaluable for further work, nevertheless allowed the big interpretive catch to escape. Ignorance rather than anti-semitism may be the overall deficiency here, though the two deficiencies are not unrelated, just as they are not in the feeling among Black folk that white scholars' ignorance of them has to do with racism. McGuinness, at the beginning of his biography, recognizes that since World War II "most families with Jewish blood, among them some of the descendants of Hermann Christian [Wittgenstein] [such as Paul of New York?], have, with whatever justification, a different attitude towards their origin and see it as the source of their energy and intelligence." He cannot extend this, however, to Wittgenstein the writer, his subject, the energetic and intelligent Ludwig, who, he says, "belonged to an earlier way of thinking, with something of *the Jewish self-hatred of Karl Kraus and Otto Weininger*" (2, emphasis added). Wittgenstein really tarred himself with the Weininger brush; not even the best-informed of scholars is able or willing to cleanse him. Why has it not been argued that he was joking when he waxed enthusiastic over Weininger, and perfectly serious when he characterized his thought as one hundred per cent Hebraic? (We have already alluded to McGuinness's view briefly, Chap. III, n.6. For the persistence of the "tarred by Weininger" effect in another major, more recent biography, Monk's, see Chap. III, n.7; this book uses a Weininger quotation as its motto. Poor Wittgenstein; it would surely appeal to his sense of humor to see his peddling of Weininger have such persistent effects!).

To our reading, the corrected understanding of the Wittgenstein-Weininger relationship is critical. Practically everybody went wrong by as-

suming Wittgenstein's self-hatred as a Jew and self-love as a Christian or ag-
nostic or Goethean pagan. This must be acknowledged to be a result of racial,
anti-Semitic attitudes; after all, given the aggressive and bloody history of the
religion, Christian self-hatred is more readily conceivable than self-hatred
among the people of the Book. Christians have converted to Judaism in Europe, though the recorded cases are limited in number because of the cruelty
such an act provoked. That Wittgenstein in his prayers as reported by Rhees
never mentions Jesus should raise some Christian eyebrows, but it hasn't. He
was somewhat of an expert in Christian prayer, though seemingly rather to
guide his Christian friends to the best prayers in their religion, Dr. Johnson's
being one of his favorites. Never a proselytizer, his praise of Tolstoy and
Kierkegaard is in the same vein—to guide Christians to the most authentic
Christianity possible. Not a word of his writings can be construed as seeking
to attract converts to Judaism.

Being an honest religious thinker does not imply blandness and neutrality
about religion. One may feel free to award the palm to the most meritorious tradition among all religions. Wittgenstein's early experiences, thinking and reading led him to favor the Jewish tradition. *This* may have in turn strengthened his
later interest in the extent of his descent, not having acknowledged it, and so on.
It is interesting that his behavior over the "confessions" was typically ambiguous. While it could surely also be seen as a public matter best resolved by formal conversion, he confined the acknowledgment of "physical" Jewishness to
an inner circle of friends and family. The concealment option thus remained in-
tact. Yet posterity had a way of learning of his feelings, and it did. Had he converted—to whatever religion—he would on the one hand not have impressed
himself, and on the other lost the psychic energy that an artist derives from evasion and concealment. Not only would he lose the valuable concealment option,
but, to recall his own metaphor, he would only acquire a tightrope walker's cos-
tume, with no evidence of his own ability to walk the tightrope. So he stayed
away from conversion, and even from any revealing act such as moving to
Palestine, emigrating to Russia and living among Russian Jews, or openly
studying Jewish texts. Many indeed are the "Jewish" writers, in any case, who
do not so much as allude to these texts.

The deep psychological rootedness of Jewish ideas, however, such as
monotheism, God the Father, law-book-writing-teaching (Talmud Torah),
difference, service to the other, human freedom and innocence, as opposed to
original sin, the ethical life of the individual as a work of art dedicated to God,
and waiting for the Messiah, derive from these texts. These ideas have been

historically embarrassing to Christian state and ecclesiastical authorities (often the same) for their potential of undermining the opposed ideas of the triune God, original sin, the resurrection of Jesus, the literality of the New Testament text, virgin birth, and the "having arrived" of the Messiah, eventually killed by the Jews. A continuing conflict made up of these elements has resulted in regular expulsions of Jews from practically every major Christian economy and society in the Old World. Wittgenstein maintained psychological rootedness not by constant reference to the Hebrew Bible which an overtly Jewish writer might make, or to the Greek myths a secular European psychologist might draw upon, but to a recurring panoply of writers in the background of his writings whom he drew on as a deconstructive textual diet, as we have seen: Augustine, Kierkegaard, Marx (through Sraffa and no doubt directly as well), Weininger, Spengler, Freud). These are thinkers on the big human issues, sex-money-morals-language-God, and though they may be psychologists, economists, philosophers *manqués* in his reading, they had tried to "know man." *He*, Wittgenstein, however, as a Jewish thinker, understood their work better than they did themselves, individually or collectively, and irrespective of whether they were Jews or not. In this sense Wittgenstein managed to put the Bible firmly in place by being silent about it, by pointing—with his signposts against linguistic traps—also to the Book of Books. With less—by waging only a battle against the bewitchment of our understanding by means of our language—he may have done more than most Jewish thinkers, and could be ranked by his own criteria as a Jewish genius and a holy man. In his own voluminous writings on psychology, however, he asks questions only of a teasingly empirical type about the puzzles of language and mind, never speaking in theoretical terms of drives, instincts, neuroses, psychoses, obsessions, and conflict.

In line with the Israeli scholar who suggested that as a small nation it was unseemly for Jews to claim what has been claimed here for Wittgenstein, one of my early interlocutors in this study observed that as a non-Jew I had the freedom to say certain things that a Jew might not. In a related way, Wittgenstein may have felt he did not have the freedom to say certain things that an observant Jew might. The freedoms he had were those of an Austrian (and later British) citizen. He might have felt he had earned them by meeting a citizen's obligations. While he could not speak as a Jew (because he had not earned *that* right), he had to be true to his Jewish perceptions. His writings consequently need not affect anyone's religious ideas if read as philosophy, nor a Jewish reader's ideas if read Jewishly. Hence also, to this extent, they do not play the insane game of writing. However, if a philosophical reader takes them as his or her religion, or a Jewish reader as his or her philosophy, they acquire a certain cross-fertilizing power, the result of a marginal man becoming a whole writer, a marginal writer a whole man; the result too of a particular reading, and not of what one may be inclined to slip into thinking of as the "original" expression. Wittgenstein, having contributed his text, is freed by us of its consequences. His work leaves the world alone. We, intervening with a reading, take responsibility for our intervention.

A word on atonement. It is a goal of any religious person, monotheist or not (though of course not only in its specific Christian sense). Wittgenstein wanted to atone as much as the next person. But the link between religion and philosophy he provides also links intellectual effort to atonement—one may atone by intelligent religious work, by *clarification*, among other ways, to use Wittgenstein's favorite word about his own activity. Yet another structure or dimension of atonement seems discernible in Wittgenstein's life. We have read the *Tractatus* as already religious and of Jewish inspiration. The completion of such an extraordinary project, despite its failure in the world of philosophy in its author's eyes, may be expected to bring a certain exhilaration, perhaps experienced in solitude in Norway. By the school teaching years, as we have seen on Hänsel's account, Wittgenstein felt he had been "called" in a dream to a mission which he was unable to take on. And this must have been a deflation of his spiritual level, as a letter to Engelmann records. One may speculate that the philosophical writing that began a few years later was atonement for the failure to rise to the mission his dream had called him to.

Appendix

This appendix is devoted to the facts of Wittgenstein's descent as they have been ascertained, and some related matters. The most precise research on Wittgenstein's ancestry appears to have been undertaken by W. W. Bartley III, to whose account the reader is referred (199–200). After surveying all relevant records for several generations and considering various (sometimes contradictory) family accounts, he confirms the account given by Wittgenstein in his confessions to friends and members of the family: "Ludwig Wittgenstein was indeed three-quarters Jewish" (200). From the confession, Fania Pascal was left with the impression that the three Jewish grandparents were active members of the Jewish community. Later she learnt that two of them had been baptized as children and one on being married (49). If indeed Wittgenstein had not foregrounded, or not mentioned at all, the matter of conversion, this may be taken as a sign of the lack of importance he attached to it, consistent with the detachment with which he greeted news of the conversion of friends and acquaintances to Catholicism, as detailed earlier.

Bartley's conclusion is reached by way of a family tree prepared in Jerusalem after World War II, in 1961, and supported by the fact that portraits of Moses Meier, Jew of Laasphe and Korbach, and his wife Brendel Simon—who by this Jerusalem family tree were the grandparents of Ludwig's grandfather Hermann Christian Wittgenstein—were in the possession of the Wittgenstein family in Vienna. (According to McGuinness, writing in 1988, these portraits "still hang in the Viennese villa of their great-great-greatgranddaughter..."). One of Ludwig's maternal grandfathers, Jakob Kalmus, a Jew of Prague, had in turn a maternal grandfather, Ernst Wehli, who had been President of the Prague Jewish community (McGuinness 21). While his mother's mother Maria Stallner, a Catholic, is counted as Ludwig's only non-Jewish grandparent, his mother herself, née Leopoldine Kalmus, was heir on her father's side to ancestors who were leading "members of the Jewish community." The status of not being Jewish by legal or traditional criteria, while having a parent who was, had already been the experience of Ludwig's mother, recapitulated in her children's generation. Bartley supposes that the family name (Meier derived from *meir* meaning "lightgiver" in Hebrew) was changed to Wittgenstein in 1808 in accordance with a Bonapartist decree that all Jews adopt surnames.

The above makes credible the suggestion, made more than once in the literature, that Karl Wittgenstein's children (i.e., Ludwig and his siblings) "thought of themselves entirely *Jewish* by extraction" (e.g., Janik and Toulmin 172). Deception, concealment or Jewish self-hatred are not indicated by this. On the contrary, Margarete Stonborough, the youngest daughter and the sister to whom Wittgenstein was closest, displayed pride and courage extraordinary under any circumstances when she "insisted upon being jailed with other Viennese Jews after the *Anschluß, over the expressed objections of the Nazis*, who were content to consider her and her family non-Jews" (*ibid.* 173). Any suggestion of lack of courage in general on Wittgenstein's part is belied by his taking on the most dangerous assignments during voluntary war service and being repeatedly decorated for bravery.

In connection with the members of his family remaining in Vienna through the war years, research of Konrad Wunsche (*Wittgenstein als Volksschullehrer*) must be mentioned, to the effect that Ludwig Hänsel, whose friendship with Wittgenstein began in an Italian POW camp after World War I, later became a leader in the Austrian Catholic youth movement, with access to powerful politicians. When the Austrian Nazis were taking over, Hänsel apparently prevailed upon their leader Arthur Seyß-Inquart, a lawyer by profession and Minister of Law—later Reich Commissioner for Occupied Netherlands responsible for the destruction of Dutch Jewry—to ensure the safety of members of the Wittgenstein family despite their Jewish descent. There is little reason to doubt this account, which to the best of my knowledge has not been noticed in the Wittgenstein biographical literature at large, remaining buried in Wunsche's book. The enforcers of the Nuremberg laws who called at the Wittgenstein residence in Vienna and were content to consider the family non-Jews may therefore have been following instructions from the Minister of Law. At the time Seyß-Inquart was referred to by the paradoxical term *Edelnazi*. Later, he accepted full responsibility for his genocidal role during the war and was executed at Nuremberg; Albert Speer records that of all the defendants there he scored highest in an IQ test administered by an American army psychologist (*Inside the Third Reich* 515, 510). Having spared the Wittgensteins resident in his fiefdom, Vienna, from the death camps, perhaps this man's only other creditable contribution to history was to extend the peace of mind of the tortured Ludwig, who had already lost three brothers to suicide. Thus may Seyß-Inquart have enabled in some small measure the completion of Wittgenstein's later writings.

The above description of Wittgenstein's descent will serve as a prelude to a consideration of how he dealt with it. The most striking component of the latter is his "confession" (*Beichte*), made serially and in at least one group session, to Moore, Pascal, Engelmann, Drury, Rudolf Koder, and members of the family. The selection of people ranges from professional colleagues, students and friends to family members, and family friends, Jewish and nonJewish, in other words a microcosm of one's actual world. In connection with this confession, some facts not often stressed are to be recapitulated. First, in general, for any of the Wittgenstein siblings, against any suggestions to the contrary, *Jewish descent was not a problem.* It was rather a source of pride, and an explanation, if unwarranted, for their energy and achievement. For some writers, however, the fact of three suicides among the Wittgenstein brothers, including two near in time to Otto Weininger's in 1903, may have become associated with the usual suspicion of "Jewish self-hatred," although I have not seen this stated anywhere. Second, in particular regard to Ludwig's "confession," there is no indication that he swore his hearers to secrecy. Certainly with his own family members this would be absurd, since he told them absolutely nothing that was not known to them, that did not apply equally to all his siblings, and that in all likelihood was known publicly in the circles that mattered in Vienna, if not in England. It is understandable that by English conventions any such conversation would be treated as confidential. But Pascal, who describes herself in recounting the scene with Wittgenstein as "a Jewish girl from the Ukraine, who had been through pogroms during the Civil War, whose childhood was darkened, branded by the anti-Semitism of Tsarist Russia," found it "embarrassing...that it [i.e. the "confession"] remained a taboo subject long after his death" (47), Engelmann having left out of his book the letter to him—presumably still in existence—containing Wittgenstein's confession. Third, according to the only detailed descriptive account we have of it, *the confession was not about greater Jewish descent than most people knew of, but of his doing nothing to prevent the misapprehension.* In other words, if I "confess" to being more Jewish by descent than people think, this may reflect on my part a poor evaluation of being Jewish, analogous to confessing one is more of a criminal, say, than people think. But if I confess to not having done anything to clarify the correct proportion of my Jewish descent, there is no implication that I am ashamed about the greater proportion of descent, only that I want to remind people of the actual record, of which some were not clearly informed—leaving completely aside the question of whether my feelings towards the record are of shame, pride or indifference. The matter only concerns one's personal search for a proper match or congruence between inner and outer, private and public understandings.

Pascal notes that "when Wittgenstein came to England before the first World War and again in the late 1920s, he had no need to designate himself a Jew" (49). With the dawn of the '30's, however, the taking of a stand might understandably have seemed necessary to any individual with pride and courage who nevertheless had the option of "passing" for a gentile. It is critically important that by Jewish law Wittgenstein was *not* Jewish. He had the option, therefore, both from the gentile side and the Jewish side, to count himself a gentile. He was thus not confessing anything out of "Jewish guilt" or self-hatred, but freely indicating in that troubled decade what his exact descent was, nothing more, apparently, and nothing less. In those times, however—and if it did not so appear before, it will now—this was a statement with reverberations perhaps not immediately clear to all his hearers, to which we will return soon.

Fourth, *the "confession" could have made no possible difference to his hearers.* They ranged from being old friends and associates to *family*—how could anyone walk away thinking differently of Ludwig, or have their world view altered in some way, after hearing that he had three Jewish grandparents and not one, something several of them in any case must have already known? This being the case, one must conclude that they were *not the intended audience.* Just as with various notebooks and manuscripts that were allowed to survive, *the intended audience for the setting straight of the record of Jewish descent was not the author's relatives or his circle of friends, but posterity.* As has been noted in the literature, it is impossible for a man who is seven feet tall not to be aware that he towers over other people. Wittgenstein knew that one day everything that he did and said would be sifted for clues to his meaning.

But what message are we as posterity to take away? No differently than his listeners, we are not concerned that Ludwig was more of one "race" than another. So one must further conclude that not only was the apparent audience not the actual audience, the apparent message was not the intended message. After all, the confession only touched on what we might call physical or hereditary Jewishness. But this concerns neither us nor the apparent audience. Here one may apply with advantage the Sherlockian saw: "When you have eliminated the impossible, whatever remains, however improbable, must be the truth." The only remaining possibility, if physical Jewishness is rejected, is intellectual and religious Jewishness. Thus *the "confession" was a means, along with the others we have surveyed, for Wittgenstein to affirm the Jewishness of his lifework*, the correct understanding of which by posterity was, as we have already seen, of fundamental concern to him, but of which he was also confident.

Wittgenstein's conduct regarding the confession bears all the characteristics of integrity, humor, economy, self-confidence, and evasive indirectness that we, along with other commentators, have already observed. By telling a selection of people that he had not one but three Jewish grandparents, he seems to have taken another rational, Maimonidean, middle-of-the-road choice between denial—never really an option—and shouting "My work is Jewish!" from the rooftops of Vienna and Cambridge.

Notes

CHAPTER I

1. *C&V*: 53ᵉ; *C&V*: 65ᵉ; Malcolm 60.

2. *L&C*: 28

3. For another important indication of Wittgenstein's thinking on history and textuality, see *C&V*: 31, last paragraph.

4. *C&V*: 21ᵉ; interestingly, as Gayatri Spivak notes, in the first published version of *de la Grammatologie* Derrida uses the word *détruire* "to destroy" and not *deconstruction*; see her translator's preface to Derrida, *Grammatology*, xlix.

5. "He was early influenced by William James' *Varieties of Religious Experience*. This book he told me had helped him greatly. And if I am not mistaken the category of *Varieties* continued to play an important part in his thinking"(Drury, "Notes," 108).

6. See Baker and Hacker 235n.: "Spengler acknowledges a debt to Goethe and Nietzsche. Of Nietzsche's 'outlook' (*Ausblick*) Spengler made an 'overlook' (*Überblick*)"; on the next page they cite Wittgenstein's remark, "How very much I am influenced by Spengler in my thought."

7. H. Aron in the *Proceedings* of the Second International Wittgenstein Symposium, 1977, Kirchberg/Wechsel, Austria, A. Hubner, ed.

8. Among these are P.K. Feyerabend and Stanley Cavell; see Kuhn xi-xii.

9. "The Availability of Wittgenstein's Later Philosophy," in Pitcher.

10. Baker and Hacker (xix) remark that "Wittgenstein's philosophy is like a stone arch; each stone supports all the others—or, at least, nothing stands up until everything is in place." Von Wright has made a similar remark about the singular "holisticity" and "integratedness" characteristic of Wittgenstein's output: see Hallett 63.

11. "Ein Buch ist ein Spiegel; wenn ein Affe hineinguckt, so kann freilich kein Apostel heraussehen."

12. The remarks from Wittgenstein's letter cited in Malcolm 36–7, and Malcolm's comments on p.62, will be of interest to all university philosophers.

13. Cf. also *L&C* 48: "Freud was influenced by the nineteenth-century idea of dynamics— an idea which has influenced the whole treatment of psychology. He wanted to find some one explanation which would show what dreaming is. He wanted to find the *essence* of dreaming."

14. This fascinating topic can be explored further in Spivak's preface to Derrida's *Of Grammatology*, especially pp. lxiii-lxv, Derrida's "Freud and the Scene of Writing" (in his *Writing and Difference*), and the relevant portions of the *L&C*. Christopher Morris's review article on Tzvetan Todorov in *Journal of Literary Semantics* XIV/3 is also helpful.

15. *Bemerkungen über Frazers* Golden Bough; on this see Norman Rudich and Manfred Stassen, "Wittgenstein's Implied Anthropology: Remarks on Wittgenstein's Notes on Frazer," *History and Theory* 1971: 84–89).

CHAPTER II

1. See Hilmy n. 494 on the "expansiveness" of Wittgenstein's foreword being a reaction to Carnap's preface of 1928. After 1929 Wittgenstein excluded Carnap from his discussions with the Vienna Circle. See Pears, *Ludwig Wittgenstein*, 71n.

2. Cf. also the Lichtenbergian remark: "He can't hold his ink; and when he feels a desire to befoul someone, he usually befouls himself most," Janik and Toulmin, 90.

3. Cf. Wittgenstein's mention of certain Indian mathematicians for whom the words "Look at this" with a geometrical figure served as a proof (*Zettel* #461, *PI* §144).

4. Cf. *Zettel* #614: "Why don't we just leave explaining alone?"

5. One commentator, uncomprehending of Wittgenstein's seriousness about his philosophical jokes, calls this an example of his having no respect for any thinking, including his own. "Does Wittgenstein mean to say that one joke cannot cover the essence of philosophy, but that a thousand interconnected jokes would do the job?" Yes! And, according to its author, the book where that has been done is the *Philosophical Investigations*.

6. "Judaism rightly understood is far in advance of Christianity; but I cannot do with a watch that gains time any better than with one that loses." This instance of the same clock metaphor by Auerbach (qtd. in Baron 248) may have an analogous bearing on the *Tractatus* vis-à-vis other writings of Wittgenstein's.

7. For examples of Wittgenstein's knowledge of "mistakes" in the *Tractatus*, see *Notebooks 1914–1916* 68, 75). Awareness of mistakes existed before, during and after the writing of the *Tractatus*. They were not something whose realization came about before creating a "new" philosophy around the *Philosophical Investigations*.

8. On the role of silence in "early" and "later" Wittgenstein, in keeping with the present reading, in 1980 Stanley Rosen already had this to say in his *The Limits of Analysis*: "Wittgenstein advises us in the *Tractatus* to keep silent about that whereof we cannot speak. I am now suggesting that this advice is meant to hold good in the case of the later Wittgenstein" (182).

9. The point is also one about the temptation in erecting theory to neglect the particular instance, the individual case with subversive potential. One of Wittgenstein's methods, early or late, is to look so minutely at the particular as to outwit our "craving for generality," which he regarded as a great disease. Cf. discussions of "rule," "understanding," etc. in the *PI*. In looking for "logical form," of course, he is taking the opposite path, a deliberate "mistake."

10. The item *ethics* is not in the fairly detailed index of Hilmy's book, and there is no treatment of the consequences for ethics of his reading of Wittgenstein. Incidentally, regarding the argument that Wittgenstein's resistance to science remained constant, David Pears says: "This resistance was a conspicuous feature of his early philosophy, and it continues, in a different form, in the later period" (*Ludwig Wittgenstein*, 186).

11. Ray Monk, Wittgenstein's most recent biographer, gives this generous and well-deserved compliment to Drury's writing: "...*The Danger of Words*, though it has been almost

completely ignored in the secondary literature, is, in its attitudes and concerns, more truly Wittgensteinian than almost any other secondary text" (403). It might justly be added that nothing like sufficient weight has been given to Drury's account of his conversations with Wittgenstein, which we have drawn upon constantly in this study.

CHAPTER III

1. "Those today who tend to dismiss Weininger as a crank must remember, if they are to understand the subterranean currents of Central European thought before and after the First World War, that many of Weininger's contemporaries took him dead seriously: between 1903 and 1923, *Geschlecht und Charakter*...went through twenty-five editions, and by 1923 the book had been translated into some eight tongues" (Bartley, 2nd ed., 27). According to Monk, Hitler "is reported as having once remarked: 'Dietrich Eckhart told me that in all his life he had known just one good Jew: Otto Weininger who killed himself on the day when he realized that the Jew lives upon the decay of peoples.' And the fact that fear of the emancipation of women, and, particularly, of Jews, was a widespread preoccupation in Vienna at the turn of the century no doubt accounts to some extent for the book's enormous popularity. It would later provide convenient material for Nazi propaganda broadcasts" (23).

2. In terms of inherent tendencies towards anti-Semitism and totalitarianism, Wittgenstein did not seem to see any clear difference between the European dictatorships and the "Anglo-Saxon" or "free world democracies." See a conversation with Rush Rhees about the architecture in Trafalgar Square in London, especially Canada House, then under construction. Waving his hand towards it, Wittgenstein said: "that's *bombast*; that's Hitler and Mussolini." Rhees comments: "And Canada House helped to show why Hitler and Mussolini *had* to work with bombast. As it showed how truly *they were one in spirit with us*" (Rhees, *Personal Recollections*, 226, emphasis added). Wittgenstein's stern and angry reaction to Norman Malcolm when he suggested that the British would never try to assassinate Hitler ("I meant that the British were too civilized and decent to attempt anything so underhand;...such an act was incompatible with the British national character"): "...you made a remark about 'national character' that shocked me by its primitiveness," Wittgenstein chastised Malcolm later in a letter. "I then thought: what is the use of studying philosophy if all that it does for you is to enable you to talk with some plausibility about some abstruse questions of logic, etc., & and if it does not improve your thinking about the important questions of everyday life, if it does not make you more conscientious than any...journalist in the use of the *dangerous* phrases such people use for their own ends" (Malcolm, *Memoir*, 32, 39).

3. There were other things they did not recognize that Wittgenstein was acutely conscious of. Here is the American philosopher Oets Bouwsma's account of a story Wittgenstein told him some thirty years after it occurred: "There had been at Cambridge an Hungarian student who when war broke out [1914] was sent home. He was killed as an Hungarian soldier [i.e. belonging to the same side as Wittgenstein in the war]. When now the war was ended a plaque was to be erected, set in the wall, with the names of all those who had died for their country. This man's name was on the list too. There was a meeting about it. And who now should protest this name in the list but the Professor of Ethics! So there is now at Cambridge, in Christ

Chapel, a plate bearing the name of this Hungarian student, set off by itself, away from all the rest. In death!" (*Wittgenstein*, 49).

4. Spengler, who refers to Weininger in his invented terminology as a "Magian," estimates his death—not necessarily in agreement with the "monster" idea—as "one of the noblest spectacles ever presented by a Late religiousness" (*Decline*, II: 322).

5. In this same "Postscript," Rush Rhees provides an account of the Wittgenstein-Weininger relationship and of the remarks about Jews that separates the two men's ideas and does not impute any anti-semitism or "Jewish self-hatred" to Wittgenstein. My reading agrees with Rhees's in both respects, but—referring to Jewish sources—it suggests further that Wittgenstein was in fact identifying with and championing traditional Jewish attitudes.

6. This attitude is shared by Wittgenstein's "official" and other major biographer, Brian McGuinness: "...Ludwig belonged to an earlier way of thinking, with something of the Jewish self-hatred of Karl Kraus and Otto Weininger" (2).

7. Monk adopts a Weiningerian epigraph from *Sex and Character* for his entire book: "Logic and ethics are fundamentally the same, they are no more than duty to oneself." If this is meant to suggest a position shared by Wittgenstein, or some sort of clear theme in his life and work, there is reason to question the thought; Wittgenstein would likely have "simply straightaway seized on it with enthusiasm for [his] work of clarification." While he did suggest that *ethics and aesthetics* are one, when Russell asked him in the famous exchange recounted by McGuinness if it was logic he was anxious about or his sins, he replied, "Both!" But logic and his ethical lapses or sins were not connected for him in the sense that one led to the other. Obviously one can be anxious about two unconnected things at the same time. There are few grounds too for taking Wittgenstein's view of ethics to be no more than duty to *oneself*, if nothing beyond oneself is indicated. Rather than such an ethical solipsism, he was inclined in all simplicity, as we shall see, to connect ethics with kindness *to others* and to living a good life as a work of art *for God*. He told Drury: "It is my belief that only if you try to be helpful to other people will you in the end find your way to God," and wrote to him: "Don't think about yourself, but think about others, e.g. your patients" (Drury, in Rhees, 110, 129). In his version of the Jewish view, Abraham Joshua Heschel tells us: "Only the egotist is confined to himself, a spiritual recluse. In carrying out a good deed it is impossible to be or to feel alone. To fulfill a *mitzvah* [see below, p. 56] is to be a partisan, to enter into fellowship with His Will" (*God in Search of Man: a Philosophy of Judaism*, 287).

Sander Gilman, relying on a secondary source here, is also off the mark when he suggests that "Ludwig Wittgenstein, confronted with his 'Jewish' nature and his Catholic upbringing, accepted and incorporated aspects of Weininger's 'philosophy' into his world view" (Gilman, *Jew's Body*,133). Against this idea, in addition to the arguments already mentioned, is to be considered Wittgenstein's own remarks of 1929: "It's a good thing I don't allow myself to be influenced!"; "No one can think a thought for me in the way no one can don my hat for me." The reflections on influence a few years later also apply: "Every artist has been influenced by others and shows traces of that influence in his works; but his significance for us is nothing but *his* personality. *What he inherits from others can be nothing but egg-shells. We should treat their presence with indulgence*, but they won't provide us with spiritual nourishment" (*C&V*: 1ᵉ, 2ᵉ, 23ᵉ; emphasis added).

8. In the German here we read: "Das jüdische »Genie« ist nur ein Heiliger", which could be rendered a little more firmly: "Only a holy man is a Jewish genius."

9. "Little Jewish genius was invested throughout the ages in the creation of great works of art...The great works of art that emerge from Jewish history are *the lives and the teachings of the greatest people it has engendered*"—belonging of course to the religious rather than to any artistic tradition (Sherwin, "The Nature of Jewish Ethics," 4; emphasis added).

10. *C&V*: 31ᵉ: "Everything that comes my way becomes a picture for me of what I am thinking about at the time. (Is there something feminine about this way of thinking?)" ("*Ist dies eine gewisse Weiblichkeit der Einstellung?*").

While Weininger equated and disparaged Jewishness and femininity, it is interesting to note that William James, in *Varieties of Religious Experience*, a favorite book of Wittgenstein's, gives the opposite equation for the Greeks, the main philosophical opponents of the Jews: "Their spirit was still too essentially masculine for pessimism to be elaborated or lengthily dwelt on in their classical literature....The discovery that the enduring emphasis, so far as this world goes, may be made on its pain and failure, was reserved for races more complex, and (so to speak) more feminine than the Hellenes had attained to being in the classic period" (125n.).

A work on *Feminist Interpretations of Wittgenstein* now exists, Naomi Scheman and Peg O'Connor, eds., Penn State University Press, 2002.

11. Along with the treatment of Weininger by Canetti and Otto Rank as analogues to Wittgenstein's, a reading of Gilman's account in *The Jew's Body* of Freud's and Sylvano Arieti's reactions to Weininger will show how they too make the same moves as Wittgenstein. All this together suggests some affinity—even though he may have been entirely unaware of them—on Wittgenstein's part with contemporary writers of various degrees of marginal Jewishness.

12. Neither *Heimlichkeit* nor *Verstecktheit* really require the translation "cunning"; the primary connotations are secrecy, covertness, deviousness at worst. There is no word too in the German justifying the introduction of *nature* in the English, with its suggestion of racial or genetic inevitability.

13. Spengler's *Decline*, a text Wittgenstein constantly used in his "work of clarification," has an acute observation on a blind spot regarding Jewish tradition in historians of religion: "...the history of Talmudic Judaism, since Hebrew philology became bound up in one specialism with Old Testament research, not only never obtained separate treatment, but has been *completely forgotten* by all the major histories of religion with which I am acquainted, although these find room for every Indian sect (since folklore, too, ranks as a specialism) and every primitive Negro religion to boot. Such is the preparation of scholarship for the greatest task that historical research has to face today" (II: 191). Spengler's complaint is that the Talmud is left out in the special field of history of religion, where its study is essential. Naturally awareness of it was even more attenuated among philosophers, linguists, or literary critics. Works have appeared in the last two decades that may bring about a change.

14. These ways of thinking are traditional. Before the "emancipation" or "assimilation" of Jews from the eighteenth century on, perhaps all members of the community would have been aware of them. There has been a great degree of secularization since that time, of course; these attitudes are now held by proportionately fewer people. But a twentieth-century writer of Jewish identity—say Canetti, or Kraus, perhaps even Freud—would be very likely affected by them.

15. Faur, *Golden Doves*, 123.

16. Wittgenstein practiced a certain caginess with regard to the prospect of his notes being read. In brief, his attitude combined a little simple hesitation with the wish to see his notes used as a "back-up," reinforcing his finished work and clarifying its direction. With regard to the vital material being considered in this chapter, McGuinness has noticed that "[o]ne of the 1930's notebooks has instructions *written in code* about how it is to be disposed off in case of Wittgenstein's death. There are also other subtler indications that *the remarks written down in the 1930s and 1940s were thought of as a kind of testament or autobiography meant to be read by others*" (212n., emphasis added).

17. In *Wittgenstein's Vienna*, Allan Janik and Stephen Toulmin relate how they were told by G.H. von Wright, Wittgenstein's friend and later one of his literary executors, that "the two most important facts to remember about Wittgenstein were, firstly, that he was a Viennese and, secondly, that he was an engineer with a thorough knowledge of modern physics" (28–29). Apparently in some contexts before World War II, because of the large Jewish population, "Viennese" meant "Jew." It is difficult to tell if von Wright was thinking of this usage.

18. Cf. also this formulation written in the same year: "A thinker is very much like a draughtsman whose aim it is to represent all the interrelationships between things" (*C&V*: 12ᵉ).

19. *Kabbalah: New Perspectives*, 215.

20. Quoting a few of the lines above, Stephen Toulmin observes in *Wittgenstein's Vienna*: "However much else changed in his actual methods of philosophizing, between 1918 and 1948, the fundamental propaedeutic never changed" (257).

21. See also the recent work by Michael A. Sells, *Mystical Languages of Unsaying*, examining "*apophatic* language as a mode of discourse rather than a negative theology. Arguing that the more radical claims of apophatic writers, dismissed by critics as hyperbolic or condemned as heretical, are vital to an adequate account of their language, he concludes that mystical 'unsaying' attempts to free human language from possession of being and closure of knowledge."

22. A medieval font of Kabbala, one kind of Jewish mysticism, the *Zohar* speaks of different levels of understanding of the Torah: "The senseless people only see the garment, the mere narrations; those who are somewhat wiser penetrate as far as the body. But the really wise, the servants of the most high King, those who stood on Mount Sinai, penetrate right through to the soul, the root principle of all, namely, to the real Torah" (qtd. in Bakan, *Freud*, 247). That Wittgenstein was directly acquainted with the *Zohar* is pure speculation, although he certainly came across secondary accounts and references in works like Spengler's; his deep interest in mystical literature is of course well known. Professor G. H. von Wright and Maurice Drury agree that the "multiplicity of interpretations of Wittgenstein's thought...have been largely without significance" (Drury, "Some Notes...", 95). This seems to be somewhat sweeping. Without a large range of guides and explanations—each with its limits, perhaps— the ordinary reader or even the philosophical specialist would hardly find Wittgenstein accessible. Personally, only after reading the texts and commentaries in conjunction did I develop the feeling at certain points that there was indeed some kind of lock or seal put on the writings which one had to get past. I cannot imagine this possible without the guidance of so-called "secondary works."

23. See p. 86 below.

24. Letter to Russell, June 22, 1912, qtd. in McGuinness, *Wittgenstein: A Life*, 129.

25. See their respective works cited in the bibliography.

26. See Shestov, Strauss on Athens and Jerusalem.

27. See J.A. Cuddon's *The Penguin Dictionary of Literary Terms and Literary Theory* (London, 1992), 402.

28. From Renan, Arnold got the idea that "the fundamental divide in world history was between Hellenic and Hebrew, Aryan and Semite" (Martin Bernal, *Black Athena*, 347). But John Murray Cuddihy says: "There is Hellenism, which is pagan, perhaps civilized, and with an eye to beauty, but greater still is Hebraism, with its concern for justice and its superior morality. From Luzatto to *Heine (from whom Arnold got it)* and beyond to Hermann Cohen (1842–1914) and the Marburg neo-Kantians, this is a major theme of alienated Diaspora intellectual Jewry" (*The Ordeal of Civility: Freud, Marx, Levi-Strauss and the Jewish Struggle with Modernity*, 183, emphasis added).

29. Wittgenstein was enormously fastidious about the translation of his German (see the *Letters to C. K. Ogden, with Comments on the English Translation of the* Tractatus Logico-Philosophicus). He maintained that the German was to be used for reference. The above translation of part of the well-known last sentence in *PI* §109 has been altered to better fit the original: "*ein Kampf gegen die Verhexung unsres Verstandes durch die Mittel unserer Sprache.*" The last word but one has been left out in the official English version. By it Wittgenstein indicates, it seems to me, our responsibility for being bewitched by our language—not "*durch die Mittel der Sprache*" ("by means of language," as the present English version reads), but "*durch die Mittel unserer Sprache*", "by means of our language". The existing version gives no hint by what agency an impersonal "language" could bewitch us. Perhaps even more significant is the consistency of Wittgenstein's phrasing and general point with the crucial *Preface* to the *Tractatus*, looked at in detail in an earlier chapter: "*die Fragestellung dieser Probleme auf dem Mißverstandnis der Logik unserer Sprache beruht*"—questions of philosophy are posed because the logic of our language is misunderstood. Both books, the *Tractatus* and the *PI*, are directed to getting us to see how we have misunderstood our language. Wittgenstein is indirectly arguing, I suggest, that this has happened because we have taken Greek philosophy for our guide.

30. In their section on Fritz Mauthner, the journalist-philosopher, author of *Contributions to a Critique of Language*, whom Wittgenstein read closely and mentioned in the *Tractatus*, Janik and Toulmin depict for us very concisely the role of "laws of nature" in intellectual history: "Mauthner spared no effort to explain the historical origin of the notion that physical laws are inexorable. He considers that the term "law of nature" is a metaphor left over from the bygone days of mythological explanation, when Nature was personified in the endeavor to comprehend it. He traces the origin of the notion back to Plato and Aristotle, and particularly to Lucretius, who first used the phrase explicitly. In the Middle Ages, the notion became incorporated into theology as the "natural law" of God, the divine providential ordering of the universe. With Spinoza's *Deus sive Natura* it became secularized, along with much else that had earlier belonged exclusively to the sphere of theology. Thus did the myth of the "laws of nature" pass down to the present time; the phrase began as a metaphor and later became reified and universally adopted by scientists"—as good an example as any of the power our forms of expression exert over us. It is worth emphasizing that this concept of the "laws of nature" is a Greco-Christian "thing"; its significant absence in biblical and rabbinic thought is discussed at several points in Faur's *Golden Doves with Silver Dots*, particularly when he expounds the Jew-

ish position with reference to the clarifications of Rabbi David Nieto, a 17th-century scientist and contemporary of Isaac Newton who lived in London. See section below on Wittgenstein and science.

31. Man. 302, 14, also qtd. in Hallett, *Companion*, 771, who adds: "Man. 111, 55, is still more negative."

32. Recall the preceding account from the *Blue Book* about differences between the uses of the word *kind*.

33. See Chapter II for discussion of the *Tractatus* as a joke on the history of philosophy.

34. In this charge against Aristotelian logic Wittgenstein is in the company of several others, including Fritz Mauthner (op. cit.), Alfred Korzybski (*Science and Sanity*, a massive work on non-Aristotelian thought), and the linguist Emil Benveniste.

35. Nicholas F. Gier reports: "In the Big Typescript Wittgenstein declares that Aristotelian logic is a language game (213, p. 260), and in a later work, agrees that "the rules of logical inference are rules of the *language-game*" [*Remarks on the Foundations of Mathematics*, p. 181)....If Aristotelian logic is a language-game, then it is just one of many ways of looking at the world, of making sense of it, and it is conceivable that more primitive 'logics' can serve just as well without following Aristotle's laws of inference." He comments: "The reason why we persist in believing that there is only one logic, i.e., the strict reason of traditional logic, is because of the dominance of this particular language-game in the history of Western thought" (190–91). In my view, any attempt to see texts as language-games, which are infinitely different, is to show them to be ordinary language, as conflicted and self-deconstructing, failing in their aspiration to be metalinguistic.

36. An extensive treatment of Augustine will be found in Susan Handelman's *The Slayers of Moses: The Emergence of Rabbinic Interpretation in Modern Literary Theory*, which I have found very useful in this study. On the parallels between Augustine and Aristotle in their thinking on signs, see especially 115–16.

37. The remarks of two other commentators on the *Investigations* on this point are worth noting: "Neither inconsistencies in his remarks nor peculiarities in some aspects of his account of language-learning disqualify Augustine as a spokesman for a certain pervasive conception of language. What interests W[ittgenstein] is Augustine's pre-theoretical, pre-philosophical picture of the working of language which informs Augustine's own remarks on language as well as a multitude of sophisticated philosophical analyses of meaning" (Baker and Hacker, *Analytical Commentary*, 22).

38. He said to Drury: "Don't think I despise metaphysics. I regard some of the great philosophical systems of the past as among the noblest productions of the human mind." Then a hint of the Kraus principle (writing, rather than not writing, shows a deficiency of character): "For some people it would require an heroic effort to give up this sort of writing" (120); here Wittgenstein, nobility apart, seems unable to resist "getting his digs in"!

39. "Believe whatever you can. I never object to a man's religious beliefs, Mohammedan, Jew, or Christian" (Bouwsma, transcript of conversation with Wittgenstein, 56). See also Drury, "Notes," 108.

40. Exactly the same spirit—understanding of another's position combined with principled criticism—is manifested in Wittgenstein's reaction to Drury's intention of becoming a priest in the Anglican Church: "I don't ridicule this. *Anyone who ridicules these matters is a char-*

latan and worse. But I can't approve, no I can't approve....I would be afraid that you would try and elaborate a philosophical interpretation or defense of the Christian religion" (Drury, "Notes," 101, emphasis added). It is significant that what he can't approve is not Christianity but its philosophical defense, or metaphysics.

CHAPTER IV

1. Paul Engelmann, an unusually astute commentator on Wittgenstein without being a professional philosopher at all, in emphasizing the primacy of religion in his work, noted that "Wittgenstein drew certain logical conclusions from his fundamental mystical attitude to life and the world. That he should have chosen to devote five-sixths of his book [the *Tractatus*] to the logical conclusions is due to the fact that about them at least it is possible to speak" (97).

2. See *C&V*: 73ᵉ and Sherwin, "The Nature of Jewish Ethics", 5 and n.

3. McGuinness gives his impression of the earliness of Wittgenstein's insights: "Again and again...we have the impression that he was comparatively little affected by new discoveries or advances made by others; and that, important though discussion and reflection were to him, their function was to enable him to articulate and clarify some initial insight, some inspiration or *Einfall* that had come to him in his earliest reading on a subject...(91–2). My reading certainly coincides with this view, provided we leave open the possibility that the early insights may have come during periods of religious concentration or prayer, such as in Norway, rather than from reading—this in view of statements discussed in Chapter III where Wittgenstein says he tried not to let himself be influenced and used the works of others for clarification.

4. Jewish virtues? See below.

5. See his article on meaning in Arthur A. Cohen and Paul Mendes-Flohr (eds.), *Contemporary Jewish Religious Thought* (New York, 1987), 587.

6. Bartley adds: "The villager was bewildered, for Wittgenstein emphasized that he did not mean that he was a Protestant (or "Evangelical"). "What Wittgenstein was trying to say cannot be determined with certainty..." (2ⁿᵈ ed., 90).

7. "The great dream of Judaism is not to raise priests, but a people of priests; to consecrate all men, not only some men" (Heschel, *God*, 419).

8. Wittgenstein once told Malcolm: "You see, when Tolstoy just tells a story he impresses me infinitely more than when he addresses the reader. When he turns his back to the reader then he seems to me *most* impressive. Perhaps one day we can talk about this. It seems to me his philosophy is most true when it's *latent* in the story" (43). This seems to me a most important pointer to Wittgenstein's own ideals as a writer.

9. Maimonides cites this passage in his *Guide*, III: 20. It is one major source for the kind of approach Wittgenstein takes to the *limits* of human understanding and natural "laws."

10. Drury 101–2. Wittgenstein also told Bouwsma that Kierkegaard "struck him almost as like a snob, too high, for him, not touching the details of common life. Take his prayers. They left him unmoved" (Bouwsma 46). These details are important because Wittgenstein has been grouped with Kierkegaard as a—Christian—religious thinker. Stephen Toulmin, for instance, told me that he thought the answer to questions about Wittgenstein's religion were to be sought in Kierkegaard and Tolstoy.

11. Maimonides touches upon the very same point towards the very end of his *Guide*: "...the reason for a human individual's being abandoned to chance so that he is permitted to be devoured like the beasts is his being separated from God."

12. "Isn't it curious that, although I know I have not long to live, I never find myself thinking about a 'future life.' All my interest is still on this life and the writing I am still able to do" (Wittgenstein to Drury, 1951; 183).

13. "Traditionally Judaism did not conceive of itself as a religion, it saw itself as the teachings and commandments consequential to the covenanted relationship between God and Israel" (Unterman, *Jews*, 7).

14. See his *Jews and German Philosophy*, 179ff., esp. 199. As to Wittgenstein's own remarks on Schopenhauer, see *C&V*: 36^e: "Where real depth starts, his comes to an end," a crude mind, "as crude as the crudest"; "he never searches his conscience."

15. Rudolf Carnap, *Autobiography*, reporting Wittgenstein's agreement on this point with Moritz Schlick. Qtd. in Hallett 426.

16. Faur says that the Greek truth *aletheia* "is static and absolute: like Euclidean geometry it transcends all contexts. Ideally, this type of knowledge ought to be thoroughly descriptive and objective. Therefore *the truth is essentially tautological*" (*Golden Doves*, 28). In exposing this tautologous nature of philosophical truth, Wittgenstein certainly alerts us to other possibilities, although there is hardly any evidence that this was his conscious intention.

17. "...the primary concern of the author of the *Tractatus* is to protect the sphere of the conduct of life against encroachments from the sphere of speculation. He sought to protect the fantasy from the incursions of reason, and to prevent spontaneous feeling from being stifled by rationalization. He was aware, as Kraus was, that reason is only an instrument for good when it is the reason of a good man. The good man's being good is a function not of his rationality, but of his participation in the life of fantasy. For the good man, ethics is a way of life, not a system of propositions: 'There are no ethical propositions, only ethical actions,' as Engelmann puts it. Thus the *Tractatus* was, first and foremost, an attack on all forms of rational systems of ethics—that is, theories of ethics that would base human conduct upon reason. It did not, of course, claim that morality is *contrary* to reason; merely that its foundations lay elsewhere. So, in contradistinction to Kant, both Schopenhauer and Wittgenstein find the basis of morality in 'right feelings' rather than in 'valid reasons.'" (Janik and Toulmin 198).

18. The *Qu'ran* or the New Testament too may deal with the human future; but they require universal conversion to their respective faiths; the Hebrew Bible and Jewish tradition do not.

19. In the popular sense of prediction, Wittgenstein may be said to have made at least two prophecies about his time to his friend Drury: "Just think what it must mean, when the government of a country is taken over by a set of gangsters. The dark ages are coming again. I wouldn't be surprised, Drury, if you and I were to live to see such horrors as people being burnt alive as witches" (152, c.1937, on the Nazis); and "England and France between them can't defeat Germany. But if Hitler does manage to establish a European empire, I don't believe it will last long" (158, 1939).

20. Appendix to *Ludwig Wittgenstein: Letters to C.K. Ogden*, G.H. von Wright, ed.(Oxford, 1983), 78.

21. *Totality and Infinity*, 78–9, emphasis added.

22. For more details on these terms and the face symbolism in the Kabbala see Adolphe Franck, *The Kabbalah*, 147, 202–3, *et passim*.

23. Faur's account (129–30) is full of intricacies, not all of which may be relevant here; anyone who wishes to be properly acquainted with the traditional account of this important issue will want to consult it directly. It may be helpful to note that the passage referred to here as Deut. 14: 12 is a misprint for Deut. 4: 12.

24. Ed. R.A. Cohen (Albany: State University of New York Press, 1986).

25. My count may be somewhat inflated by the inclusion of *countenance, expression,* and one or two related terms, and by the fact that some of the occurrences of these words may not have to do with what I am calling "the face theme" as such. But I wish only to give a rough indication that can easily be made precise.

26. See Bakan, *Sigmund Freud*, 246–47.

27. These developments are clearly explained in a book by Morris Kline, significantly entitled *Mathematics: The Loss of Certainty*.

CHAPTER V

1. The second occurrence of "Moses hat existiert" in *PI* §79 is mistranslated as "Moses did not exist" in the standard edition (p.37ᵉ).

2. Hilmy 253 n.216. Discussion by Wittgenstein of Moses and his name occurs also in the *Lectures 1932–1935* edited by Alice Ambrose (pp. 32, 47).

3. My reading is to be distinguished from Staten's in this, that for him only the so-called "later Wittgenstein" is allied to Derrida and postmodernism.

4. The writings of Handelman, Schneidau, Atkins, Rapaport, Aronowicz, the Yale critics, and others have contributed to understandings of the relation of Derrida and Levinas to Judaism. The latest work devoted to Derrida alone is Gideon Ofrat's *The Jewish Derrida*, 2001.

5. On Wittgenstein's use of the "darkness" metaphor, see remarks by Ira Nadel, *Joyce and the Jews*, 270n.

6. According to Malcolm, Wittgenstein suspected "that his friends regarded *him* as 'Vogelfrei': that is, as an outlaw, a bird at whom anyone had a right to shoot" (57).

7. On Beethoven's composing procedure, see Barenboim, *A Life in Music*.

8. Ms. 160, qtd. in Hallett 9.

9. See the chapter "Postmodernism is a Jewish Movement" by Stanley Tigerman in his *Versus*. For some background on postmodernism and Jewish theology, see Peter Ochs, ed. *Reviewing the Covenant: Eugene B. Borowitz and the Postmodern Revival of Jewish Theology*. For some rather dry but useful observations on Wittgenstein, Nietzsche and postmodernism, see Michael Peters and James Marshall, *Wittgenstein: Philosophy, Postmodernism, Pedagogy*.

10. "The Recognition Scene of Criticism," *Critical Inquiry*, 4 (1977), 410, qtd. in Atkins 771.

11. There is evidence that Foucault and Lyotard were influenced by Wittgenstein. On Foucault, see Aron.

12. See Monk 417 for a useful account of Wittgenstein's "unsophisticated" language in discussing mathematical logic, for instance; the author rightly thinks that the lack of sophistication had a "propagandist" purpose.

13. For a reading of Wittgenstein's attitude to theory compatible with the present one, see Monk 304–306.

14. Some other writers are aware of Wittgenstein's anti-theoretical convictions, although they do not necessarily use them to illuminate his other concerns; Monk will again serve as an example: "Again and again in his lectures Wittgenstein tried to explain that he was not offering any philosophical *theory*; he was offering only the means to escape any *need* for such a theory" (301). But why escape the need for theory? In the present view, theory is related to idolatry; it obscures the focus on God and ethics.

15. On Wittgenstein and Buddhism, see Chris Gudmunsen's *Wittgenstein and Buddhism*; there are numerous works on deconstruction and Buddhism. On the appeal of Buddhism to contemporary Jews, see Rodger Kamenetz, *The Jew in the Lotus*.

16. *Dictionary of Literary Terms* (Cuddon), 735.

17. *Ibid.*, 735–36.

18. I refer those interested in the question of Wittgenstein and education to my unpublished paper, "The Battle for Intelligence: Wittgenstein as Educator."

19. Derrida translates Walter Benjamin's phrase, *ein neues geschichtliches Zeitalter*.

20. See the rather unadorned account of the effect of the Holocaust on Western intellectual tradition in Byron Sherwin's essay in *Shoah*, citing Isaac Bashevis Singer among others.

21. The Dalai Lama has taken a keen interest in Judaism; Thurman has written on Tibetan Buddhism and private language; see also Kamenetz.

22. Ira B. Nadel, *Joyce and the Jews* (University of Iowa Press, 1989).

23. In the "Movements of Thought" diaries as published in Klagge and Nordmann, eds., Wittgenstein's positive apostrophe to the Jews is glossed as *a departure from earlier anti-semitism*. In our reading it is completely in keeping with Wittgenstein's lucid analyses of the Jewish predicament, discussed above mainly in Chapter III. My argument throughout that there is an integrity to all Wittgenstein's religious and philosophical thought—its main ideas, as he said, came to him early in life—does not require us to see him as veering within a few years from rabid anti-Semitism to a quiet affirmation of Israel's glorious destiny.

Bibliography

Certain works such as Klagge and Klagge and Nordmann appeared close to the time of completion of the manuscript. I have been able to use them to a limited extent in the text. Among recent treatments of questions such as Wittgenstein's 'Jewishness' and 'was Wittgenstein a Jew?', the essays of McGuinness and Stern may be mentioned as divergent from the present reading. My interpretation of Wittgenstein's remarks about Jews as outsiders in Europe appears most closely to match that of Béla Szabados, whom Stern cites.

Ambrose, Alice, ed. *Wittgenstein's Lectures, Cambridge 1932–1935.* Totowa, NJ: Rowman and Littlefield, 1979.

Aristotle. *On Interpretation.* In *The Organon.* 2 vols. London: Heinemann, 1960.

Arnold, Matthew. *Culture and Anarchy.* London: Smith and Elder, 1869.

Aron, H. "Wittgenstein's Impact on Foucault." *Second International Wittgenstein Symposium,* Kirchberg, Austria, 1977, 58–60.

Aronowicz, Annette. Introduction to her trans., in Levinas, *Nine Talmudic Readings.*

Atkins, G. Douglas. "Dehellenizing Literary Criticism." *College English* 41 (1980) 769–79.

Augustine. *Confessions.* Trans. Henry Chadwick. New York: Oxford University Press.

Bakan, David. *Sigmund Freud and the Jewish Mystical Tradition.* Boston: Beacon Press, 1958.

Baker, G. P. and P.M.S. Hacker. *An Analytical Commentary on Wittgenstein's* Philosophical Investigations. Chicago: The University of Chicago Press, 1985.

Barenboim, Daniel. *A Life in Music.* New York: Charles Scribner's Sons, 1991.

Baron, Joseph, ed. *A Treasury of Jewish Quotations.* N.p., Aronson, 1985.

Barret, Cyril. *Wittgenstein on Ethics and Religious Belief.* Cambridge, MA: Blackwell, 1991.

Bartley, William Warren III. *Wittgenstein.* Philadelphia: Lippincott, 1973. 2d ed.: LaSalle, IL: Open Court, 1985.

Bernal, Martin. *Black Athena.* New Brunswick, NJ: Rutgers University Press, 1991.

Bernasconi, Robert, and Simon Critchley, ed. *Re-Reading Levinas.* Bloomington: Indiana University Press, 1991.

Boman, Thorleif. *Hebrew Thought Compared with Greek.* Trans. Jules Moreau. London: SCM Press, 1960.

Bouwsma, Oets. *Wittgenstein: Conversations 1949–1951.* Ed. J.L. Craft and Ronald Hustwit. Indianapolis: Hackett, 1986.

Brown, Cecil H. *Wittgensteinian Linguistics.* The Hague: Mouton, 1974.

Brown, Norman O. *Life Against Death: The Psychoanalytical Meaning of History.* New York: Vintage, 1959.

Brudner, Alan. "The Identity of Difference: Toward Objectivity in Legal Interpretation." In *Deconstruction and the Possibility of Justice. Cardozo Law Review* 11: 5–6 (1990) 1133–1210.

Cavell, Stanley. "The Availability of Wittgenstein's Later Philosophy." In Pitcher, 151–85.

Chatterjee, Ranjit. "Linguistics and Rule Skepticism." *Journal of Literary Semantics* XIV/3 (1985) 174–85.

Cohen, R. A., ed. *Face to Face with Levinas.* Albany: State University of New York Press, 1986.

Cuddihy, John Murray. *The Ordeal of Civility: Freud, Marx, Lévi-Strauss and the Jewish Struggle with Modernity.* New York: Basic, 1974.

Danford, John. *Wittgenstein and Political Philosophy: A Reexamination of the Foundation of Social Science.* Chicago: The University of Chicago Press.

De Mauro, Tullio. *Ludwig Wittgenstein: His Place in the Development of Semantics:* Dordrecht, Reidel, 1967.

Derrida, Jacques. *Of Grammatology.* Trans. Gayatri Chakravorty Spivak. Baltimore: Johns Hopkins University Press, 1976.

——. "Violence and Metaphysics: An Essay on the Thought of Emmanuel Levinas." In his *Writing and Difference.*

——. *Writing and Difference.* Trans. Alan Bass. Chicago: The University of Chicago Press, 1978.

——. *Glas.* Trans. John P. Leavey, Jr. and Richard Rand. Lincoln, NE: University of Nebraska Press, 1986.

——. *Edmund Husserl's* Origin of Geometry: *An Introduction.* Trans. John P. Leavey, Jr. Lincoln, NE: University of Nebraska Press, 1989.

——. "Force of Law: The 'Mystical Foundation of Authority'." In *Deconstruction and the Possibility of Justice. Cardozo Law Review* 11: 5–6 (1990) 919–1039.

——. "Some Statements and Truisms About Neo-Logisms, Newisms, Positivisms, Parasitisms, and Other Small Seismisms." In *The States of 'Theory.'* Ed. David Carroll. New York: Columbia University Press, 1990.

Drury, Maurice O'C. *The Danger of Words.* New York: Humanities Press, 1973.

——. "Conversations with Wittgenstein." In Rush Rhees, ed. *Ludwig Wittgenstein: Personal Recollections,* 112–89.

——. "Some Notes on Conversations with Wittgenstein." In Rush Rhees, ed. *Ludwig Wittgenstein: Personal Recollections,* 91–111.

Eagleton, Terry. *Against the Grain. Essays 1975–1985.* London: Verso, 1986.

Elman, Benjamin. "Nietzsche and Buddhism." *Journal of the History of Ideas* XLIV: 4 (1989) 671–86.

Engelmann, Paul. *Letters from Ludwig Wittgenstein, with a Memoir.* New York: Horizon Press, 1968.

Erlich, Bruce. "The Aesthetics of True Naming: On the Judaic Tradition of Wittgenstein, Lukacs, and Walter Benjamin." R. Haller, ed. *Aesthetics* (= *Proceedings of the 8. International Wittgenstein Symposium,* Part I), 203–07.

Fann, K. T. *Wittgenstein's Conception of Philosophy.* Berkeley: University of California Press, 1971.

Faur, José. *Golden Doves with Silver Dots: Semiotics and Textuality in Rabbinic Tradition* Bloomington: Indiana University Press, 1986.

———. *In the Shadow of History: Jews and Conversos at the Dawn of Modernity*. Albany: State University of New York Press, 1992.

———. *Homo Mysticus: A Guide to Maimonides's* Guide for the Perplexed. Syracuse: Syracuse University Press, 1998.

Feyerabend, Paul. "Wittgenstein's *Philosophical Investigations*." In Pitcher, 104–50.

———. *Science in a Free Society*. London: NLB, 1978.

Finch, Henry L. *Wittgenstein: The Later Philosophy*. Atlantic Highlands, NJ: Humanities Press, 1977.

Franck, Adolphe. *The Kabbalah, or the Religious Philosophy of the Jews*. Trans. I. Sossnitz. New York: Kabbalah Publishing, 1926.

Giddens, Anthony. *New Rules of Sociological Method*. New York: Basic Books, 1976.

———. *Central Problems in Social Theory*. Berkeley: University of California Press, 1979.

Gier, Nicholas. *Wittgenstein and Phenomenology*. Albany: State University of New York Press, 1981.

Gilman, Sander. *The Jew's Body*. New York: Routledge, 1991.

Glatzer, Nahum, ed. *Franz Rosenzweig: His Life and Thought*. New York: Schocken, 1961.

Grayling, A.C. *Wittgenstein*. New York: Oxford University Press, 1988.

Greisch, Jean. "The Face and Reading." In Bernasconi and Critchley, ed. *Re-Reading Levinas*.

Grunfeld, Frederic. *Prophets without Honor: A Background to Freud, Kafka, Einstein and their World*. New York: Holt, Rinehart and Winston, 1979.

Gudmunsen, Chris. *Wittgenstein and Buddhism*. New York: Barnes and Noble, 1977.

Hallett, Garth, S.J. *A Companion to Wittgenstein's* Philosophical Investigations. Ithaca, NY: Cornell University Press, 1977.

Handelman, Susan. *The Slayers of Moses: The Emergence of Rabbinic Interpretation in Modern Literary Theory*. Albany: State University of New York Press, 1982.

Hartman, Geoffrey, and Sanford Budick, ed. *Midrash and Literature*. New Haven, CN: Yale University Press, 1986.

Heschel, Abraham Joshua. *God in Search of Man: A Philosophy of Judaism*. New York: Farrar, Strauss and Giroux, 1976.

Hilmy, S. Stephen. *The Later Wittgenstein*. Oxford: Basil Blackwell, 1987.

Hoffman, Edward. *The Way of Splendor: Jewish Mysticism and Modern Psychology*. Boulder: Shambhala, 1980.

Hunnings, Gordon. *The World and Language in Wittgenstein's Philosophy*. Albany: State University of New York Press, 1988.

Idel, Moshe. *Kabbalah: New Perspectives*. New Haven, CN: Yale University Press.

Jacobs, Louis. *Jewish Mystical Testimonies*. New York: Schocken, 1977.

Jacobson, Arthur J. "The Idolatry of Rules: Writing Law According to Moses, with Reference to other Jurisprudences." In *Deconstruction and the Possibility of Justice. Cardozo Law Review* 11: 5–6 (1990) 1079–1132.

James, William. *The Varieties of Religious Experience*. New York: Collier, 1961.

Janik, Allan. *Essays on Wittgenstein and Weininger*. Amsterdam: Rodopi, 1985.

—— and Stephen Toulmin. *Wittgenstein's Vienna*. New York: Simon and Schuster, 1973.

Jeans, James. *The Mysterious Universe*. Cambridge: Cambridge University Press, 1948.

Kamenetz, Rodger. *The Jew in the Lotus: A Poet's Re-Discovery of Jewish Identity in Buddhist India*. San Francisco: Harper, 1995.

Kaufmann, Walter. *Critique of Religion and Philosophy*. New York: Doubleday, 1961.

Kerr, Fergus. *Theology after Wittgenstein*. New York: Basil Blackwell, 1986.

Klagge, James C., and Alfred Nordmann, eds. *Ludwig Wittgenstein: Public and Private Occasions*. Lanham, MD: Rowman and Littlefield, 2003.

Klein, Dennis. *The Jewish Origins of the Psychoanalytical Movement*. Chicago: The University of Chicago Press, 1985.

Kline, Morris. *Mathematics: The Loss of Certainty*. New York: Oxford University Press.

Korzybski, Alfred. *Science and Sanity: An Introduction to non-Aristotelian Systems and General Semantics*. Lakeville, CN: International Non-Asristotelian Library Publishing, 1958.

Krailsheimer, A. J. "Introduction" to Pascal's *Pensées*. Harmondsworth: Penguin, 1966, 9–29.

Kripke, Saul. *Wittgenstein on Rules and Private Language*. Oxford: Basil Blackwell, 1982.

Kuhn, Thomas S. *The Structure of Scientific Revolutions*. 2d enlarged ed. Chicago: The University of Chicago Press, 1970 (= vols. I & II, *International Encyclopedia of Unified Science*).

LaCapra, Dominick. *Rethinking Intellectual History: Texts, Contexts, Language*. Ithaca: Cornell University Press, 1983.

Levinas, Emmanuel. *Totality and Infinity: An Essay on Exteriority*. The Hague: M. Nijhoff, 1979.

——. *Nine Talmudic Readings*. Trans. Annette Aronowicz. Bloomington: Indiana University Press, 1990.

Lyotard, Jean-François. *The Differend: Phrases in Dispute*. Trans. Georges van den Abbeele. Minneapolis: The University of Minnesota Press, 1988.

Maimonides, Moses. *The Guide of the Perplexed*. 2 vols. Trans. Shlomo Pines. Chicago: The University of Chicago Press, 1963.

Malcolm, Norman. *Ludwig Wittgenstein: A Memoir, with a Biographical Sketch by G.H. von Wright*. London: Oxford University Press, 1958.

Mauthner, Fritz. *Beiträge zu einer Kritik der Sprache*. 3 vols. Stuttgart: Cotta, 1921.

McGuinness, Brian. *Wittgenstein: A Life*. Berkeley: University of California Press, 1989.

——. "Wittgenstein and the Idea of Jewishness." In James C. Klagge, ed. *Wittgenstein: Biography and Philosophy*. Cambridge: Cambridge University Press, 2001. Pp. 221–236.

Meese, E. A. *(Ex)tensions: Re-figuring Feminist Criticism*. Urbana, IL: University of Illinois Press, 1990.

Monk, Ray. *Ludwig Wittgenstein: The Duty of Genius*. New York: Penguin, 1990.

Moore, Barrington. *Privacy: Studies in Social and Cultural History*. New York: Random House, 1984.

Murti, T.R.V. *The Central Philosophy of Buddhism*. 2d ed. London: George Allen and Unwin, 1960.

Nadel, Ira. *Joyce and the Jews: Culture and Texts*. Iowa City: University of Iowa Press, 1989.

Nietzsche, Friedrich. *The Twilight of the Idols* and *The Anti-Christ*. Trans. R. J. Hollingdale. Harmondsworth: Penguin, 1968.

Norris, Christopher. *What's Wrong with Postmodernism?* Baltimore: Johns Hopkins University Press, 1990.

Nyíri, J.C. "Wittgenstein 1929–1931: Die Rückkehr." *Kodikas-Code Ars Semeiotica* 4–5 (1982) 115–36.

Ochs, Peter, ed. *Reviewing the Covenant: Eugene B. Borowitz and the Postmodern Revival of Jewish Theology.* Albany: State University of New York Press, 2000.

Ofrat, Gideon. *The Jewish Derrida.* Trans. Kidron Peretz. Syracuse: Syracuse University Press. 2001.

Pascal, Blaise. *Pensées.* Trans. A.J. Krailsheimer. Harmondsworth: Penguin, 1966.

Pascal, Fania. "Wittgenstein: A Personal Memoir." In Rhees, *Recollections*, 26–62.

Pears, David. *Ludwig Wittgenstein.* New York: Viking, 1970.

Perloff, Marjorie. *Wittgenstein's Ladder; Poetic Language and the Strangeness of the Ordinary.* Chicago: The University of Chicago Press, 1999.

Peters, Michael, and James Marshall. *Wittgenstein: Philosophy, Postmodernism, Pedagogy.* Westport, CN: Bergin and Garvey, 1999.

Pitcher, George, ed. *Wittgenstein: The Philosophical Investigations.* New York: Doubleday, 1966.

Pitkin, Hanna Fenichel. *Wittgenstein and Justice On the Significance of Ludwig Wittgenstein for Social and Political Thought.* Berkeley: University of California Press, 1972.

Putnam, Hilary. *Renewing Philosophy.* Cambridge: Harvard University Press, 1992.

Ramsey, Frank. "Letters to Wittgenstein." Appendix to *Ludwig Wittgenstein: Letters to C.K. Ogden.* Ed. G.H. von Wright. Oxford: Basil Blackwell, 1973.

Rapaport, Herman. *Heidegger and Derrida: Reflections on Time and Language.* Lincoln, NE: University of Nebraska Press, 1989.

Rhees, Rush, ed. *Ludwig Wittgenstein: Personal Recollections.* Totowa, New Jersey: Rowman and Littlefield, 1981.

Robertson, Ritchie. "'Jewish Self-Hatred'? The Cases of Schnitzler and Cannetti." In Robert Wistrich, ed. *Austrians and Jews in the Twentieth Century*, 82–96.

Rorty, Richard. Review of Derrida's *Margins of Philosophy. London Review of Books*, February 16–29, 1984, 5–6.

Rosen, Stanley. *The Limits of Analysis.* New York: Basic Books, 1980.

Rosenzweig, Franz. *The Star of Redemption.* Trans. William Hallo. Notre Dame: University of Notre Dame Press, 1985.

Rosten, Leo. *Hooray for Yiddish!* New York: Simon and Schuster, 1984.

Rotenstreich, Nathan. *Jews and German Philosophy: The Polemics of Emancipation.* New York: Schocken, 1984.

Rudich, Norman and Manfred Stassen. "Wittgenstein's Implied Anthropology: Remarks on Wittgenstein's Notes on Frazer." *History and Theory* 1971, 84–89.

Samar, Vincent J. *The Right to Privacy: Gays, Lesbians and the Constitution.* Philadelphia: Temple University Press, 1991.

Scheman, Naomi and Peg O'Connor, ed. *Feminist Interpretations of Wittgenstein.* University Park: Penn State University Press, 2002.

Schneidau, Herbert. *Sacred Discontent: The Bible and Western Tradition.* Baton Rouge: Louisiana State University, 1976.

Schoeman, F. D., ed. *Philosophical Dimensions of Privacy.* Cambridge: Cambridge University Press, 1984.

Schwarzschild, Stephen. "Wittgenstein as Alienated Jew." *Telos* 40 (1979) 160–65.

Sells, Michael. *Mystical Languages of Unsaying*. Chicago: The University of Chicago Press, 1994.

Sherwin, Byron. "Primo Levi and Arnošt Lustig on Moral Implications of the Holocaust," *Shoah* 1: 4 (1979) 24–29.

———. "The Nature of Jewish Ethics." *Occasional Paper no. 4*. Dworsky Center for Jewish Studies, University of Minnesota, 1986.

Shestov, Lev. *Athens and Jerusalem*. Trans. Bernard Martin. New York: Simon and Schuster, 1968.

Speer, Albert. *Inside the Third Reich*. Trans. Richard and Clara Winston. New York: Avon, 1971.

Spengler, Oswald. *The Decline of the West*. 2 vols. Trans. Charles F. Atkinson. New York: Knopf, 1945.

Spiro, Rabbi Jack. "Meaning." *Contemporary Jewish Religious Thought*. Ed. Arthur A. Cohen and Paul Mendes-Flohr. New York: Scribner, 1987, 565–71.

Spivak, Gayatri. Translator's Preface. In Jacques Derrida, *Of Grammatology*.

Staten, Henry. *Wittgenstein and Derrida*. Lincoln, NE: University of Nebraska Press, 1984.

Steiner, George. *After Babel: Aspects of Language and Translation*. London: Oxford University Press, 1975.

———. "Real Presences." *Leslie Stephen Memorial Lecture*, November 1, 1985. University of Cambridge.

Stern, David. "Was Wittgenstein a Jew?" In James C. Klagge, ed. *Wittgenstein: Biography and Philosophy*. Cambridge: Cambridge University Press, 2001. Pp. 237–272.

Strauss, Leo. *Persecution and the Art of Writing*. Chicago: The University of Chicago Press, 1988.

Szabados, Béla. "Was Wittgenstein an Anti-Semite? The Significance of Anti-Semitism for Wittgenstein's Philosophy," *Canadian Journal of Philosophy* 29 (1999): 1–28.

Thurman, Robert. "Philosophical Nonegocentrism in Wittgenstein and Candrakirti in their Treatment of the Private Language Problem." *Philosophy East and West* 30 (1980) 321–36.

Tigerman, Stanley. *Versus*. New York: Rizzoli, 1982.

Timms, Edward. "The Kraus-Bekessy Controveersy in Interwar Vienna." In Robert Wistrich, ed. *Austrians and Jews in the Twentieth Century*, 184–98.

Unterman, Alan. *Jews: Their Religious Beliefs and Practices*. London: Routledge and Kegan Paul, 1981.

Viertel, Berthold. *Karl Kraus ʒum 50. Geburtstag*. Vienna, 1924.

Vohra, Ashok. *Wittgenstein's Philosophy of Mind*. LaSalle, IL: Open Court, 1986.

von Wright, G.H. "Biographical Sketch" (of Wittgenstein). In Malcolm.

Weininger, Otto. *Sex and Character*. New York: G.P. Putnam's Sons, 1908.

West, Cornel. "Nietzsche's Prefiguration of Postmodern American Philosophy." In Daniel O'Hara, ed. *Why Nietʒsche Now?* Bloomington: Indiana University Press, 1985. 241–70.

Winch, Peter. *The Idea of a Social Science and Its Relation to Philosophy*. New York: Humanities Press, 1970.

Wistrich, Robert. *Revolutionary Jews from Marx to Trotsky*. New York: Barnes and Noble, 1976.

———, ed. *Austrians and Jews in the Twentieth Century*. New York: St. Martin's Press, 1992.

Wittgenstein, Ludwig. *Philosophical Investigations*. Trans. G.E.M. Anscombe. New York: Macmillan, 1953.

———. *The Blue and Brown Books*. 2d ed. New York: Harper and Row, 1960.

———. *Lectures and Conversations on Aesthetics, Psychology and Religious Belief*. Compiled from notes taken by Yorick Smythies, Rush Rhees and James Taylor. Ed. Cyril Barrett. Berkeley: University of California Press, 1966.

———. *Remarks on the Foundations of Mathematics*. Ed. G.H. von Wright, Rush Rhees and G.E.M. Anscombe. Trans. G.E.M. Anscombe. Cambridge, MA: M.I.T. Press, 1967.

———. *Zettel*. Ed. G.E.M. Anscombe and G.H. von Wright. Trans. G.E.M. Anscombe. Berkeley: University of California Press, 1970.

———. *On Certainty*. Ed. G.E.M. Anscombe and G.H. von Wright. Trans. Denis Paul and G.E.M. Anscombe. New York: Harper and Row, 1972.

———. *Tractatus Logico-Philosophicus*. Trans. D.F. Pears and B.F. McGuinness. With an Introduction by Bertrand Russell. London: Routledge and Kegan Paul, 1961. Reprinted with corrections, 1972.

———. *Letters to C.K. Ogden*. Ed. G.H. von Wright. Oxford: Basil Blackwell, 1973.

———. *Bemerkungen über Frazers* Golden Bough. Ed. Rush Rhees. Trans. A.C. Miles. Atlantic Highlands, NJ: Humanities Press International, 1979.

———. *Notebooks 1914–1916*. 2d ed., ed. G.H. von Wright and G.E.M. Anscombe, trans. G.E.M. Anscombe. Chicago: The University of Chicago Press, 1979.

———. *Culture and Value*. Ed. G.H. von Wright, in collaboration with Heikki Nyman, trans. Peter Winch. Chicago: The University of Chicago Press, 1980.

———. *Remarks on the Philosophy of Psychology*. 2 vols. Ed. G.H. von Wright and Heikki Nyman. Trans. C.G. Luckhardt and M.A.E. Aue. Chicago: The University of Chicago Press, 1980.

———. *Last Writings on the Philosophy of Psychology*. 2 vols. Ed. G.H. von Wright and Heikki Nyman. Trans. C.G. Luckhardt and Maximilian Aue. Chicago: The University of Chicago Press, 1982.

———. *Denkbewegungen*: Tagebücher 1930–1932, 1936–1937. Ed. Ilse Somavilla. Innsbruck: Haymon, 1997.

Wright, Crispin. *Wittgenstein on the Foundations of Mathematics*. Cambridge, MA: Harvard University Press, 1980.

Wünsche, Konrad. *Der Volksschullehrer Ludwig Wittgenstein: mit neuen Dokumenten und Briefen aus dem Jahren 1919 bis 1926*. Frankfurt a.M.: Suhrkamp, 1985.

Zahavy, Tzvee. "Midrash and Medieval Commentary." *Johns Hopkins Guide to Literary Theory and Criticism*. Ed. Michael Groden and Martin Kreiswirth. Baltimore: Johns Hopkins University Press, 1994, 81–84.

Index

STUDIES IN JUDAISM

Yudit Kornberg Greenberg
General Editor

Studies in Judaism draws together scholarly works in philosophy, history, biography, and culture. The series includes all historic periods, with a particular focus on modern and postmodern interpretive perspectives and practices.

For additional information about the series or for the submission of manuscripts, please contact:

Yudit Kornberg Greenberg, General Editor
c/o Dr. Heidi Burns
Peter Lang Publishing, Inc.
P.O. Box 1246
Bel Air, MD 21014-1246

To order other books in this series, please contact our Customer Service Department:

800-770-LANG (within the U.S.)
(212) 647-7706 (outside the U.S.)
(212) 647-7707 FAX

Or browse online by series at:

www.peterlangusa.com